WOMEN
WHO
impact

WOMEN
WHO
impact

A COLLECTION OF POWERFUL STORIES TO RECONNECT, EMPOWER & IMPACT YOUR SOUL'S JOURNEY

kate butler
B O O K S

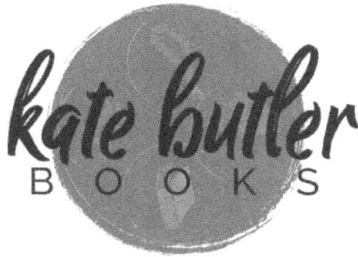

First Edition

Copyright © 2018 Kate Butler Books

www.katebutlerbooks.com

All rights reserved.

Design by Margaret Cogswell
margaretcogswell.com

WOMEN
WHO
impact

A COLLECTION OF POWERFUL STORIES TO RECONNECT, EMPOWER & IMPACT YOUR SOUL'S JOURNEY

kate butler
B O O K S

First Edition

Copyright © 2018 Kate Butler Books

www.katebutlerbooks.com

All rights reserved.

Design by Margaret Cogswell
margaretcogswell.com

This book is dedicated to you. We see you, we feel you, we relate to you, and we connect with you, because … we are you. At the core we are all the same. We are beings of light and love who deeply desire to make a positive influence on the world with our unique type of brilliance. The pages of this book promise to fill you with the wisdom, insights, and inspiration that will align you further with your soul's path. Our hope is that the vulnerability and authenticity of these stories will remind you deeply of who you are and inspire you to share your impact with the world.

It is your time. It is our time. It is time.

enjoy the unfolding …

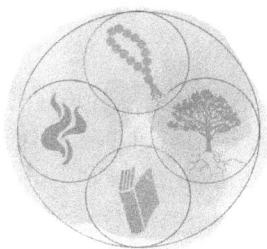

FOREWORD

Lisa Nichols

With $11.42 in the bank, there wasn't even enough money to buy diapers for my son, Jelani. I remember putting my hand on his little tummy and making a promise to him and myself that I would never be that broke or broken again.

What shifted for me in that moment was that I was willing to completely cut off any form of me that had been, so that I could fully birth the woman I was becoming. I knew I was here to make a greater impact. I knew this deep down, even if the path to get there wasn't exactly clear.

The reason that most people won't become who they want is because they are too attached to who they have been. You hear it all the time; people will say, "Well, I have always been this way," or "I have always done things this way." And if that version of you is working for you, then great, please keep it going. But I knew it wasn't working for me anymore. I had hit my version of rock bottom. So I was willing to let go of everything and everybody in order to step into my greatness.

Another reason I believe people don't arrive at who they want to be is because the doorway that you need to walk through is just big enough for you to walk through, but often times we are trying to carry everyone along with us. We need to recognize that we must rescue ourselves first before we can begin to rescue others. I am much more valuable to my family and my community because I was willing to let them go, and go through the door myself so that I could teach myself, learn myself, condition myself, and then come back again.

I am much more valuable to them now, but I had to go through ten years of judgment, lack of understanding, and pain before I came through the other side. I had to be willing to allow my conviction to make me inconvenienced. You see, we want to grow, but we all want to be liked by everyone. Social media is a perfect example of this in our culture now, every single day. I was willing to be my own rescue at the risk of your approval. It had to be enough for me that I woke up and liked myself this morning, and I decided that your like is extra. My job is to like me first. I was willing to say everyday, "Lisa, do you like you? Lisa, are you proud of you? Lisa, are you playing full out?" Every single day, I would ask these questions before I checked in with anybody else as I was growing through this time.

This process can test you. This process can be lonely. This process can be scary. This process will test your limits. So I forced myself to go beyond any previous limits. I forced myself to find people who had what I didn't have, who were living lives I wasn't living, who believed things I didn't know about, and I was willing to become their student. I got up every day and I ate a piece of humble pie. I just knew I never wanted to get caught up in my bio. I never wanted to feel like I had arrived. I'm not interested in resting on the accomplishments of my past, I'm only interested in the impact I am creating for the future.

What I learned as a student was that success was on the other side of service. I had become successful, because I was serving more and more people. But even though I was seeing success, I knew there was more. I knew there was more to learn and more people to serve. I was hungry for it.

When I say I became a student, I mean I really became a student. So much so that I attended the same conference forty-two times. Yes, forty-two. Some people would stop and say, "Oh, I've been there and learned that already." But I was not going to stop. I wanted to master these teachings. I knew that success was leaving clues for me, but I also knew it was my responsibility to pick them up, regardless of the challenges in my way. I was the only African American person and one of only two females who attended this conference. I did not let this challenge me, I allowed this to open up opportunity for me. As a result of the mastery I developed, the last twenty-nine sessions of this particular conference I no longer sat in the audience, I led the conference instead. This was because I was willing to be the student first and because my truth was coming from a place of serving others.

I was willing to inconvenience myself, I was willing to learn, and I was willing to invest in myself, because we are not supposed to get up every day and tuck our dream back under our pillow. We are not supposed to leave our dreams at home. We are not supposed to spend our whole life going out and working to fulfill someone else's dream. This is not what we are wired to do. Your human spirit is designed for you to soar. When you get to the edge your brain will always tell you to step back because you can fall. It will tell you to step back because your brain is designed to keep you safe and it remembers when you have fallen before. It also remembers watching others fall and fail. And because of this, if you desire to make an impact on this world, you need to be willing to play between your brain and your soul. Some days, you just have to listen to and honor your soul. You have to make the decision to get to the edge and take that leap. Most people are at the edge right now and you are standing there watching everyone else fly. You are standing there wondering what it's like to jump without ever jumping.

I am here to tell you: JUMP. Only three things can happen:

1) You jump and fly.
2) You jump and land on something soft.
3) You jump and land hard.

In either fall, it doesn't matter because you already know you have what it takes to pick yourself back up again. Your greatest fear is not that you will fall, your greatest fear is that you will live your entire life and never fly. Your greatest fear is that you will get to the end and will have never taken that leap. You are not afraid of dying, you are afraid of dying before the world sees who you really are, before the world knows your unique fingerprint, before they breathe in your breath, before they really receive your contribution. The biggest fear is that you will leave and the world will never have known you were here. This is why you MUST give your dream a chance. This is why you must be inconvenienced. This is why you must learn and do what it takes to put the pieces of your dream together. This is what it takes to show up and make an impact on this world.

It's time.

Lisa Nichols
NY Times Bestselling Author
Inspirational Speaker
Chief Executive Officer of Motivating the Masses, Inc.
www.motivatingthemasses.com

table of contents

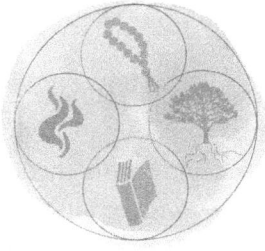

INTRODUCTION

Kate Butler

I t was the summer of 1993. My parents had just given us the surprise
of a lifetime when they shared that they had bought a house at the
Jersey Shore. We spent summers vacationing there, but only for a
week or two at time. What a dream come true to be able to live at the
beach all summer long.

My parents had only one request, which was more like a requirement;
if we wanted to live at the shore for the summer, we would need to find
a job. Since I was fourteen at the time, and did not have a driver's license
yet, I needed to find something within walking distance to our home.
I was hired at a local ice cream parlor making $5.05 per hour. Jackpot!
I was over the moon!

Since I was the new girl in this ice cream operation, they started me
off with only a few hours a week. Even though I had worked limited
hours during that first pay period, when I received my first paycheck,
it was like I received my first taste of freedom.

I began picking up extra shifts, working when others didn't want
to, filling in for others when they were sick, and offering to pick up
doubles on holidays. My paychecks grew and so did my motivation.
I was beginning to realize that I had more control over my pay than I
originally thought.

I also began to realize at that very young age that hard work and honest effort wasn't easy to come by. While all the other teenagers I worked with were ditching work to hang with their friends on the boardwalk or go see a movie with their summer squeeze, I was more than happy to pick up all the extra hours. I still did all those things; I just met up with them a few hours later... and with a few more zeros in my pocket.

The next summer, I returned to the ice cream parlor when they offered me a raise to come back. I was thrilled to be making more than minimum wage and began my now normal routine of "filling in" when everyone else had something better to do.

But, one afternoon that summer I received a call from my boyfriend. He and his family were going to go sailing. It sounded so regal and fancy to me at the time. Growing up, we had a ski boat that we would take out on the lake, but I had never been sailing. I couldn't wait to go.

The only problem was, I was scheduled to work. I figured it would be no problem for someone to fill in for me. I had been covering shifts for two summers by this point; surely someone would return the favor. I was wrong.

I was left with the decision to go to work and keep my job or go sailing and get fired.

It didn't feel like much of a choice to me. It actually felt like I had no good options.

It was the first time I felt stuck like that in my life. And I did not like that feeling. I decided at this point that would not happen to me again.

I had never been one to follow the path most traveled. And even when I did, I ended up doing things my way. I ended up working more hours, picking up shifts and creating the experience I wanted with the job. But, I didn't like the idea of only having one option. So I decided to create my own path the next summer.

I came across a customer service position at a local bank. They were paying me more, to work fewer hours, and I got to actually sit down in air conditioning while I worked. *What were all those kids doing working*

on the boardwalk all day? I asked myself.

I was fascinated by how this all worked.

As much as I enjoyed the bank position, I was not willing to give up the ice cream job. At that point I had received my third raise in three years. I was a supervisor and I was adamant about having more than one option of income. I did not realize until later that this was the point in my life that I began to create multiple streams of income and never stopped.

When I went off to college, I had several different jobs, including a waitressing position. I'll never forget the last day on that job. It was a pivotal moment for me in more ways than one.

I had a customer who came in weekly, the same day each week. She would order the same meal. We would talk about life, her family, and my family. She never had children, but said that I reminded her a lot of her niece. We developed a beautiful relationship. This particular day was approaching graduation. When the customer left that day, along with the money to pay her bill, she also left a card. When I opened the card, I found a $100 bill, along with a note that said,

"Dear Kate, It has been such a pleasure coming in here every Monday and being greeted by your kindness. I have enjoyed getting to know you. Thank you for spending more time with me than necessary and thank you for showing me such warmth. It meant more to me than I can say. My family left this area many years ago, and spending time with you each week was like spending a little time with my family, which means more to me than you'll know. I have felt more love in our time together than I have felt in a very long time, and you have touched my heart. Congratulations on your college graduation. You will go on to do great things."

I sat down with tears dripping down my face.

Her heart may have been touched, but in that moment, my heart was broken wide open.

The money meant nothing. It could have been $1 or $10 in there, or nothing at all. It wouldn't have made a difference. What mattered were the words she wrote and the moments we shared. My life was forever changed.

That was the moment I realized, it was not about the income, it was about the IMPACT.

A few moments later, I dropped a ketchup bottle off of my tray and it shattered all over the floor.

After the mess was cleaned up, the manager came over and told me he would be taking money out of my tips that night to account for the ketchup bottle I broke and also the work that went into cleaning it up.

I didn't quite understand since other waitresses had accidents before and were never docked pay as a result of it. The manager informed me that they needed to start somewhere and I would be where they started with this new policy.

I quit on the spot.

It was so interesting. I had spent years doing everything in my power to have options, so if a moment like this ever came I wouldn't feel trapped. I did have options. I did have other means of income. But I realized it wasn't any of this that made it so easy to walk away. It was that I had received what I had come there for; I had received my lesson.

It was my time to start somewhere, too.

After college, I went on to work in corporate recruiting and loved finding people new jobs and companies new employees. I loved it so much, I went on to open my own recruiting company after my first daughter was born.

The company did very well, but after a few years, I realized I was not getting the feeling that my dear, diner customer had taught me on that pivotal day.

Then I remembered, I didn't have to do things the way everyone else did them. I did not have to stay in a job that wasn't fulfilling me anymore, even if I was the one who owned the company. Maybe it was crazy to begin a whole new career that I knew nothing about, but I felt like it was even crazier to stay on a path that, in my heart, I knew wasn't mine anymore. I remembered that I had to make my own rules, take the roads that feel best to me, and remain open to options.

I sold the company.

I followed that knowing and because I did, the universe provided me a platform to spread inspiration around the world.

I followed that calling and it allowed me to create a sacred space where women could gather, share, and conquer. It allowed me to create a space where inspiration overflowed and making an impact was not a choice, but a way of life.

I followed that feeling, and it led me to write this Inspired Impact™ Book Series, as well as inspirational books for children.

Seven #1 Best-selling books later, the feeling is still there.

The impact is the core of it all.

Impact is connection.

Impact is love.

Impact is sacrifice.

Impact is making shifts.

Impact is inviting in change.

Impact is innovative.

Impact will illuminate the world.

Impact is for the greatest good of all involved.

The pages of this book will reflect moments of impact that have shifted lives forever and also commitments to impact that will forever shape lives moving forward.

The chapters that follow will provide you ways you can make massive impacts in your life, in your business, in your community, and in turn, the world.

I am committed to positive impact in this world, and I invite you to join me. Are you in?

ABOUT KATE BUTLER

About Kate Butler

Kate Butler is a #1 Best Selling Author, Certified Professional Success Coach and International Speaker. Kate has been featured on HBO, in the Huffington Post and many other televisions, news, and radio platforms.

Kate's children's books, More Than Mud and More Than Magic, have received the prestigious Mom's Choice Award for Excellence®, the Readers Favorite International Book Award® and have also been endorsed by popular children's brands, Kidorable® and the Garden State Discovery Museum™.

Kate received her degree in Mass Communication and Interpersonal Communication Studies from Towson University, MD. After 10 years in the corporate industry, Kate decided it was time to fulfill her true passion. Kate then went onto to study business at Wharton School of Business at The University of Pennsylvania and received her certificate in Entrepreneur Acceleration.

Kate now follows her soulful mission to guide people to activate their core brilliance so they can impact people's lives and ignite their own. In pursuit of this mission, Kate has impacted thousands of lives through her books, keynote speeches, live events, and coaching programs in her business as a Certified Professional Success Coach.

Ways to work with Kate:
Coaching - From 1:1 Coaching to Online Group Coaching, Kate offers a programs that facilitate guaranteed success in both your personal and professional life.

Publish a Book - If you have always dreamed of sharing your story or publishing a book, then let's connect and discuss how we can make this happen for you! We take care of all the logistical work, so you can just enjoy the writing process! You are guaranteed to become a Best-Selling Author in Kate's Publishing Programs.

Speaking - Whether you are hosting an intimate women's circle or a massive seminar, Kate would love to support your work by speaking at your next event. Kate is not just an inspirational speaker, but also an experiential speaker, bringing the audience through exercises that will create energy shifts and mindset expansion right there on the spot. The audience will leave feeling inspired, empowered, uplifted and with a renewed sense of clarity. Kate's main mission is to inspire women to align with their soul's path and she would love to partner with you in order to impact more people!

Author Visits - Inspiring children is where it all begins, and Kate does this through her school visits. Kate travels around the world to share her books with schools, often times with her daughter, Bella, who co-wrote More Than Magic. Through reading their books and sharing the writing and publishing process, they encourage children to believe in themselves and their dreams.

To connect with Kate or to learn more about her work, we welcome you to visit www.katebutlerbooks.com.

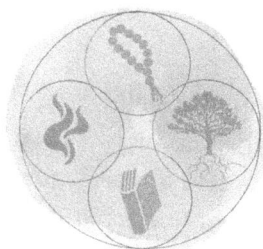

NEXT GOOD STEP

Enna Aujla

always believed it was the things you don't choose that make you who you are. Your city, your neighborhood, your family."

If there was a line out of a movie that could describe what I was thinking as a very young adult, it would be this line from the movie *Gone Baby Gone*. I can only describe the feeling of knowing who I did not want to be. Thus, coming into adulthood meant choosing the exact opposite of who I did not want to be. There are those who would say you need to know where you are going and to clearly know what your goals are, but the expectation of knowing these things was overwhelming for me at the time. It was simply easier to walk away from what I knew, to start walking along a path and see where it might lead ... I simply chose not to wait for the next bad thing to happen. It was as basic as this.

Thirty years after starting this walk, I find myself as a career professional pharmacist, leading teams as a National Director of Operational Excellence, while raising two wonderful girls with an amazing life partner. How did I get here? As I connect the dots in retrospect, I realize it all began with books, and the stories of characters who lived such different lives than mine. As a young girl, I read six or seven books a week as a means of burying myself, as a means of escaping a difficult family dynamic that created feelings of fear and shame. I can only describe my childhood as a series of intense feelings rather than actual activities or events. More than likely, this was simply a mechanism of survival for me. From watching my mother stuck in what she perhaps felt was her 'lot in life,' coupled with her fears of not being able to financially support her three children, I knew I never wanted to feel that way. I have learned that my mother gave me the gift of resilience. Through the most difficult of circumstances and her perceived barriers, by maintaining her courage and faith, my mother was able to successfully raise her three children and contribute financially to the family.

As a child of parents who had emigrated from India, I felt the burden of cultural expectations; I would finish high school, get married, have kids and, somehow, that was supposed to make me happy. I knew I wanted to be happy, but was filled with doubt that these steps would create the life I wanted for myself. I decided I was going to educate myself. I turned my love of reading into a "way out." I enrolled in a diploma program for Nuclear Medicine Technology, because I believed the cultural expectation that, as a girl, there was no need for me to pursue a bachelor's degree at university. As I came close to completing the program, I did not feel confident this diploma would give me the financial freedom I was seeking, nor was it satisfying the desire I had to go to university. Had I just wasted the last two years? The white light in this program was a professor of Nuclear Pharmacology, who had a passion for what he taught. It was this passion that peaked my curiosity to ask myself, *Is that passion what I want?* I decided I had not wasted two years ... going through the program had led me to my next step; had shown me that learning could open me up to a new idea ... that I could have a career that would allow me to be financially independent and that I could also passionately enjoy.

I graduated from university with a bachelor's degree in Pharmacy and became a pharmacist. The feeling of accomplishment was coupled with a feeling of self-doubt; I wasn't supposed to be here, this place in life wasn't the expectation for me. The messages and feelings from childhood kept popping up. I delved into my practice to avoid dealing with the negative self-talk.

The pharmacy where I worked was in the downtown core of the city, with patients from all walks of life, from the executives in business to the homeless who peddled outside the pharmacy. As I served my patients, I recognized that helping others was helping me. In particular, there was one gentleman (we will call him John for the sake of this story) who became a catalyst for my turning point. John was a businessman who came to the pharmacy every day in a suit and tie to receive his methadone, a medication he used to control his addiction for heroin. He would wait every morning at the front door for the pharmacy to open, so he could take his daily dose and then go to work. He was always friendly and positive, and he never missed a day. On the days when other patients were also at the pharmacy early, I noticed he was less talkative and waited off to the side for me, away from the others. I sensed his feelings of shame and embarrassment. One morning I asked if he would like to come into the pharmacy a few minutes before official opening each morning to get his dose, suggesting maybe it would help him to get to work a little earlier. His eyes lit up and he was so grateful. I understood that his gratitude was for recognition of his feelings.

John's commitment to come to the pharmacy every morning fueled my curiosity to better understand mental health issues and addiction in an effort to help him stay on his chosen path. In helping John, I began to develop feelings of joy, gratitude, and purpose. My life had started moving in the right direction. It seemed that each window I opened would lead me down a path where there was another window, and it was up to me whether I opened that window or not; it was my choice. Maybe I was supposed to be here.

I was beginning to notice a pattern: learning was the key for me. Learning by reading through books as a young child, learning in university, learning about mental health issues as a young professional ... learning was what brought me joy. This was my "a-ha" moment; I carry

11

that lesson with me to this day, and pass it on to my teams, and my family and friends.

I am committed to being a life-long learner. The challenge came to me as a mother of two young children, working full-time, with a husband who was a career Naval Officer and was often away from home for prolonged periods. I was constantly exhausted and taking a course seemed overwhelming. I did not have the time to learn anything new. I changed companies so I could work fewer evenings and weekends to be with my girls, and noticed that I learned many new things just by changing companies. My learning did not have to come from a certified course, but could come from everyday opportunities to learn new skills within my current profession, to learn about the different market sectors and the niches that existed within the pharmacy world. The learning did not have to stop, it just had to happen in a different way.

It continues to this day with my recent completion of a Certificate in Applied Positive Psychology. As I endeavor to become a flourishing change agent, someone who is always growing, always questioning, always moving towards self-improvement, I consistently encourage and support my teams to join me on this journey. Through the PERMA-V model developed by Dr. Martin Seligman, the founder of Positive Psychology, I have learned the pillars that support human flourishing, including Positivity, Engagement, Relationships, Meaning, Accomplishments and Vitality. I was already doing some of the things that contributed to my own well-being, I just did not know it. Learning the science behind the theory showed me I already had inside of me the resilience to achieve what I wanted.

In cultivating a love for learning in others, I use the same approach with my children as I do professionally, with my colleagues and my teams. We seek answers together, no matter who is asking the question. I encourage "question thinking," especially when we cannot find answers to a problem. If we cannot find the answers, perhaps we are not asking the right question, so chasing the right questions become a crucial part of learning. I also place a high value on reflection as a method of spurring further learning.

I enjoy encouraging others in pursuit of their personal interests. I recognized that, in making time for interests unrelated to my professional world, I would show up to work with that extra boost of energy and openness that only comes from having spent time with my family or doing something that truly stimulated me. I wanted others to experience this as well. Ironically, I learned this approach to learning from my two daughters, having placed them in a Montessori-based school. They have taught me how to share the joy of learning.

Very early in my career, I moved into a management position and managed my own pharmacy team, and perhaps unconsciously, became the one who spoke up for those who felt they could not speak up for themselves, those who felt they were not being heard. I easily recognized this learned helplessness in others as it was a reflection of my own up-bringing. I was the one who had listened so much that I became attuned to hearing what was not being said. I learned to watch for cues in body language. I could hear the emotions of others. As I progressed in my career, I came to see this as a valuable skill. I was able to hear what my patients were reluctant to say when they came to visit me at the pharmacy. I was able to hear when my staff were uncomfortable speaking in front of their co-workers. I knew I did not want others to feel helpless. Speaking up for others was an easier step perhaps than speaking up for myself, but it did eventually propel me in the right direction. Listening to others' opinions, ideas, and thoughts helped me to continue on my learning path. The power to listen has helped me build strong and trusting relationships, both professionally and personally.

In translating this talent to my teams, I always make myself available to listen and respond, whether it's a phone call, email, or text. Listening to concerns of managers and front-line staff has allowed me to detect the early identification of problems, and listening to their solutions has driven their performance and their overall job satisfaction. Listening to others has become a leadership responsibility for me. Truly, listening without interruption and being engaged and mindful of what others are saying or not saying has been critical to my success. Every conversation is approached with a commitment to listen and learn.

As a young pharmacy graduate navigating my first professional role, I had no idea what to expect and, really, no one to ask. I was lucky enough to have joined an organization that used mentorship as part of their corporate training. My mentor had been a manager for more than thirty years, and, needless to say, he had lots of experience; but more important than the experience was his genuine desire to see me succeed. He told me that when I became a manager, I needed to remember that my staff were "my" customers. If I treated my staff well, they would treat the customers well. I was stunned that he thought I would become a manager one day and I remember his advice to this day. He exemplified this value daily: that everyone deserves to be treated with dignity and respect.Since that time, I have always sought out mentors or role models to learn from, to seek out encouragement and to help me see all the possibilities. From each mentor, I would take away a lesson and I began to build my "mentor toolkit." So far, I have shared two out of the three most important tools in my toolkit, learning and listening … laughter is the third.

Humor and laughter is the bow that helped tie the shoe string for me; it has tied it all together. Laughter is my key to learning. It has helped me to remember and to learn. Laughter has always helped to create an emotional distance from overwhelming events, and it helped me to hold onto a perspective that made moving forward possible. It was a way of building resiliency. Putting a smile on at least one person's face every day has become an imperative for me. It has been said that laughter serves the development of leaders, not in spite of, but because of the vulnerability it exposes. The more my teams shared laughter, the more we trusted each other and the more we built a bonded community. Similarly, the more my family shares laughter, the more we build a bonded family.

I have come to realize that I have become a mentor in my own right, as my teams share their stories with me and let me know that I am the voice in their head that guides them as they face their own challenges. As I have moved into this mentorship role with my teams, my career has become more of a calling as it has become the most enjoyable part of my role. I revel in bringing positivity, engagement, and joy to my teams.

Do I have it all figured out? Absolutely not; there is still so much to learn, and perhaps the line from the movie *Gone Baby Gone*, "I always believed it was the things you don't choose that make you who you are. Your city, your neighborhood, your family," was partly true. It is where I came from that drove where I wanted to go. So maybe I was supposed to be there, so that now, I can be here … and what a great place this is to be, waiting for the next good step.

ABOUT ENNA AUJLA

Enna Aujla has been a pharmacist for twenty-five years and is the Director of Operations for a Specialty Pharmacy operating across Canada. Practicing in a profession that is experiencing rapid and continuous change, Enna coaches pharmacists to become resilient leaders, to remember the core purpose of their work is patient care, and to honour the trust that has been placed in them.

Enna is a Positive Psychology Practitioner, empowering her teams, colleagues, friends, and family to use their core strengths to achieve new heights. She is passionate about helping companies build an organizational culture that encourages and fosters strong relationships and connections, celebrates successes, nurtures trust, and creates team cohesion through creating a sense of purpose and a safe space for vulnerability. This helps build resilient teams that are innovative and creative.

As Enna continues her own journey of self-discovery and self-impact, she believes in the unshakeable hope that something better awaits each of us, and that everyone already possesses the ability to choose positive outcomes to create personal and professional success.

Enna has been married for twenty-three years to a now-retired Naval Officer, and lives in Victoria, British Columbia. She has two beautiful daughters who remind her to learn, listen, and laugh every day. She enjoys spending time with her family, reading, and yoga.

Connect with Enna: www.linkedin.com/in/ennaaujla

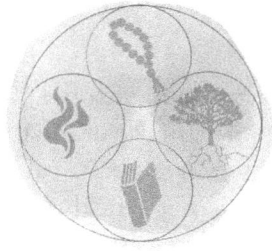

EVIDENCE OF MAGIC

Laura Husson

'll never forget how hearing that sentence felt upon the delivery of my first child. A daughter?! I was old enough when my mum had each of my younger siblings—both boys—to remember wishing that they were girls.

I was immediately head over heels and felt like I had everything I'd ever wanted. I had a newborn baby girl, I was on maternity leave from my teaching job, and we lived in a house that we loved. Life was good.

During one particularly long nap session when my daughter, Ellen, was around six weeks old, I stumbled into an accidental online business. I was a prolific poster in a mother-and-baby forum and had suggested in there that instead of each of us buying the latest much-lusted-over baby carrier that was perfect for taking a tiny baby on a sunny holiday, that I buy one and then loan it out. The idea being that, after I made my investment back, I'd donate the continuing loan donations to a baby loss charity.

The crowd went wild (or something along those lines.) When I came back a few hours later there were more than 120 replies from mums wanting to book in for their specific holiday dates. Without knowing it, I had uncovered something that people really wanted. So I sprang into action.

One thing led to another, and with the baby carrier manufacturers loving this idea, within 10 days of the original suggestion I found myself with more than £1,500 of donated baby carriers on my doorstep.

When things got underway it quickly turned out that once people borrowed their carrier, they started asking if they could buy them. "Sure, why not?!" I said, and without even pausing to breathe, I launched an e-commerce website where I sold the carriers and associated products.

Things were crazy and before I knew it, maternity leave was over and I was going back to teaching. The prospect of being part-time felt exciting … I hadn't factored in a whole new business, endless trips to the post office, and missing my baby girl.Around six months after going back to teaching, I found myself standing in the deputy head teacher's office just before 9 am one morning..

"Hi, Laura, what's up?"

"Um … I think I'm here to hand in my notice."

I don't know which of us was more shocked. I had zero awareness that was coming. I heard it happen almost as though I was in a dream, or like I was watching someone else do it.

I went home that night absolutely exploding with excitement. Fear and anxiety were also making a pretty significant appearance, but underneath all of the feelings was a deep knowing that this was the right move.

As a child, when asked the age old, "What do you want to be when you grow up?" my answer was, "My job hasn't been invented yet!"

Obnoxious? Maybe.

True? Without question.

I started 2011 with the crystal clear reality of no salary and a drastically different life altogether than the one I had been living only a few short weeks ago. But I was 100 percent committed. To all of it.

I spent vast amounts of time lost in my online mother-and-baby forum where my online business had all started. I was sharing my journey as it unfolded in a safe, non-judgmental space. I felt understood and supported.

One afternoon, one of the mums reached out to me privately and asked if I would consider building her website. I was so confused … "But I don't build websites?!' I told her when she asked what my rate would be.

"You do! I've seen the different ones you've created for yourself and I love how they feel. None of the agencies I've spoken to can understand what I want to build. Send me your bank details and I'll transfer the deposit right now. I don't care how much it is."

What this mum didn't know was that same morning, I had been digging around in the sofa for a coin. Any coin. I'd been agonising on whether to spend the only remaining coin I possessed on either playgroup or milk.

I chose playgroup. Trusting that something would work out later.

Later, not only did I magically have money for milk, I had my very first website client.

If you're detecting a theme here, you're catching on quicker than I did. I was again responding to the opportunities that presented themselves to me. I was being matched by what felt like divine appointment to the people and situations I needed most at the time they most needed me.

By mid-2013, my husband left his increasingly demanding job in the movie industry and came into my business full time. I had sold the baby business after knowing it had been a perfect stepping stone. Everything flowed beautifully. Happy clients were rolling through our hands and we seemed to have it all.

Websites were our bread and butter. And we were able to afford the finest bread at the bakers, thanks to the way business was booming. But the niggling feeling was still there.

I had this guilty feeling of wondering … how am I making an impact or changing the world through building websites?

It didn't feel like enough.

I began resenting it and the needs of our clients. None of that felt good.

I started thinking there was something wrong with me. I had changed my entire life and yet I still felt there was something missing.

I had everything I had always said I wanted AND by this time we had also welcomed our beautiful baby boy, Finn, into the world.

Would I ever be happy?

Who even was I?

As if by magic, the same day that I was beginning to wonder if I'd ever find my 'thing', my friend sent me a link to a transformational coaching experience that she felt had been created for me. When I read the page I wept with relief. I immediately signed up and couldn't wait for the first session.

That first session didn't disappoint. We went deep. And it was apparent within just a few minutes that I had truth ready and waiting to bubble up and out of me.

That same familiar feeling from 2010 was washing over me again. The lights had been turned on. Only this time they were shining on the absolute core of who I was and the work I was here to do in the world.

The only question now was   how ready was I?

Doing this essential, deep work was providing me with all the opportunity I needed in order to reflect on my life with so much understanding.

It was all FOR me.

I had spent a great deal of time running around telling everyone "everything happens for a reason," and a bunch of other clichés that I was just hoping could be true. But now, I knew that every seemingly 'random' decision I had been making my whole life truly was all for me.

I was free.

I was able to acknowledge that I had unknowingly already cleared the way for magic. I didn't know what that looked like yet, but I no longer felt the need to search for answers. I was ok with just knowing that I was on the path.

As with all things we've been holding, when I let go it all began to become clear. I started following what simply felt good. One of the first examples of this was when I followed the nudge to enroll in a class about psychic mediumship.

I had no motivation for enrolling other than it seemed like fun. That was my guide. During the first group call, I was irritated because I had been caught up in prolonged bedtime and came late to the call. The group were looking at a photo of someone's passed loved one and saying what they saw. Once I got past the impulse to hang up, I said what I saw. A lilac handbag with a shiny object inside that would be of no value to anyone who hadn't seen it created. One of the girls from that call fetched her lilac handbag and found inside a ring folded from aluminum. It was her grandmother in the picture. The ring was something she had folded for her granddaughter before she passed.

Needless to say, I found this 'game' all kinds of fun and I 'guessed' the most random things about people. It was like a new party trick. When the creator of the class I had been taking announced a Florida-based retreat that coincided perfectly with an already planned speaking engagement in NYC, I was in.

Shortly after arriving at the house for the retreat a few months later, we all met in the living area and shared what had called us to attend. Hearing the other ladies share stories of deepening their mediumship connection, learning to communicate with a child who had passed and seeking connection with others who understood, I had to take a deep breath before sharing my truth. "I came because the house looked insanely beautiful."

In that moment I knew that I had already hit a new level. It would have been so much easier to have created a deeper reason as to why I was attending. Instead, I dug deep and spoke from a place of integrity. In hearing my voice speak its simple, bare truth, I laughed at my audacity.

Who was I becoming?

I didn't care … I loved this girl.

I lost myself in the experience of the retreat and was fortunate to connect with a spirit guide who was ready to guide me to greatness. Following the beat of his drum, I gained all kinds of trust in my ability to channel guidance for myself and act on what I had received.

Another deep breath was required just a couple of months after tapping into this spiritual connection when I publicly shared the story of how I channel guidance from my spirit team. I started a livestream and simply told the story of what happened at the retreat and how I've trusted and followed that connection ever since. I had my largest and most captivated audience ever.

I was shedding the appearance of Laura "The Website Girl" and showing who I truly was. What I believed in and the way I had lived my whole life was finally stepping forward to run the show.

One of the comments that popped up on my screen made me smile. It read, "Where do we book a session with you?!"

This was where the penny finally dropped.

I'd grown a whole business and made every decision my whole life based on following the clues … the signs … the nudges. And here was the mother of all nudges calling me to show up and serve in a way that I had been doing for myself since I arrived on this earth.

Of course, my typical reply came: "I don't do sessions for other people! I do them for me!" And as you probably guessed, this livestream viewer kindly offered, "But you could?! Send us a link!"

I created a link thinking it would be fun if a few sessions got booked in. Imagine my surprise when forty-six different people all handed over money to get on my calendar to receive channeled guidance from yours truly.

FINALLY! The hunt for my purpose was over. It felt so good. It felt so easy and I was so clear. I could see the undeniable evidence of the magic that had been around me all along. It had been right there the whole time waiting for me to be ready.

So my question to you can only be … how ready are YOU?

Are you ready to live in a place of truth? Are you ready to live in a place of flow and fun? Are you ready to show up as all that you already are and shine your light no matter what people could think/say/do?

When you are, know you have a friend over here cheering you on.

Everything really is always working out for us.

Your feet are already walking the right path. Let them lead the way.

ABOUT LAURA HUSSON

Host of the Business Beyond Belief podcast and founder of the Evidence of Magic online community, Laura Husson travels the world providing energetic support to transformational leaders, and speaking on the topic of living in total truth.

Through the unique blend of her pure connection to Spirit and her 10+ years of experience as an online entrepreneur, Laura delivers channeled guidance for the members of her community "Spirit Lounge." Those members learn how to trust their own intuition and trust Laura to be their bridge between realms. Laura's clients profess to experience deep peace after working with her and "mind-blowing life changes in the best of ways."

Laura believes passionately in supporting every person at all stages on their journey of spiritual discovery and connecting each individual to the truth that is at their heart's center.

Join Laura's Evidence of Magic online community here:
www.evidenceofmagic.com
Business Beyond Belief Podcast: www.businessbeyondbelief.com
Laura on Facebook: www.facebook.com/laurahussondotcom
Laura on Instagram: www.instagram.com/totallylaura

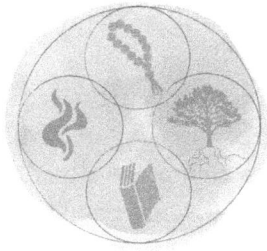

JUST A VISITOR

Stefanie O'Polka

> "*I am responsible. Although I may not be able to prevent the worst from happening, I am responsible for my attitude toward the inevitable misfortunes that darken life. Bad things do happen; how I respond to them defines my character and the quality of my life. I can choose to sit in perpetual sadness, immobilized by the gravity of my loss, or I can choose to rise from the pain and treasure the most precious gift I have—life itself.*"
> ~Walter Anderson, American Painter

For as far back as I can remember, my life was pretty freaking great. I lived in a happy home, was healthy, had lots of friends, was good at school, and had a family who adored me. After high school, I went to an excellent college and eventually started a marketing career in the same company where my dad worked. Things continued to progress when I got married, relocated to a new city for my husband's job, and landed an exciting new position in a marketing agency. It was hard leaving my family with whom I was so close, but the personal and professional opportunities in front of both me and my husband made the sacrifice worthwhile.

At this point, I was twenty-seven years old with the world in the palm of my hand, living a charmed life and thinking it was never going to change. My biggest concerns were being scared of the dentist and worrying over my sister who had recently separated from her husband. I was one of the fortunate ones—I was happily, albeit somewhat blindly, moving forward on a comfortable path that I believed had been predetermined for me. I was going to advance in my career, buy a nice house, maybe have a kid or two, go on vacations, and live happily ever after with my husband. As an added bonus, I always knew that in the almost impossible event that anything went wrong, I had the safety net of my loving and supportive parents to fall back on.

And then the phone rang. It was 11:30 on a Tuesday night, and my husband and I had just gone to bed. It was my dad's best friend on the other end, and he said rather hesitantly, "Steve shot your mom."

Let me explain who Steve was. Steve was the estranged husband of my sister, who I previously mentioned, and the father of my three-year-old niece. Steve had a good job, a nice house, and plenty of friends. Steve was also someone I had always liked, and I had even written him a letter telling him that he would always be a part of our family, regardless of what ultimately happened between him and my sister.

So when I heard that strange sentence over the phone, my first thought was that my mom must have walked in while Steve, being a hunter, was cleaning one of his guns and that the gun had gone off accidentally and shot her in the knee. The knee?! I have no idea why the knee, that's just the story that popped into my head. I asked if she was okay, and that's when it got really weird. My dad's friend said, "I don't think so. I think it's really bad."

"Bad" is a relative term, so for someone like me whose only experience with loss had been my grandfather's death a few years prior, I began feeling a few twinges of panic that my mom's injuries might be slightly more serious than just her knee. Of course, she was going to be okay, though, because everything was always okay, and Steve was a nice guy. He wouldn't purposely hurt anyone, especially my sweet mom. It then struck me as odd that it wasn't my dad who called was calling to tell me this news, so I asked his friend where my dad was. He told me he didn't know, which made absolutely no sense to me.

I honestly don't remember how I ended that phone conversation with my dad's friend, but I know something clicked in me, and I had to get some answers. I placed a couple of phone calls to family members who were either completely in the dark or didn't answer the phone. Still operating under the accidental-knee-shooting theory, I called the local hospital to see if my mom had been brought in for treatment, which would explain why my dad hadn't been the one to call me. He would be at my mom's side while the doctors were fixing her.

My life changed forever, in ways that I could never have even begun to imagine, when an emergency room nurse picked up my call. She told me that my mom had died of her wounds and that she was going to pass the phone to my maternal grandmother. My grandma, who I had always looked up to as a pillar of strength, said three simple words to me in a broken voice that I hardly recognized: "Honey, she's gone."

The weight of those words nearly crushed me, and as I was trying to wrap my mind around them, my grandma proceeded to deliver more and more incredulous news. My dad was also dead, and my paternal grandmother, who had been visiting my parents' house in Pennsylvania from South Carolina, had also been shot and was being flown by helicopter to Shock Trauma in Pittsburgh.

Between the utter shock of what we knew for sure, which was that Steve had murdered my parents, and the confusion of what was still unanswered, my recollection of the exact details of the events over the subsequent couple of hours is somewhat cloudy. Two things, however, stand out very clearly in my memory of that night:

1. The feeling of pure rage that washed over me when I got off of the phone with my grandma. I grabbed my husband's college fraternity paddle from the bedroom wall and started smashing holes in the drywall.

2. The image of standing in my closet looking at my clothes and

realizing that I had to pack for my parents' funeral. What would be appropriate? I had only been to one or two funerals in my whole life, and now I was packing for the funeral of BOTH of my parents. My dad was fifty, and my mom was forty-nine.

To this day, twenty-one years later, there are questions surrounding this tragedy that will never be answered, the biggest and most unanswerable of those questions being, "Why?"

In the absence of that answer, I'll recount the facts that we do know. After my sister finished work that Tuesday evening, she went to Steve's house to pick up their daughter. My sister and Steve argued, and after my sister left with my niece to go to their apartment, Steve left his house and drove the couple of miles to my parents' house. My dad had just returned from a motorcycle ride and was putting his motorcycle away in the garage as Steve pulled in their driveway and shot him three times, killing him instantly. He was still wearing his motorcycle helmet. Steve then entered the basement through the garage, met my mom coming down the basement stairs and shot her three times, also killing her instantly. He continued up the stairs into the kitchen, where he shot at my grandma three times, hitting her twice. One of the bullets hit her spine and paralyzed her from the waist down. She spent a month in Shock Trauma, endured multiple surgeries, and required 24-hour care for the rest of her life. She died two years later from complications.

Steve was still not finished. He drove to my sister's apartment, kicked in her door, grabbed her and my niece (his own three-year-old daughter,), held the gun to my sister's head, and told her she had to decide which one of them he was going to shoot first. For reasons unknown, Steve thankfully left my sister's apartment without physically harming her or my niece. He drove to the hospital, walked into the emergency room carrying the gun, then turned around and went back out into the parking lot. He stood beside his car, shot and killed himself, taking the answer to the "why" question with him.

28

The reality is it doesn't matter why Steve chose to do what he did. There is no reason that would ever be good enough to justify such actions. I've come to believe in karma, and I have faith that he is not escaping it, which gives me some level of comfort. And I will not let him win. As overcome with shock and grief as I was, I made a choice in the early days of dealing with this horrific situation that I was not going to allow him and this to ruin my life. My parents would not have wanted that, either. They loved my sister, my niece, and me more than life itself and would have willingly given theirs for us to have ours. Their deaths—and my grandmother's—could not be in vain.

I believe what fueled my determination to move forward initially was a combination of anger at Steve, the desire to make my parents proud of me, and sheer grit. I powered through the first few years, but later accepted that it was ok—even better—to reach out for help, and I found a therapist, who, to this day, I still see on a regular basis. I learned that it is actually necessary to go to the grief, and fury, and resentment, and all of the other dark places. But it is my decision whether I become a resident or just a visitor. The visitor angle provided a much better view.

Over the next eighteen years, I worked hard at building the best life I could. My husband and I became very successful professionally and financially and had three amazing children. We lived in a beautiful house, I was able to stay at home with the kids, and I gave back by volunteering. That is not to say there weren't challenges; life happens, and there always are. But remembering that it could always be worse helps keep things in perspective.

Perspective became my best friend in April of 2015. At the time, I was healthy, active, and forty-five years old. I came down with a serious case of pneumonia that hadn't responded to several courses of oral antibiotics, so my general practitioner sent me to the emergency room to be admitted for IV antibiotics and rest. After the first chest x-ray, I began to suspect something might be wrong when a seemingly abnormally large number of doctors and specialists came to see me just for a case of pneumonia.

They all kept saying they "saw something in the lung and had to rule things out." I spent several days in the hospital having multiple tests and procedures done, wondering the whole time if I was going to be okay. On about the third day, I had a bronchoscopy, where an instrument is inserted down the throat into the lungs. I remember waking up with a doctor at my bedside. Through the fog of anesthesia, I clearly saw the word that was embroidered in blue on his white lab coat—"Oncology"—and I knew without hims saying a word. I had cancer.

Horror is how best to describe what I felt when the doctor confirmed that it was lung cancer. I had never smoked a cigarette in my entire life. My first thought was a memory of reading that Dana Reeves, also a lifelong non-smoker, had died of lung cancer just a few months after her diagnosis. Unlike when my parents were murdered, my life wasn't just about me anymore. I now had three children to raise. I knew what it was like to have to learn to live without my parents at the young age of twenty-seven. My kids were only eight, eleven, and fourteen at the time.

I allowed myself a bit of room to be scared and sad and angry about this newest development in my life. I felt sorry for myself, but only for a bit, because just like I chose to not let Steve win, I wasn't going to let lung cancer win—even though the odds were stacked against me. You see, lung cancer is the deadliest of all cancers, killing more people each year than breast, colon, and prostate cancers combined. The five-year survival rate of those diagnosed with lung cancer is only eighteen percent.

Not great odds, but then I started thinking about the odds of being dealt these crappy life situations, and I made a big decision. What are the chances that my brother-in-law would murder my parents and grandma? Pretty fucking slim. What are the chances that a 45-year-old non-smoker would get lung cancer? Pretty fucking slim. If I defied the odds in these negative ways, I was going to choose to defy the odds in positive ways, too. Why not? Somebody has to be in that eighteen percent survival rate, and why shouldn't it be me? I had already proven to be a survivor. This was going to be no different.

I put on my big girl pants and began doing research on which doctors and hospitals were going to cure me. I am so fortunate to live in the Baltimore area, with its plethora of truly amazing medical professionals and facilities. I chose a compassionate and talented thoracic surgeon at the University of Maryland Medical Center, who removed the majority of my right lung, and I chose a progressive oncologist at the renowned Johns Hopkins Hospital, where I completed four months of weekly chemotherapy. I also researched alternative treatments and made a decision to actually stick to the ones I believed would truly help me, including acupuncture, supplements, nutritional support, and alternative medicine. I'm proud to say that I was one of only two (the only female) of all of my oncologist's patients to ever complete all sixteen weeks in a row of the intense chemo regimen prescribed for me. A small accomplishment, but also one to note: Somehow, I did not lose my hair, much to the surprise of my oncologist!

What's more, I chose not to be viewed as a cancer patient, because it wasn't something I wanted to ever get comfortable with. When I was diagnosed, I was slated to serve as the Parents' Association president at my kids' school, a demanding and almost full-time position. A dear friend and mentor asked me if I was still up for it. Without hesitation, I said, "Yes," and she believed me, because she knows me. I would show up most days at the school and do my job, and on Fridays—chemo day—I'd set up my "office" in the infusion chair and work until my body told me it was time to rest. The nurses complimented me each week, because I always arrived dressed nicely with my hair and makeup done. That might seem unimportant, but for me, it made me feel like less of a patient and more like just a visitor.

As I write this, I'm beyond grateful to say that I'm three and a half years cancer-free. I don't think the thought of cancer will ever be completely erased from my mind, but I honestly don't want it to be, just like I don't want to ever forget what happened to my mom, dad, and grandma, because I've grown and evolved and become stronger as a result of each of these challenges and the others I've faced. I will handle whatever life throws at me with more courage and dignity because of them. I choose to find a silver lining in every cloud.

I've waited a long time to figure out what to do with these stories. I always knew it couldn't just be that my parents were murdered, and I survived lung cancer—the end. I HAD to do something with them to make a positive impact on others. It is my intention that, by telling them, someone realizes that they have the ability to face life's challenges, whether big or small, and respond to them with strength and positivity. Stop by the dark places and the heartache, but don't move in. Choose to be just a visitor. I did it, and I'm just a girl from a small town in Northwestern Pennsylvania who chose one way rather than the other. You are responsible for your choices in every situation.

ABOUT STEFANIE O'POLKA

Stefanie O'Polka has survived one of life's greatest challenges: a lung cancer diagnosis with a staggeringly low survival rate. She also endured a tragic loss of lives that few can comprehend. Stef is now focused on sharing her story so that others going through any challenge in life may benefit from her incredible journey.

Born and raised in Western Pennsylvania, Stef is the proud daughter of Richard and Sharyn Freer. After earning her bachelor's degree in Economics from Allegheny College, she settled in the northern suburbs of Baltimore, Maryland. She built a career in marketing, working her way up to Vice -President & Management Supervisor of a global marketing firm, before stepping out of the daily grind for her most important role—raising her three children. Owen, Carter, and Spencer emulate Stef in many ways, from her positive outlook on life to her wit and her sense of style. Never one to be idle, Stef has continued to provide marketing consulting services to many local businesses in varied industries, including fitness, food and beverage, and even farming.

In addition to being a mom and a badass cancer survivor, Stef is personally rewarded by volunteering in the community and her children's school. Her philanthropic spirit was ignited years ago when a neighbor was diagnosed with cancer, and she chaired a benefit that raised $75,000 for the family. Since then, she has served as Vice President, President (while going through four months of chemotherapy), and Past President of the Parents' Association at St. James Academy, and currently serves as Treasurer of the Chershine Foundation, an organization that provides college scholarships to local high school seniors.

As a lung cancer survivor, Stef has become determined to do everything she can to increase survival rates for others diagnosed with this deadliest of all cancers. She recently partnered with the Lung Cancer Research Foundation and personally raised more than $30,000 for a yoga-thon in Baltimore. Moving forward, ten percent of all of her sales of *Women Who Impact* will be donated to the Lung Cancer Research Foundation.

Stef truly believes that you can choose to be just a visitor in the inevitable heartache that life hands us on our journeys, and that we all have the ability to move out of that dark space and turn it into something positive.

To learn more about being just a visitor, go to www.justavisitor.com, or email Stef at stefopolka@cs.com.

STRONG GIRL SPIRIT

Terrie Peters

Inspire … Empower … Encourage … Embrace

We believe that better is always possible.
We believe that YOU DO make a difference.
We believe in revealing the superhero in YOU.

What is Strong Girl Spirit? It's a positive movement for girls and women to inspire, encourage, empower, and embrace the strong girl in you! Every girl and every woman deals with insecurities sometimes. That being said, I have some news for you; you are more amazing than you believe, you are stronger than you know, and you are smarter than you think.

My passion is to drive a positive message of strength and confidence into girls and women everywhere. To help you see the real, the fun, the flawed, the quirky, the amazingly beautiful strong girl that YOU ARE!

Let's put on our "Cape of Confidence" together and reveal the superhero in You.

Take a trip with me to a time before I was a Strong Girl, and before I had a "Cape of Confidence." I was an insecure girl, plain-looking and bullied. I can still remember that time like it was yesterday. The kids used to make fun of my hair, my glasses, and my clothes. I wondered how they could make fun of me without knowing my heart. I started to withdraw from activities, from friends, from anything that meant I had to be in a group. Being in a group was painful as the negative words from people stung twice as hard.

A time that sticks out to me in particular is when I made a skirt (as required) in a Home Economics class. I was so proud of my skirt and probably even prouder because I was the one who made it. I was happy with my "A" grade and so excited to wear the skirt to school the next day.

What a mistake! I can't recall anyone being nice. It was a day of mean and hurtful comments about how ugly my skirt was, and worse, harsh comments about how ugly I was in the skirt.

I was mortified and never felt worse about myself and my beloved "A" project. I never wore the skirt again. What some people don't realize is just how painful these comments are and how they stick to you for years! I also recall attempting to climb that dreaded rope in gym class. I just knew I wouldn't be able to do it. I felt so fat and was worried the rope wouldn't hold me (all a made-up story in my head, now that I look back). When I couldn't climb the rope, a lot of ridicule and teasing ensued. Everything from laughter to, "you're too fat to ever climb that rope." From that point on I did everything in my power to avoid gym class.

Just as my self-image was rapidly fading, the silver lining showed up in the form of my Grandma Ruby! Turns out, she had always been there, but it took me a long time to pay attention.

During my childhood, we used to make the two-hour drive to my Grandma and Grandpa's every other week or so for a visit. My Grandma Ruby was an amazing Grandma/woman/friend/inspiration, and though she's gone to be with God, she is always in my mind and spirit.

Those Saturdays at her house were my happy days. Grandma Ruby would hug me, love on me, and speak positive words of intention to me. Her attitude was always positive. She called me her "Strong Girl." Thinking back now, I know that her intuition told her I was sad and struggling. Her words and strength are why I can write this today. She was my "Cape of Confidence."

In addition to her words of faith, strength, and empowerment, some of my fondest memories were of us washing our faces together at night with Noxzema. She would always say, "Strong Girl, we must take care of the beautiful skin that God gave us."

During the early daylight hours we tended to her giant garden. She would tell me that when you take care of the seeds, watering them daily, they will become a beautiful vegetable or fruit. I now use that metaphor for Strong Girl Spirit and in my daily life. When we plant positive words of strength, we will reap the rewards of a positivity filled life.

Every weekend when we left Grandma Ruby's, my head was full of affirmation that I was a Strong Girl, that I will always be a Strong Girl. I know this saved my life, and as time went by, shaped me into who I am today.

It wasn't until I was an adult that I realized the impact and influence Grandma Ruby had on me. As a child I had never realized that she was considered the premiere "Cheer Lady" among locals. She loved to dance and attend potluck dinners and parties at her local senior center. She made an amazing impact on not only me, but a small town in Montana, too.

Something else I didn't know about Grandma Ruby was that she had both the systemic and discoid forms of lupus. This meant that she was allergic to almost everything: junk foods, alcohol, perfumes, prints, inks, pens, pencils, and chemicals of most types. The sun was her enemy as well, which explained why she always carried an umbrella (which I just thought was fun) when she went walking. She never complained; she always said what a full life she had. Talk about a woman of impact!

She was the walking, talking, living, breathing example of a Strong Girl. Thinking back now she always had on her Cape of Confidence and her attitude was ALWAYS UP, ALWAYS POSITIVE; she was ahead of her time. The feelings and intentions that came with her words are what I carry today as an adult.

You, too, may have a strong woman in your life who provides this message of strength to you. But if you don't, I'm here to tell you, we are here for you.

You are a Strong Girl. You are amazing, you matter, and you DO make a difference.

That's why I started this Strong Girl Movement. We ALL have a Strong Girl in each of us. Strong Girl Spirit wants to be there for you, to support you and help you realize that at any age, you are awesome. The Strong Girl Movement wants to help you see the real, fun, flawed, quirky, amazingly beautiful, strong YOU!

As I turned fifty-five this year, this project just flowed from me. I can tell you that at times I thought, *Why I am doing this now, why am I even going to take this path? Is it too late for me?* Well, ladies, let me tell you, age doesn't matter; it matters what your story is, when and if you are ready. I now realize that I wasn't ready at twenty, at thirty, or even at forty. I was still working on developing myself and making this path the right path with the right experiences to share.

About eleven years ago, in my new role at my corporate job, I was asked to deliver an hour and a half presentation. I delivered this hour and a half presentation in about twenty minutes flat. I never looked at the audience even once; all I did was read the slides, or should I say, speed-read the slides. In no time at all, the presentation was over and I quite literally thought I would never work again. I just knew my new role would now be my ex-role. To make it worse, my new boss was in the audience to observe me; perhaps that's why I went so fast. I wanted to show her my auctioneer skills. Kidding (glad I can kid about that now.)

Afterward, she said to me, "Terrie, now that you know what that feels like, just don't let that happen to you twice."

Great advice, because I decided in that moment I would get really good at this skill, and I did just that. It has and will continue to serve me well with this positive movement. The lesson here is to learn from your mistakes. We all make them, but if we grow and learn from them, then they weren't mistakes.

I had an "a-ha" moment this year. As I reflected over my life, everything—and I mean everything—that has happened in my life was meant to bring me to you, to this movement of Strong Girls.

Push higher, live higher, be higher … exceed your expectations. Fill your soul and your mind with positive words of encouragement. Be the example other Strong Girls can follow.

Do you have a superhero you admire? I challenge you to take a look in the mirror. Who you see staring back is the only superhero you will ever need to admire. I want you to think about the times when life surrounds you with obstacles, negative circumstances, and roadblocks. Now imagine you have a cape you can put on: your Cape of Confidence.

When life gets too heavy, you can put on your Cape of Confidence. This is how you will fight the negativity, the sadness, and the obstacles staring you down. You are a Strong Girl. Whatever you may be going through is meant to be part of your plan. Your plan to grow you and make you stronger.

While what I went through as a young girl and even as an adult was tough, I can only imagine what our girls go through today. So when life gets too tough to stand, kneel and pray, because God is always listening and he is always there for you.

As I close this story, let me share one last thing with you about Grandma Ruby. She would say anyone can have a great attitude. I get that sometimes that can be a tall order, so that being said, on your next tough day or when you're feeling down, just try humming "Zippity Doo Dah," and after a minute or so you will feel better. We can't always choose our physical state, but we can choose our mental state. We can choose a positive attitude!

I think you can all see how a positive approach to life, people, and situations can be a benefit in your everyday journey to being a Strong Girl.

Let's all try to adopt it for ourselves. You remember how to hum, don't you?

Inspire … Empower … Encourage … Embrace

ABOUT TERRIE PETERS

For more than forty years, Terrie Peters has built her brand and credibility through her "boots on the ground" life experiences. Working with and building up people is her passion. She has held several roles including coaching, teaching, and training individuals and store teams across the U.S. and Canada. She currently serves as an Associate Advocate in her role as HR Director for a Fortune 500 company.

Terrie Peters has teamed up with her daughter, Monica, and granddaughters, Rylee and Desi, to help move forward the message of positive power within each girl and woman. Together they are working to create daily positive journals to inspire, empower, encourage, and help plant and grow their individual seeds of strength.

To further spread the positive seeds of strength, Terrie speaks to girls and women in churches, schools, and business groups.

Strong Girl Spirit is about sharing our passion for people through inspiration, empowerment, and embracing the importance of daily positive reinforcement in our own lives and the lives of others.

There is nobody else on earth just like you. Accept and love your Strong Girl ways, your body shape, your hair, your voice, your laugh, your walk, and your sense of Strong Girl style.

Go out and be AWESOME.

How can you become a part of this Strong Girl Movement?

Please share your positive stories regarding your "Cape of Confidence" moments.

Check our website out at: stronggirlspirit.com

Follow Strong Girl Spirit on Instagram, Facebook, or Twitter

Email us at: terrie@stronggirlspirit.com

SLOWLY SHIFTING

Cristina Rodriguez

I remember the waves gently clapping against the sand at low tide one fall afternoon. Sitting on the beach in Santa Cruz is one of my favorite pastimes, and on this particular afternoon I found myself there, barefoot with my toes digging in to the layers of warm sand beneath me. I closed my eyes and hugged my knees close to my chest, taking in the sun and sound while pondering where I was in life and how the hell I got there. Something about the ocean has always calmed me and made me feel at home. I have often thought it was due to my zodiac sign being a Cancer, however, I feel it goes much deeper than that, and, in truth, I still do not know what it is. There is an energy and a wholeness about the ocean that comforts me. It feeds my soul and connects me back to my true self, a woman I lost touch with many years ago.

I found myself on this sunny, perfect fall day at thirty-four years old, a single mom living with my parents, and in recovery for co-dependency, anxiety, and depression. I had been living at home with my parents and my two children for four months, gently caring for my son and daughter with the smile on my face I had crafted many years before. It was sweet and glowy, like a delicate stream of honey flowing off of a spoon into a cup of tea. I knew this smile well, and it was completely inauthentic. To many it was the face they always knew. The face I allowed them to

43

see. I knew exactly when to turn this face on to certain people, making subtle changes only I could detect to accommodate who I was spending time with. "Who do they want to see today?" I would ask myself. Yet deep down in the core of my being there was a dark space that I found myself living in. On the surface, I appeared strong. Independent. Happy. Inside, I felt lost. Hopeless. Abandoned. I felt like a failure to my children and to myself.

"Who am I?" This was the question I asked myself while wiggling my toes deeper in the hot sand, letting the grains fall every which way across my skin, eventually settling into the crevices between my toe nails. They reminded me of my life experiences. Some would fall right off my feet and back into the vastness of the beach. Experiences I allowed to fall away from my being with no second thought. Those that stuck to my feet I stared at, wondering which ones would stay the longest and which ones would eventually wear out their welcome and disappear. I closed my eyes and looked up at the sun, feeling the heat on my face and seeing the red glow behind my eyelids. It filled me with a sense of wholeness, something I had not felt in a long time. All of a sudden, a flood of memories filled my mind with the same intensity as the waves that were hitting the shore. Memories that would, ultimately, erupt within me a drive to begin a life-changing journey.

Over the years, I mastered the art of people pleasing. I learned how to reinvent myself based on who I thought people wanted me to be. Growing up with three older brothers, I learned how to be tough and adapt my personality to be able to participate in their games and adventures. As their only little sister, I created a story in my mind that I had to prove I was strong enough to be a part of the action. I remember times when I would get hurt as a result of the roughness of our play. Wrestling and jumping from tall tree branches filled our afternoons, and oftentimes resulted in some pretty gnarley bruising. I smiled to myself as I remembered this time in my life. My brothers would surround me as I began to cry, telling me to breathe and repeat the mantra, "Be tough,

Key! Be tough!" Key was the nickname they had given me when I was a baby and they still call me that today. As Key, I learned how to be tough and take pain. I learned how to internalize it, feel it, and create a relationship with it that was very accepting. In many ways, I appreciate my brothers teaching me how to tolerate physical pain. It definitely came in handy during childbirth! The internal battle that I created as a result is still ongoing. I learned in those moments how to be tough. Ultimately, however, I created an identity that I connected with and held on to for my entire life.

This identity held a belief that other people and how they felt was more important than how I felt. A belief that told me time after time, experience after experience, that I needed to swallow my pain when I felt I was mistreated because the other person was hurting, too. Hurt people, hurt people, I would tell myself. I began to integrate myself fully into the identity of a martyr. My beliefs and feelings were not as important as someone else's. I believed this so completely, that I found myself throughout the years in situations where I began to allow abuse, neglect, and manipulation fill my life. "Hurt people, hurt people, Cristina. Help them. You will be fine. It isn't that big of a deal. Don't overreact and cause a problem. Suck it up. You know who to be to fix this."

Tears streamed down my face and fell into the sand beneath my legs. Therapy had been very beneficial to me in the months prior to my day on the beach. I began to deconstruct every identity I had created for myself and allowed myself to begin to feel my feelings, something I had not allowed for more than fifteen years. The flood of emotions kept coming up from my core, seemingly in sync with the crashing of the ocean waves in front of me. With every heave and gasp I expelled pain and breathed in love.

Love was always something I desired and still desire. I spent many years believing that I would receive this love from someone else. I gave so much power to another person, telling myself that I needed to be perfect in order to earn from them the love I wanted so badly. Thus,

I found myself in the constant pursuit of perfection. People called me the "perfect girlfriend." I would never get mad; I accepted being lied to, cast aside, told I wasn't smart and needed someone to go with me to college in order to graduate, stood up on dates, and gaslighted. So many toxic behaviors from different people that I felt were acceptable. I would convince myself that it was my fault, that I wasn't trying hard enough and needed to work on being better so they would love me and want to be with me. Only the more I tried, the more I was either ignored, made to feel like I was inadequate, or dismissed. The dark hole in my heart grew with each experience, and all the while I kept that honeydew smile plastered firmly on my face. It became like a shield of armor protecting me. It was the only thing I knew how to control.

The cycle continued through the years until I finally began to listen to and pay attention to my intuition. In that moment on the beach, with the tears and the heaves and the gasps flooding my being like a ritualistic drum, I began to feel the little girl inside of me again. The little girl was crying with me, asking why I left her. She was scared, hurt by me, and felt alone. I decided in that moment to never leave her again. I promised her that I would love her, listen to her, and care for her for the rest of my life. I hugged my knees tighter to my chest and cradled my inner child like I would cradle and comfort my children. I found myself again on the beach that day, and that experience was the doorway I needed to walk through to begin a spiritual journey of transformation and empowerment.

The journey along the path of depression is long, dark, and arduous. In the months that followed my inner child experience, I struggled through every day and every step I took. For six months, the realization that I truly had abandoned myself for what seemed like my entire life spawned a period of depression that, at the time, I felt would never end. My days were a repeat of the same behaviors and activities: wake up with the kids, feed kids, play with kids, nap with kids, wake up, bathe kids, feed kids, read and play with kids, go to bed. Every. Day. My only interruption to this routine was my hour therapy appointment each week. My sessions were filled with tears, release, and asking why I wasn't getting better. "I've discovered so much and I want to be better, why don't I feel better yet?!" I would ask my therapist. I was so frustrated day in and day out because I wanted so badly to laugh again, to have the desire to go outside and feel the sun. I knew there was light at the end of the dark tunnel I found myself navigating, and I was trying to rush to the end. Depression doesn't work this way, however, and until I leaned into it and truly let myself be in that deep, dark place, I wasn't going to find a way out.

One night, as I was lying in bed, I felt the pang of emptiness overcome me. A loneliness that resonated throughout my entire body. In the past I would put on headphones and listen to music to distract myself from feeling it. This time, however, I decided to shake its hand. That hand shake turned into a hug, and a night that was so scary and transformative I will never forget it. By morning my eyes were red-rimmed and puffy. I felt like I'd been through a battle of wills to unleash myself from the grip depression had on me. I conquered it by loving it. I looked at it like an angry child. A child who did not feel loved and was punishing me, demanding that I see it and feel the pain it was feeling. It did not want to be ignored any longer. I gave light and presence to it and it hurt so much. I told it I appreciated it, for I knew that when it was time to be released from me I would be a stronger person. The result was something I hadn't felt in a very long time: hope. A lightness had entered into my chest. I rolled out of bed and looked at myself in the mirror and knew the day would be different. Oh, how different it was.

The first change to my day was small, and enormous. I ate breakfast. A good breakfast. I made myself eggs and bacon and savored every bite, slowly eating and noticing how good it felt to enjoy food again. I showered, and spent an extra five minutes in the heat, allowing myself to breathe deeply and feel the water rinse the toxins off of my body. I spent time blow drying my hair and doing my makeup, something I had not done in a long time. I put on a cute top and stared at myself in the mirror. I didn't recognize the woman in front of me, and I knew I liked her a lot.

I left the house and decided to go for a walk in Campbell. It's a cute little suburb outside of San Jose with a quaint downtown strip. It was springtime, and it happened to be a very crisp, sunny day. The sky was spotted with white puffy clouds, the kind that looked like fluffy marshmallows you wish you could jump in to. There was a slight breeze through the newly sprouted leaves and flower buds on the trees. The air smelled sweet and the concrete was still wet from rain the night before. I began to notice the beauty of my surroundings and my heart started to feel different. I started to feel warm. Interesting, I thought. As I made my way through the stores I found myself standing in front of a small metaphysical shop. I had always felt intuitive growing up, and was often drawn to the Tarot and crystals. I abandoned that part of my being for a long time, and then there I was, standing in front of a store that represented a large part of myself that I ignored for a long time, on a day that had started out different from the get go. I decided to embrace it and walk in. *What do I have to lose?* I said to myself.

The first thing I noticed when I entered was an incredible aroma. Incense was burning and it filled my lungs with a comfort that flooded throughout my body. The energy from the crystals in the store was magnetic. I wandered the aisles with an awe and interest that must have shown on my face, like a child in a candy store. I noticed that the store offered psychic readings and Reiki healing, and I immediately asked for one. The man working had availability, so I did a reading. It was life changing. I was so inspired that I booked another session for a few days later.

I had never heard of Reiki or energy healing before, and something inside of me felt pulled to it. As I parked the car and walked in to the shop for my session, I felt a mix of emotions. I was scared, nervous, apprehensive, and excited. I knew that this would shift something in my life, and I was so ready for it. I laid down on the table and closed my eyes, breathing deeply in and out as the session began. I remember feeling warm and comforted as the practitioner healed and balanced my chakras and my energy flow.

Chakras and energy were two things I knew nothing about at the time. I was led there feeling a sense of loss and I left the session that day feeling whole and full of hope. I went home and began to research Reiki and the chakra system. I found myself over the next few months with a new-found interest in different forms of healing. I began to see my friends again, enjoy reading and shopping again, and I began to experience and take in the world around me with a newfound appreciation for life. The blessings and healing that came as a result of my Reiki session led me to dig deeper into what I wanted to do with my life. I started to allow myself to think about all the possibilities that were in front of me, and began to have faith in a better, brighter future. I knew that everything was going to be ok.

Since that initial Reiki session, many changes have occurred in my life. I found the inspiration to apply for my Master's degree in Holistic Counseling Psychology. It had always been a dream of mine to be a therapist, and so I made the decision to go for it. I was so shocked and excited when I received my acceptance letter. Going back to school at thirty-five with two small children has been such a rewarding and challenging experience. There are still times when I question if I made the right decision and if I am doing the right thing. I accept that these questions will pop up from time to time, and I shower light onto them with appreciation in reminding me why I made the decision in the first place. I have moved out on my own with my two kids, and we have created a happy home for ourselves that is bathed in love.

Recovery from depression, anxiety, and co-dependency is a continual process. Self-doubt creeps back in from time to time. Reiki has helped me in overcoming fear and doubt. So much so that I decided to learn, train, and become attuned to Reiki. I am a certified Reiki Master Healer and now have my own business as a Reiki practitioner and Life Coach. I am dedicated to helping and supporting others heal and discover their true calling, just as I did.

A client who was enveloped in grief and loss said to me after her first Reiki session, "I don't know what to say … I just feel like after all this time everything is going to be ok. I finally feel at peace."

These are the special gifts Reiki gives, and this is what drives my soul. It has been two years since that day on the beach. Two years since I dared to feel what I was so scared to feel. I look back on what I have gone through with gratitude and appreciation. I honor every moment, no matter how painful. For if I had not gone through it, I would not be where I am today. There's a whole lot of love, support and hope in that, friends. A whole lot.

ABOUT CRISTINA RODRIGUEZ

At thirty-four years old, Cristina Rodriguez embarked on a life-changing journey of healing. This journey took many twists and turns, ultimately guiding her to discovering the benefits of Reiki energy healing and a rediscovery of her spirituality. In March of 2018, Cristina became a certified Reiki Master Healer. Upon completing her Reiki certification, the doors to her company, The Blossoming Lotus, opened for business.

Cristina services clients from all aspects of life, healing their energy through Reiki as well as guiding them with Spiritual Life Coach services. She takes an individualized and empathic approach to healing for each client. She prides herself in her ability to reach others on a personal level, emphasizing to each client that they are the expert of their life. This ultimately fosters a deeper sense of ownership for her clients in their own healing process as they navigate their life path and create the life they have always dreamed of having.

Cristina is located in the San Francisco Bay Area. She is available for in-person consultations, as well as phone consultations and video conferencing sessions. Reiki energy healing is also available at a distance, allowing Cristina the ability to help her clients from all over the country.

For more information on Cristina, Reiki healing, coaching, and her contact information, please check out her website at www.theblossominglotus.org.

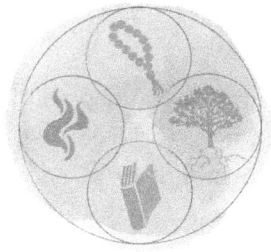

THE WOMAN BEHIND THE MASK

Patty Staco

Thirty years. Thirty years … how had that happened? How had time been so fleeting? Thirty years ago I graduated from high school, and here I was the night before the reunion, busy with the business of life—work, child, and husband. Just five years earlier, at my 25th year reunion, I was a total wreck, painfully deliberating over every wardrobe choice. Everything had to be perfect. I was going to walk in there with my husband and son on my arms, exude confidence and project an image of a rock star woman, owning her power. Little did I know that I had not yet become that woman, or perhaps more accurately, I had not yet remembered her. The minute I stepped into the reunion and locked eyes with that boy who used to poke fun at me back in the day, I reverted back to that insecure 14-year-old who had already disconnected from her own sense of self-worth. I spiraled down into my old story and once again became the scholarship kid, not worthy of being around these children of privilege, the one who had to earn her right to be there.

Fast forward five years. The night before my 30th reunion, with a load of laundry in the washer, I was wrapping up some work while dinner was being delivered. I looked down at my un-manicured hands, dry cuticles and all, and then down at a two-and-a-half-week-old pedicure. For a split second I pondered how I could possibly squeeze in a mani-pedi in the few hours I would have the next day. That thought only lasted a few seconds. "Nope, not going to do it!" I said. No new outfit, no mani-pedi; there was no need.

For so much of my life, I was a master of showing a good face, all while struggling on the inside to live up to what I thought was expected of me. And here I was at forty-seven years old, deciding that my manicure would be me slathering my cuticles with my secret weapon, Neosporin! My feet would be just fine in the enclosed boots I intended to wear with the black pant suit that was already in my closet. SHUT THE FRONT DOOR ... REALLY?! Could life be that easy? Could I really have not one concern in the world about confronting my past and showing up as me? Could I actually be THAT woman? DAMN SKIPPY!

It was never about the clothes, the perfect nails, a flawless face, or any of that. It had always been about how I felt about myself. I was finally in a place where I RE-MEMBERED who I truly was. I had reclaimed all of the parts and pieces of me I had given away or allowed to be taken away. I was feeling WHOLE, content, and so comfortable in my own skin that this 30th, albeit a blip on most people's radars, ended up being my own personal debut! I walked into that reunion with my head held high, authentically me, feeling an inner peace and confidence that, it turns out, only I could ever give myself. There were no triggers, no flashbacks, no insecurities, just me, 100 percent me, fully present, owning who I was and blessed to realize that I had become the woman I so longed to be just five years earlier. I was my own source of acceptance, love, and confidence. I was at home within myself and regardless of what was happening around me, this feeling was unshakeable.

When I look back now, I realize that this pivotal night was at least a decade in the making, but even before that, I must acknowledge where I once was and where it all began. Too often, my focus has been on the end, the goal, reaching the peak of the mountain. In those moments when I questioned my ability to carry on, my focus was always on how far away it seemed, instead of honoring where I was and appreciating how far I had come.

I invite you to look back with me as I honor the gift of the climb and how far I have come. I was born in 1970 to Haitian emigrants. For any of you who may be first generation Americans like me, you're familiar with the expectations. For those of you not blessed with firsthand experience, let me give you a peek. The purpose of life was to create stability and security, in the form of exceptional grades, advanced degrees, a good job with great benefits, including a 401K, preferably as a doctor or lawyer, since, as my father put it, "There will always be sick people and people suing each other in this country." There were great expectations placed upon me and being the good little girl that I was, I took them on and made them my own.

At the age of twelve, I was actually still in touch with that part of myself that knew who she was and what brought her joy. I wanted to be an actor. I wanted to touch people's lives by performing, and from that place of immense fulfillment have an impact on their lives, if only for one night.

I remember as if it was yesterday: my father, in his most sincere, loving way said, "Do you really think that out of a thousand people going for a part, you would get it?" I remember feeling anger, then sadness, then discouragement, and finally resignation. My own father didn't think I could do it, so maybe I was crazy for allowing myself to believe in this "dream." And there you have it ... the day I quietly tucked away that truest, most pure part of me. That girl with big dreams and a deep connection to the light within her, discovered that listening to others and denying her power and her gifts was a way to survive and be safe.

Since calculus was not my strong suit and an unfortunate requirement for the pre-med track, my only other approved option was to become a lawyer. And so I did just that ... I graduated from law school, passed the bar, and went into corporate America, working for a large tech company. I had checked all of the boxes, and yet there was something missing. It wasn't something I could identify, simply a nagging feeling, but nothing that happy hours, hanging out with friends, and making money couldn't fix—or more accurately, silence.

Everything after that became about playing it safe, doing the "right" thing, being practical, living up to impossible standards of self-imposed perfection; in essence, being whoever everyone else expected or wanted me to be. I systematically began losing more and more of myself in those roles and expectations.

Don't get me wrong: this isn't about placing blame on my parents, but about honoring their courage, strength, and fearlessness by building upon it and daring to be ME! You see, they took that initial leap of faith. They came to this country seeking more opportunities. They came with their dreams and visions, and when we were born, it was as if they vowed that all of their sacrifices would not be in vain; their children would go far beyond their own achievements.

A noble intention indeed! But the catch was that our achievements and what they should look like were suggested out of fear. So, doctor or lawyer, accountant or engineer, we picked up the dreams of our parents, made the "smart and practical" choices and, for some of us, started down the path of a life half lived. Practical, YES. Stable, probably. Fulfilling, NO.

When I was younger, I couldn't see that this was LOVE. It felt like a part of me was being denied, ripped out. Yet, as I now know, it was a love whose purpose was to shield me from pain, disappointment, and having to rely on anyone else. It was a love that plagues every parent ... a love whose purpose is to prevent our children from taking risks and getting hurt. But it was also a love that stirred up self-doubt, denial of and disconnection from my true self—and resulted in buying into their fear and playing small.

All was good. I was living life ... nothing extraordinary, but nothing to complain about. Until, that is, I gave birth to my son. Motherhood broke me and then it broke me wide open. I discovered fairly quickly that I could not live up to this mythical creature called "Mom" who I had created in my head. I hit my own personal rock-bottom. Turns out, this person I had convinced myself I was my whole life was a paper-thin façade. I had become a master shape-shifter, wearer of masks—masks of competence, reliability, "stick-to-itiveness," "I've got this," "no help required." But get this: throw in hormones, sleep deprivation and the presence of a little being, sans instructions, and once tested, this made-up persona could not bear the weight and the impossible standards that I had placed upon her. With one crack, this "being" I had fashioned from all of the desires, labels, wishes, fairy tales, and expectations of others began to crumble. Who was I if I wasn't perfect? Who was I if I couldn't even PRETEND to be perfect? I was brought to my knees after having suffered in silence. Three words came forward during my darkest hours … Who AM I? I had been so many things for so many people that I had failed to see that I had lost who I was. Here I was with this baby, needing me to give of myself for his every need, and there was nothing left to give.

And so the journey back to me began. I had completely lost myself somewhere along the way, somewhere within the expectations, some-where within the need to be perfect. I had lost myself and I knew that I needed to be able to take back all of those pieces and reclaim them as my own. I needed to go back and REMEMBER who I was before everyone told me who I was supposed to be. I realized that I wasn't going to be able to do this alone. Instead of silently suffering, I allowed myself to be vulnerable. I wanted to share my pain, my confusion, my doubt. I wanted safety in asking for help. I needed someone who could hold space for me as my self-judgment whirled around me.

By chance, I stumbled upon an amazing woman who ended up being a coach. I worked with her and through her I discovered an incredibly unique university. Within months, I was enrolled in a Master's program and two years later, at the age of forty, fourteen years after getting my law degree, I got my Master's in Spiritual Psychology and began rediscovering the answer to that question, WHO AM I?

One life skill at a time, I gained awareness of why I made the choices I did. I learned to own my part in the life I had crafted. I took responsibility for making different choices. I did my forgiveness work, self-forgiveness. I tuned into my inner voice. Turns out, the actor was alive and well. For our second year project, we were asked one question: "What would you do if you could not fail?" I heard that little girl inside of me loud and clear: ACT, of course!!! I not only wrote a one-woman show as part of my Master's program, but also had the opportunity to perform it in a festival in NYC in front of my whole family! That night, my father was in the front row holding a bouquet of flowers, and the man who I thought would not understand the humor in my show was the first voice I heard break into laughter. That night I introduced myself, my real self. to my family. And although my mother was no longer with us in the physical realm, I felt her smile and her warmth.

There would never be any awards or nominations for my performance, but there was a wellspring of joy that I connected to by honoring myself, my dream, my vision. The light I felt that night wasn't the spotlight beaming on me from the theatre, it was the light from within. I had never felt so alive. From that pure place, my calling, my purpose became so clear. This taste of freedom I had allowed myself was meant for all to experience for themselves. And so I took all parts Patty, the attorney, the woman trained in both Spiritual and Positive Psychology, the actor, the mom, the sister, the daughter, the wife, the shower singer, wedding dancer, and air guitarist, and embraced ALL parts of me and set out to bring this journey of remembering to every woman who is awakening to that call from deep within her.

There was a time when what held me back was guilt ... guilt around somehow rejecting my parents and wanting to be different, wanting more. But through my work, I arrived at a place where I thank them for going first. I have come to acknowledge that my bravery comes not in the form of living out their dreams, but in the form of DARING TO BE ME and living out my own dreams. I honor them by being courageous enough to simply be me ... and after all, isn't that the ultimate prize in this lifetime?

One of my favorite quotes is from Neale Donald Walsch: "To lead does not mean follow me, to lead means I'll go first." To me, that means it all started with me, the woman behind the mask, really seeing her, all of her and making peace with the reflection staring back at me. The truth of the matter is that when I did look in the mirror, I didn't know who was staring back at me. A little girl lost, I began my quest to find my way back to me. So on this look back, I celebrate how far I have come in order to honor where I am in this very moment.

When I first discussed being a contributing author in this book, I could feel the resistance within me about the title: *Women Who Impact*. Truth is, I am a woman in progress. Writing this chapter was a journey of its own for me, an opportunity to practice what I preach and to continue to grow as a Whole, Remembered Woman. Me, a woman who impacts? Immediately the echoes of an old story came back. "What have you done? What charities have you founded? What are you doing in the world, Patty, to make a real difference in the lives of others?" Knowing that comparison is the death of self, I silenced the intruders, stood in front of the mirror and called on what I know to be true.

I AM A WOMAN WHO IMPACTS, not only because of what I can do, but because of who I choose to be. I am a woman who impacts because I listened to that still, small voice years ago that called me back to my truth. I am a woman who impacts because in my darkest hour, I was courageous enough to be vulnerable and ask for help. I am a woman who impacts because I choose to connect to the intuition that is my superpower as a woman. I am a woman who impacts because I have chosen to go on this journey of remembering who I am, and by doing so, show other women the way back to themselves.

If you are reading this book, you are a woman who impacts. You are a woman who impacts because you are open to seeing the possibility that lies ahead of you. You are aware that your thoughts and choices determine your life and that as you awaken, you have access to creating more choices for yourself. All of the answers are within you. You are not broken and you do not need fixing. You are a woman who impacts because you are a woman remembering. Welcome to the tribe!

ABOUT PATTY STACO
Founder of Unleash Your Bold™

Patty is a Women's Empowerment and Spiritual Life Coach. As a first generation American, Patty carried the debilitating weight of people-pleasing and chasing perfect at the ultimate expense of trading in her dreams for a life of stability, security and obligation. It was through the struggles of early motherhood that she broke down and broke through to the forgotten woman staring back. It was in that moment, choosing to honor the woman in the mirror, that her path became her purpose.

Patty founded her coaching practice in 2012, after feeling compelled to share these life-transforming skills and tools with other women. She had to "take it to the streets" as her own personal journey had now imbued her with a sense of purpose that extended well beyond just herself. Patty leads by going first, and so her purpose is rooted in her own continued growth and evolution. It's what makes her so relatable, approachable, and impactful in the lives of the women who work with her.

Patty is a skilled transformational coach and empowerment expert who is passionate about creating confident and self-aware leaders in business and in life. She leverages both positive and spiritual psychology principles to inspire and empower her clients to own their unique strengths fully. Patty stretches clients to confront and eradicate limiting beliefs, dance with fear, and create a new awareness that supports a creative versus a reactive approach to their personal and professional lives.

Patty helps strong, accomplished, and evolving women reclaim all parts of themselves and step unapologetically into the world because a woman remembered is UNSTOPPABLE!

Patty works with clients through 1:1 coaching programs, day intensives, and group programs under her signature program, Unleash Your Bold™! You can connect with Patty at www.pattystaco.com

Patty holds a B.A. in Psychology and French from Duke University, a J.D. from the University of North Carolina at Chapel Hill, a Master's degree in Spiritual Psychology from the University of Santa Monica, is Certified in Positive Psychology (CIPP) – Certified by Professor Tal Ben-Shahar of Harvard University and Kripalu Center for Yoga and Health, and trained in expressive arts.

FOUND

Stacey Friedman

I dedicate this story to all of you beautiful mothers out there.
May you continue to shine love and light on your little
ones while remembering to leave a little for yourself, too.

Some of my most vivid childhood memories were made down at the shore. My family and I spent the hot days jumping salty waves and the cool nights playing games on the boardwalk. I can still see the vibrant lights, hear the ringing arcades, and smell the aroma of fresh funnel cake. This sensory carnival overwhelmed me as a small child, so my mother always held my hand while we zig-zagged our way through throngs of tanned bodies. Her hand was my anchor. As long as I held on, I knew I'd be okay. Then one summer, without knowing it, I let go. Searching the crowds for my mom's familiar face, I grew frantic as the sound of hungry seagulls hovered overhead. Minutes passed like hours while I stood there all alone, praying I'd be found.

***

This is the first time I remember getting lost, but it certainly wasn't the last. About ten years ago, I switched hats from teacher to stay-at-home mom. As bittersweet as it was to leave my career behind, I embraced the change with eagerness and joy. Like a good perfectionist, I spent months carefully planning for my baby's arrival. I read parenting books, memorized milestones, and learned baby sign language. I studied nursing photos, compared reviews on baby monitors, and reorganized every closet in the house. When my daughter broke my water on her due date (that's my girl!), I was more than prepared.

The first year of her life was miraculous. The milk freely flowed, she quickly slept through the night, and twenty-five of the fifty-five pounds I'd gained during pregnancy easily melted away. I was so in love with my daughter, so happy as a new mother, and so satisfied that all the planning had paid off. I napped when she did, took pictures each month to chart her growth, and followed a schedule for feedings, baby activities, and even some "me time." Our lives were in sync. It only seemed logical to try for another, so just shy of my daughter's second birthday, a perfect little boy was born.

Shortly after we arrived home with my son, though, the sturdy life I'd so carefully built began to wobble. I was in a lot more pain after the second Cesarean, and everything felt much more frantic. It was *unbelievably* hard going from one child to two. I was torn between my children's needs: constant reassurance for my daughter whose world had been rocked, and non-stop kisses and frustrating attempts at nursing for my son. The demands of having "two under two" quickly squashed any old notion of self-care: out it went with the dirty diapers.

As time marched on in my baby-proofed world, I stopped being able to distinguish one day from the next. Though I was madly in love with all the cuddles and coos, every day was Groundhog Day. It was prepping snacks, patting bottoms, and picking up toys all day long. Every day was the same. I tried so hard to focus on giving my kids equal attention, yet somehow the scale always seemed unfairly tipped. To soothe my mom guilt, I did what any good mom would: I gave them even more of me. More playtime. More snuggles. More reassurance. A mother's well for her children runs infinitely deep, but she must take the time for replenishment.

As I made less time for me, I grew more disconnected, finding comfort in unhealthy habits. I'd mindlessly eat from the kids' plates and goody bags, grab extra birthday cupcakes "for my daughter" at parties, and buy bags of tater tots I knew no one would eat but me. Some days I'd sneak away to the bathroom while the kids watched *Peppa Pig* to read a magazine or just sit in silence. Each night brought immense relief after tuck-in. Once my little angels had dozed off, I'd tip-toe down the stairs and sink into the couch like it was the greatest joy in the history of life itself. Then sure enough, as soon as my feet went up, my husband would slide in beside me. Or my mom would call. Or I'd realize that there were still a dozen toys littering the carpet. Instead of telling my husband I needed alone time, instead of letting the calls go to voicemail, instead of embracing my messy home, I'd tell myself tomorrow would be another day, a new chance to take care of me. It was official: I had dropped to the bottom of my to-do list. My spirit withered there, buried under piles of unfolded laundry.

By the time pre-school arrived, so much of the life I'd led before having children had changed. It felt as though I had divorced my former self. I no longer read stimulating books, wrote in my journal, or ate healthy meals. My marriage was suffering, too. I'd grown proficient at thickening the protective shield that kept my husband out. All he wanted was to get closer to me, to know me again, but the truth was I didn't know myself anymore. So many nights I went to bed lonely, knowing that at any moment I could just reach out in the darkness and touch him. That it was safe. That he loved me. Becoming a mom had changed me in every way, though, and I was too afraid to admit that the woman we both once knew and loved was gone.

I felt weighed down in every way, and the symptoms began to show. Lower back pain became a familiar friend of mine. When I'd get a shock from lifting my kids or chasing them around the basement, it was a shameful reminder of my self-neglect. I muscled through it, though, until the day came when denying my own needs was no longer an option.

One morning while pulling on my sweatpants, I was stabbed with searing pain that radiated down my lower back. My entire body seized up. Hunched at a 45-degree angle, I tried to breathe deeply. To relax. Holding on to the wall, I tried to get anchored, but I couldn't. Each time I attempted to straighten, the pain shocked me again. I was terrified. Tears poured down my face as I screamed for my husband, praying my kids wouldn't hear my cries. He rushed upstairs to find me stuck in that position. "I can't do this anymore," I cried. "I need help!" I had finally said it aloud.

After several hours of IV treatment at the emergency room and a lecture on the causes of inflammation, the doctor sent me home with a prescription. As I held the blue slip of paper on the car ride home, I realized there was no pill that would save me. Drugs would only mask the symptoms of a much deeper issue: I'd lost myself.

Once the babysitter left, I sat down on a kitchen stool and took inventory. Dishes still sat in the sink. A garbage bag sagged by the door. Mega Blocks were everywhere. On any other night I'd start straightening up, but on this night, I just let it be. I inhaled. In that deep breath of surrender came the crystal-clear realization that I spent more time taking care of my house than I did of myself. I had endless energy to nurture my kids, but none for me. I thought I was being a good mom, doing all the things a good mom does. But when I flashed back to my children's fearful faces when I'd hobbled out the door hours earlier, two haunting questions stared me dead in the face: *How could I take care of my kids if I couldn't take care of myself? How could I teach them the importance of self-love and self-worth if I didn't show them what that looked like?* Becoming a mother was the greatest gift of my life, and I felt overcome with gratitude that I still had the chance to make things better.

That evening in bed, I thought about all the ways I would begin to reclaim myself. I wanted to nourish my body by exercising and eating well. I wanted to read books again, to connect with nature, and to stop worrying so much about all the shit that didn't really matter, like having a spotless house. It was a start. I drifted off to sleep with hope in my heart for what was possible. Tomorrow, I thought, I would hit the reset button.

When I woke up the next day, I dug out my old journal and made a long list. Then, I called a friend who had once invited me to Pilates and told her I wanted to go. Even though I was out of shape and terrified, I went to class the next day. Then again the next week. For months, I showed up. The slow and controlled movements, the focused breathing, and the mental energy needed to perform Pilates forced me to connect with my body. To be present. Each time I left the studio, my limbs felt longer, my spirit lighter, and my heart fuller. Before long I found myself giggling while fearlessly lifting my kids into my arms. The pain was subsiding. My hard work was paying off.

As the connection to my body grew, so did my desire to eat healthier. I'd survived on Goldfish and fruit snacks for far too long and knew my body was starving for nutrition. I remembered an old friend who offered whole food cleanses and signed up to do one. It felt foreign to load my shopping cart with so many colorful fruits and vegetables rather than the lifeless boxes of processed food I was used to. I bought kale, kohlrabi, and collards, foods I'd never tried. At first, eating only whole foods felt unfulfilling. Then after a few days, I grew to enjoy it. I felt lighter. Clearer. More energetic. I absolutely loved knowing I was feeding my body the nutrients it needed. Even the cravings began to disappear. I learned how to savor the taste of real food and appreciate the way it was healing me. Each time I washed a vegetable, I pictured the farmer who grew it and silently offered thanks. When the cleanse ended, so did the brain fog, bloating, and mental exhaustion. I felt free. I committed to clean eating from that point forward, and I never looked back.

Not much later, my best friend invited me to a New Year, New You retreat. She told me we'd do three days of yoga with a focus on our chakras. Even though I had no clue what a chakra was, a soft voice inside me said "Go!" It was so outside my comfort zone, but the idea of spending two nights with my best friend in a hotel was enough to say yes. The universe had been steadily rewarding me for listening to these whispers, so I convinced my husband he'd do great with the kids, packed a bag, and kissed my family goodbye.

At this retreat, I was given a safe space to tune in, breathe, and reflect on why I was there. We did yin yoga poses, set intentions, and listened to the healing sounds of crystal bowls. It was amazing to have so much time for myself—to have the support and permission to focus on myself. All of this led to an incredibly powerful breakthrough. While folded over in child's pose, placing awareness on my second chakra, I was struck by intense sadness. Tears began to roll down my face, only I had no idea why. When I opened myself up with a deep breath, clear as day, I received the answer. I became keenly aware that the grief was coming from deep inside my center. Instantly, I flashed back to the molar pregnancy I'd had many years ago, before I'd had my daughter. I could not believe it. Even though I had gone on to have two perfect children, my womb was still crying from that loss. In this sacred awareness, I knew exactly what I needed to do. I wrote a letter giving my center permission to let it go. I told her it was not her fault and that I loved her completely. That she was perfect. That she had done a beautiful job creating, nurturing, and supporting my two precious children while they grew to term in her loving embrace. I forgave her.

It was exactly what she needed to hear. Later that day, though it was not my time of the month, I began to bleed, shedding the pain of my past. It lasted for two days, and when it stopped, I felt whole.

Nothing felt the same when I returned home. I was changed. New energy pulsed inside my body. I felt like I was hovering on some higher plane of existence. The world looked so new, so bright. I wondered how on earth I would keep this feeling going. I needed to keep it going—for my kids, my husband, and me. I committed to waking up earlier every day so I could honor this new relationship I'd begun with myself. My morning routine came to include a variety of rituals like yoga, meditation, journaling, diffusing oils, wearing mala beads, planning my meals, drinking tea, setting intentions, writing letters, and practicing gratitude. Embracing these practices helped me cultivate a deep sense of appreciation for my life. I found my voice again. I found my passion. I found my freedom.

My journey doesn't end here. There is *so much more* to discover. I am still learning, expanding, and creating every day. I am forty-two, and it feels like my life has only just begun.

I invite you, dear reader, to view where you are right now in this very moment as the beginning of something bigger. Something better. Something more aligned with who you truly are.

Find your courage. Honor your whisper. Lean in and listen. Then take the first step. Leap. The universe is waiting to catch you.

***

The seagulls swooped down at once, competing for a mess of curly fries. And just as the victor flew off into the night, I felt it. My anchor. The warmth of my mom's hand brought breath back into my body. I looked up at her through tearful eyes and saw the worry on her face relax into a beautiful smile. Everything would be all right again.

I'd been found.

ABOUT STACEY FRIEDMAN

Stacey Friedman is one lucky girl. She has a supportive husband, two huge-hearted kids, and one crazy dog. She loves writing, cooking, connecting deeply with others, and showing up fully in her life each day.

Stacey earned her Master's in Education from the University of Pennsylvania and taught Reading & Writing for more than ten years. She also earned her Master's in Keeping It All Together and, most recently, her PhD in Self-Care. She is the grateful recipient of many distinguished awards from her kids including Most Loving Mom, Most Helpful Mom, and Expert at Making Really Good Cheesy Eggs.

Stacey is incredibly proud of her new business, Lucky Girl Health and Wellness, where she works as an Integrative Nutrition Health Coach. A graduate of the Institute for Integrative Nutrition, she offers knowledge from top experts in the field of holistic nutrition and wellness. She also brings real life experience, enthusiasm, and authenticity to all of her client relationships.

Her passion is to help those who are ready to take the first step on their journey to healthier, happier living. Stacey's programs are designed to inspire, educate, and motivate her clients. She empowers others with the tools they need to live with balance and joy, both on and off the plate. Life is too short to settle for anything less!

You can e-mail Stacey at luckygirlhealth@gmail.com. Learn about her coaching and cleanse programs, read her blog, enjoy free recipes, and follow her upcoming projects at www.luckygirlhealth.com. You can also connect with her on Instagram (@luckygirlhealth) and Facebook (luckygirlhealth). She can't wait to hear from you!

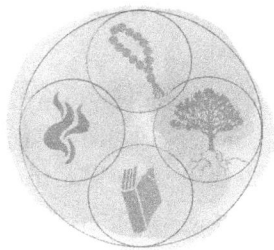

THE POWER OF MONEY ON AN ORDINARY DAY

Katie Jefcoat

On an ordinary day, a moment at the checkout counter at the local grocery store changed the way I lived my life—forever. I was seven years old.

My family had recently moved to a suburb of Kansas City, Missouri—miles away from our extended family and where I had grown up in Minnesota. A new school, a new city, and new friends.

We had a cart full of groceries: boxed mac-and-cheese (it was the '80s after all), potatoes (my mom made the best mashed potatoes), lots of hamburger, canned corn, and canned green beans—none of the fancy stuff like name-brand breakfast cereal, chicken nuggets, or sweets.

We pulled into the empty checkout aisle, my mom loaded the groceries onto the conveyor belt, and took her place at the pay area as the checkout lady rang up the items. I stood impatiently to the right side of my mom as I watched the cashier slowly key in the items, listening to the clicks of the keypad on the register.

As the last few items were rung-up, everything changed. A mother from my new school pulled up behind us in the checkout aisle. My mom gave a nod, a smile, and a quick hello, but at that moment, shame overcame her. And I felt it, even at seven years old. I felt the embarrassment pouring out of my mom's soul. She looked like she wanted to escape.

71

Her body became smaller, her shoulders turned down, her eyes focused toward the ground, and her bright smile became an anxious grin.

I had never seen or felt anything like this from her. My mom is a classy woman; she's a warrior, a fighter, a career woman who is steadfast in her convictions. She's the one you want on your team—every single time. In that moment, this woman standing next to me was not the person I knew.

When the cashier gave the total for the groceries, my mom looked me in the eyes and asked me to move from her right side to the left side, positioning me between her and the mother from my school, suggesting I talk with and distract her, which I did. And then my mom fumbled in her purse and pulled out colored food stamps—which looked like play money—to pay for our groceries. I emotionally absorbed her shame. She stoically paid, and we hurried to the car.

Looking back, there is no doubt my mom was trying to get through that moment the best way she could. Who knows what any of us would do?

From that day on, we never shopped in our town again. We would drive thirty miles one-way to the grocery store. My mom went to great lengths to never put herself, my sister, or me in that type of situation again.

As a child, I had no idea we financially struggled. I believed we had everything we could ever want and need. We didn't have the name-brand clothes or the name-brand breakfast cereal, but I thought that was out of principle, not because we couldn't afford it. My parents worked. For a short period of time, we just needed a little bit of help. It was humiliating for them, especially my mom, who had to use those food stamps at the grocery store. She didn't look like a person who needed help.

This was my first introduction to how powerful money can be. Something shifted in me that day. I decided I would always have enough money. Not just enough—*more than enough.*

Because of my conviction to choose abundance over scarcity that day, I never entertained a scarcity mindset. Over time, this shaped me. In my 7-year-old mind, money would equal my security, so the situation at the grocery store would never happen to me.

I knew I would need a career path that allowed me to make more than enough money. I told everyone I knew that I was going to be a lawyer, get a good job, make a good living, and be secure. I set my mind to it, and I 100 percent believed I would do it. For the next eighteen years I never once—not for a minute—wavered in my ambition and dedication to becoming a lawyer. I knew if I could be a lawyer, and pave my own way, I could make more than enough money, feel safe, independent, and have financial security.

I was told, time and time again, that my dreams were too big and being a lawyer was not in the cards for me. I never believed the doubters. Their skepticism fueled me. I was on fire. I was out to prove the naysayers wrong. I stayed the course despite my circumstances and the critics. I believed in myself and my dream to be a lawyer and be financially secure.

Unwavering belief can be a powerful thing.

Of course, there were easier career choices, easier paths, but I knew if I created this life for myself, it would provide for me. My financial dreams were never about what money could buy. They were always about the feeling of security that comes along with having money.

In the grocery store, I felt my mom's shame and how desperately she wanted out of that situation. I was sure, as a woman, making my own money would bring me the security—and, frankly, the control—I thought my mom deserved in that moment.

* * *

About ten years later, I was tested. I was back in Minnesota attending college and working at a restaurant to help pay for school and living expenses. I was waitressing and facilitating a weekly classic car show. Owners would drive the classic cars to the restaurant and showcase them in the reserved VIP section of the parking lot. It was a fun job. I recorded advertisements and live spots on the local radio station, and each week—in my poodle skirt with a scarf tied around my neck—I would warmly greet and register the guests who drove up in their shiny, perfectly detailed classic cars.

One day, an executive for the radio station stopped by in her brand-new car. Unlike the men from the radio station who I usually encountered, she was a woman. I was so impressed by her. She was dressed to the nines. She wore big chunky jewelry and high heels. She radiated power.

It just so happened that I was in the market for a new car myself. I made a poor attempt at small-talk—anything to connect with this influential, powerful woman in my community. I mentioned how nice her new car was, and added, "Maybe I'll get a car like yours someday."

She replied in the most dismissive voice, "Oh, honey, you will never be able to afford a car like this."

I turned and walked away, doubts immediately assailing me.

Was she right? Maybe I would never have more than enough. Had I been fooling myself? Was my dream to become a lawyer and have financial security just a lie I spent more than a decade telling myself? I certainly didn't have the pedigree, I was waiting tables at a '50s restaurant. She was a very influential woman. She must know a thing or two. Does she not think I'm smart enough? Capable enough? Am I good enough to go to law school? Was this the sign from the Universe telling me not to waste my time and money on law school tuition?

Like I said, unwavering belief can be a powerful thing.

My self-doubt, while real and visceral in the moment, lasted for one hot second. And then I told myself, *She doesn't know what she's talking about. She doesn't know me—I'm about to go to law school. I am more than capable. I will have a nice car like hers someday when I'm a lawyer. I made this decision when I was seven years old, nothing has changed.*

The beat inside of me, my personal mantra.

I'm going to law school.

I'm becoming a lawyer.

I'm making my own money.

I'm going to be self-sufficient.

I'm going to be independently successful, all on my own.

These are the only things I am available for. I am not available for anything less.

My abundant mindset had been forming over the previous decade, manifesting in self-belief that I would have more than enough—that I was worthy of having more than enough. That belief outweighed any doubts that crept into my mind.

* * *

By the skin of my teeth, I graduated law school. I was proud. After graduation, I followed my now husband, Kyle, to Washington, D.C. I took the New York bar exam as a non-resident of New York, which has a reputation as one of the hardest bar exams in the country. I added the Connecticut exam, an extra day to the already two-day exam, as a backup, just in case. I may have a ton of belief in myself, but I'm still pragmatic, and I wanted to give myself the best chance I could. I passed both, which allowed me to also practice law in Washington, D.C.

I didn't have a top-tier school pedigree. My grades certainly didn't help my job search. I was in a huge city where I didn't know a soul—and where most lawyers had never heard of the law school I attended. The cards were stacked against me. That didn't matter. I never stopped believing I was on this path to being a lawyer and achieving financial security.

I found a good job—who am I kidding?—a great job as a paralegal at a prestigious, big law firm in Washington, D.C. I was making more money than I could as a lawyer at a small firm down the street. I wasn't going to be a lawyer right out of law school. Did my dream just implode before my eyes? No. Did I want to be a lawyer? Of course, I did—I worked hard to be a lawyer!

Still, I felt good about my decision. I was able to add value to the law firm and contribute financially at home. Even with the enormous student loan debt, I felt financially secure and in control.

So, I worked and I hustled. For years, I put in 40+ hours a week as a paralegal, with hourly overtime. I worked to prove myself as a valued member of the team and to prove I could be a lawyer at this prestigious law firm. In reality, I had no business thinking I could be a lawyer there. Top tier law firms like this had "recruiting seasons" where they would receive hundreds of applications for only a few coveted spots in the entering class of associates. But I wanted it and believed I could do it.

One day, the firm's managing partner walked into my tiny office. He shimmied around the bankers boxes of documents, removed the pile of papers from the lonely chair across from my desk, and sat down. This is the guy who makes you nervous in his presence. Why was he in my office? What did I do? Was I getting fired? Why wasn't I warned? No one warned me! I must have turned three shades of white. I wanted to crawl into a hole and pretend like I was invisible. My heart was pounding out of my chest.

Then he started to speak. The first minute or two I could not process his words. I finally got it together enough to understand that he stopped by to offer me a staff attorney position with a salary. Seriously? It was happening. I was going to be a lawyer. This was the moment! Fireworks were exploding in my mind, I was already celebrating. My passion for our clients, working late, arriving at the office early, extra hours as the go-to person on the case, the grit, and determination had been noticed.

The managing partner knew this position was what I had always wanted. I had taken the bar exam. I was licensed to practice law. I worked in a law firm. Then, he told me what my salary would be. Without hesitation, I told him that it wasn't enough money and that I could not accept the position at that salary. I explained that with my current workload and overtime as a paralegal, I would make more money as a paralegal than as an attorney at his current offer. I asked him to reconsider his offer.

In my mind, there was no *decision* to be made. I innately knew my worth. He left my office, stunned at my request to reconsider the offer.

I called Kyle to tell him how excited I was that I got the offer and that I asked for more money. I think Kyle dropped his phone. He thought I was nuts. What was I thinking? That's just it, I didn't think. I also didn't leave any time for my mind to talk myself out of what was coming out of my mouth. In my core, I knew I was worth more.

The next day, I was offered the same staff attorney position with a higher salary.

About a year later, I was promoted to a full-fledged associate at one of the largest law firms in the world. In all of my dreaming, I had never envisioned I could have *this* job. There is no way I could have ever dreamt that big. This was so far outside of my wildest dreams.

I'm a girl who grew up in a town so small that it didn't even have a stoplight. I went to the nearby state college and a small law school within driving distance of my parents' house. And, there was always someone along my path who told me I could never do this. I was not worthy of this life. I was ordinary.

But I believed in this. I believed in me. And, in 2006, I was standing in a life beyond my wildest dreams.

* * *

At the top of my game, my husband and I got pregnant. The moment our daughter was born, I realized I would never practice law again.

Looking back, this was the biggest test, and the most impactful decision, of my life. All of this grit and hustle to achieve this dream of being a lawyer, was because in my 7-year-old mind, lawyer (good job) = money = financial security. But in reality, it was never about the title.

I was financially secure. But suddenly, I realized I'd found security in something else: my family. Stability came in the form of a family and not a job. Security wasn't in the form of money, but the form of love.

For the next six years, I lived in the moments of staying at home raising my daughter and later my son. Kyle reminded me: "We're the Jefcoat Enterprise. It's our money and I value your commitment to our family." He poured this into me for so long, that it became my truth. I believed then, and believe now, that my worth at home with our children is of equal value to my husband's job. Still today, he reminds me that we are a team and my worth far exceeds a salary.

Since I was seven years old, I had a goal of being a lawyer. That goal became an identity. Later, I had an identity as a wife. Then a new mom, a mom of two, and a mom of toddlers. When my oldest was in elementary school and the youngest was right behind her, I became restless. Life had settled in around me. What was next? Was this *more than enough*?

My whole life, I had been driven by an idea of what money represented. My drive and ambition didn't disappear when I chose to stay home and raise our children. But money earned simply for a life of security wasn't driving me anymore—not like before. I was sick to my stomach thinking about reigniting my law career or starting a new career with no flexibility for my family. The career I had always wanted, I didn't want anymore.

I was still dreaming big, but this time, for the first time in my adult life, I didn't have a plan—not yet. It was time to figure out my next chapter.

I grew up in a family of entrepreneurs—my parents owned brick and mortar stores—and when I was introduced to my current network marketing company, my entrepreneurial curiosity was sparked. The lawyer in me was skeptical, but the determined dreamer was intrigued. The potential of not trading time for money was attractive. I created a system within my company where I felt comfortable as a professional. I am now a leader who supports a growing global team of dedicated entrepreneurs around the world—coaching them to reach their personal goals and in some cases, change their lives.

* * *

I have a new goal, a new unwavering belief. Showing women that they are not defined by their financial history. In fact, you can re-write your story.

I'm still this 7-year-old kid on food stamps who doesn't take a single thing we have now for granted. Helping my children understand the emotional power and responsibility that surrounds money is a cornerstone to our parenting. I don't know what moment will shape my children. I don't know what money story they will tell someday, but I know for sure they will have one. We all do.

My children will likely never fully understand what made me who I am and why this mission of financial self-worth is so important. Even when you're living on food stamps, you still get to be the hero, like my mom. She worked hard, managing a full-time job plus two side jobs. Her work ethic is stronger than anyone I have ever known. My mom showed me you can get through hard times.

Regardless of where you start, the bumps in the road, the tests, the trials, the ups and the downs, you can always choose to be great. You can accomplish amazing things. You have the power within you to take charge of your thoughts and re-write your story. You deserve a healthy relationship with money. I'm living proof that you can do it.

I still want money, but it's for different reasons now.

Looking back, I realize now it was always about creating a secure environment. I practiced an abundant mindset I created in an instant when I was seven years old. At the time, I had no clue what I was actually doing. How could I? But I have continued to develop and recommit to this throughout my life. It evolved, it grew, and it changed from shame, to determination, to a life beyond my wildest dreams, and finally to a life that is more than enough.

I feel honored and humbled to share my story in the hopes of inspiring you to discover your story, and perhaps, re-write it.

ABOUT KATIE JEFCOAT

Katie is a recovering lawyer and the founder of Kickstart With Katie. As a speaker and workshop facilitator on money and self-worth, her system guides audiences in discovering their money mentality story.

Imagine one trip to the grocery store changing your entire perspective about money, forever—that's what happened to Katie. It wasn't until years later that she realized as women, we tie so much of our self-worth to our net-worth.

Her incredible life story demonstrates for her audience what living an abundant mindset looks like and how they can have it, too. She shares the life lessons that challenged her belief about money, security, and self-worth. Her audiences leave with a renewed feeling of worthiness to show up in their businesses and lives with more confidence.

Katie's warm and inviting nature allows her to connect with women in person and online. As a "big personality" she brings the party and loves to celebrate the wins.

A small-town girl from Minnesota, she exceeded her career goals as a young adult, and then unexpectedly left it all behind. As a dedicated entrepreneur, passionate about showing others how to create the life of their dreams, Katie empowers others to build wealth through her expanding global network marketing businesses.

She lives with her loving husband and two children in the Washington, D.C. Metro Area. Most days, you can find Katie sipping a steaming cup of coffee and creating a color-coded to-do list. To learn more about Katie and access resources to shift your money mentality, visit www.KickstartWithKatie.com.

Connect with Katie on social media:
Facebook: @katiejefcoat and @KickstartWithKatie
Instagram: @KickstartWithKatie
LinkedIn: Katie Jefcoat
Pinterest: Kickstart With Katie

ENOUGH

Michelle Lee

To all the little girls who feel broken and damaged, and are told you don't matter. You are beautiful, smart, and amazing. Your past does not define your future, nor does anyone else. YOU ARE ENOUGH, you are loved, and you matter to this world more than you even realize.

I sat there nervously on an epically uncomfortable wooden bench in court, fidgeting with my sweaty hands, waiting to face my abuser for his crimes. This was THE moment I had been waiting for—the justice I spent more than fifteen years looking for and not getting. I was nervous and scared. I looked at my parents sitting next to me, and suddenly every single time I was abused came rushing back.

I was nine, in the cold shower at my abuser's home crying my eyes out, knowing at THAT moment I had finally realized what I had endured then and the years before. I was washing the filth off of me and asking myself why had I been so stupid before and why didn't I know sooner? Did I ask for it at some point? Was this my fault? Did I like it and I didn't know? Was I the guilty one? Yes, yes, this was my fault, I had to have done something for this to happen. This was the moment I told myself things like this only happen to dirty little girls who are unlovable, unworthy, and disgusting. This is what I told nine-year-old me after the flashbacks of the abuse at the hands of our family friend from the ages of three to six until they moved, and then again at nine when I traveled to stay with them for a gymnastics competition. I felt guilty and ashamed. I had stayed quiet so I must have been guilty. I knew differently. After I spent three hours in their cold shower with the door locked trying to wash it off of me, I got out, dried off, and continued with my trip. I returned home, not saying ONE word, thinking, *how can I face my parents and tell them I did this?* Staying silent only made my suffering worse.

By the time I was twelve, we had moved to a different county, and I felt like I was going to have a fresh start. A girl in my neighborhood took me to a party with older guys where there were drugs and cheap beer. I felt that this must be what it was like to be "older" and I tried to fit in. One guy who was much older than me was showing me all sorts of attention. My 12-year-old little girl mind was having exciting thoughts of first kisses and him being "the one." He asked if I wanted to go for a walk. Of course I trusted him, he was "the one," remember? We were walking in the dark, and suddenly I looked up just as his elbow made impact with my face. I flew back and hit the ground hard. Dazed. Bleeding. In pain. Confused about what just happened. Next thing I knew, my idea of "the one" was on top of me, with a rock in his hand and bashed me over the head. I don't remember much of what happened next. I thankfully blacked out for most of it. After coming to, I got up, stumbling around looking for my jeans, and tried to find my way back to the party. What happened after was a blur. All I know is that I was shattered into a billion pieces.

I kept silent. This was my punishment, I thought, for what happened to me as a child. So there was no comfort, no healing, and no justice. Just darkness and pain. This began my love affair with the only thing I could count on to help me not feel. Drugs. Not only was I doing everything I could to punish myself—pushing myself to the limits, including drugs, overdosing, and suicide attempts—I also suffered from severe anorexia and bulimia. Cutting binges left me raw, bleeding, and in pain. Pain I thought I deserved. I see those scars every day, and they used to remind me of the pain, the embarrassment, and the shame. I was only drawn to those who treated me poorly and hurt me physically, emotionally, or mentally.

At fourteen, I was at a party where people were passing around a needle filled with God knows what. I had one small glimmer of thought, *this can't be my life.* The next day I told my dad that I needed help. My parents knew I was struggling, didn't know why, and didn't know how to help me. I was admitted to a treatment center. Thankfully, both my parents were supportive. My mom even stayed with me on my first night at the treatment center. That is where my drug addiction, depression, and anxiety were revealed. It took several trips for me to admit what had happened when I was a child, face my parents, and tell them the truth. It took several years for me to then subsequently forgive my parents. I blamed them for the abuse, especially my mom, even though I knew she hadn't known. Had she known, she would have stopped it, she would have gotten me the help I needed, HAD SHE KNOWN. But they didn't. They only saw my self-destruction of cutting, drugs, suicide attempts, aggression, and teenage angst in addition to my depression.

My path of self-destruction continued for a few years of yo-yoing back and forth between sobriety and addiction. I began dating yet another guy who was controlling from the start, so I knew he was the right one. In the year we dated he beat me at least three times a week, daily reaffirming my FALSE belief that I wasn't enough and that I deserved the beatings. One night he pushed me out of a moving car and then tried to run me over. Most sane people would have walked away well before that, but he told me no one would want me, and I believed him. In my heart I knew I was nothing and deserved to be treated as such.

One special night I came home from work to find him angry because I was thirty minutes late. He began to beat me with a golf club and scream how worthless I was and that no one could ever love someone like me. I was sure I was going to die that night. I lay in the fetal position, covering my face and head the best I could. He got up and I saw a straight line from my foot to his face and I went for it. I have never kicked anything so hard in my life. He went down hard. I didn't wait, I didn't think, I just ran out of there.

He chased after me, pulling me and hitting me. Miraculously, neighbors from across the hall opened their door and began yelling at him to let me go, and then THEY started pulling me! It felt like a tug of war. He finally let go, spouting horrific things to me and them. They brought me in and locked the door. While one was on the phone with the police the other offered me a cup of tea. The cops came and he was charged.

Sounds like this was going to end in triumph, doesn't it? Finally getting justice? This punk finally going to jail for domestic violence? Let's get back to that wooden court bench where I was nervously ready, and surprisingly confident he was "going down."

The prosecutor informed us that my abuser was prepared to plead "No Contest," which means he isn't admitting or denying he did it. I have never felt so hot in my entire life. I flat out refused. There was no way I was letting him talk his way out of this I had proof, I had pictures, and he was going to answer for what he did. So, court continued. He testified, spewing lies. I am still thinking I have this in the bag. *How could he NOT be punished for this?* I thought.

Then I took the stand. Feeling for the first time, I'm getting to tell MY story. What happened next I could never have prepared myself for. On cross-examination his lawyer brutalized me. It was like I was being violated all over again, telling the whole world and my parents all my failings as a person. Telling why all of this was my fault, especially since I was a cutter, I could have done this to myself. I left that stand shattered. Did I win that case? No. The last I knew he was married with three little girls, which is a terrifying thought.

So, here I was, my one big stand for all the injustices and abusers who hurt me, and I was told it was my fault. I was DONE. I was so pissed off that a court of justice thought I deserved to be abused. In that moment I knew if I was going to live to see another birthday I needed to change my WHOLE life, to become a person who others valued more than a junkie punching bag.

The first step was getting clean. I had been in rehab before and it never worked, mainly because I didn't care enough about myself for it to work. This time I was so pissed off I was determined to make it work. I spent several grueling weeks at home in complete withdrawal, shaking, sweating, vomiting, crying, screaming, hallucinating, and being violent with my parents while they tried to keep me from hurting myself, and them. It wasn't my finest hour. But, one day I woke up, and I realized I knew where I was, why I was there, and that I was hungry. The fog had cleared. I was past the worst of it, but it still wasn't easy after that.

Finally, after sixteen years, it is easy.

I found myself in a corporate job that moved me out of state, which further helped with my goal to change my life. I had a great job where I wore suits and went to board meetings. I was "important." I started to slowly gain confidence in who I was. I ultimately moved back home a few years later and surrounded myself with people who believed in me. I just still didn't believe in myself. It took years of making mistakes, learning, discovery, finding and losing friends and career paths. My validation was all external. My value was directly proportional to external validation, nothing internal. Despite efforts, I always seemed to find myself on the losing end.

No matter what I did to prove my worth, it was never enough. Until I became pregnant. I was fighting so hard for the little life inside me, and he didn't have to prove anything to me for my love, he didn't have to jump through any hoops for my support or me fighting every day to love him. It wasn't just me anymore. I was fighting for his life as well as mine. I was fighting for his well-being and mine. We were one being and the love and protection I felt for the little body growing inside of me started to transfer over to myself as well. I realized by loving him, I was loving me! I also knew it wasn't as simple as saying "Oh, I love myself." I was going to need years of reprogramming, reframing, up-leveling my life, and getting rid of that which didn't serve or support me and my Jack. I knew so much had to change.

What I finally figured out—it was ME. I needed to change ME. My thoughts, my behaviors, my habits, my environments, my everything. It wasn't the abusive guys. It wasn't abuse as a child. It wasn't the rape. I wasn't my mistakes. It was ME allowing people to treat me however they pleased, because I didn't have the self-worth, or self-esteem to think I deserved better. But growing that baby inside of me, protecting and fighting for him, I realized I was just as worthy and loved as he was and no matter what, I would become the best me I could be. I knew it was going to take some SERIOUS work, and I AM committed to being the best me I can be.

This is just a glimmer of my life; I still make mistakes, still have days when I fall apart. Self-worth is not a destination, it takes constant loving attention, grace, and compassion for yourself to manifest and last.

I have battled with self-worth since I was a child. It is a lifelong journey to reframe the habits, and most importantly, the beliefs I had in myself. Once I became consistent in my practices, shifts started to happen. One of my biggest shifts recently was reframing my thoughts. Instead of saying to myself, "Why did you eat that, it's just going to make you feel like crap," I show gratitude for the food I do have. It is about facing my limiting beliefs and letting them go. I am focusing on me, the real me, and figuring out who I really am.

I have continually surrounded myself with people who are uplifting and encouraging, and walk away from those who are not. I have been blessed to have had some incredible people in my life and still do.

I have continued to grow, learn, adapt, attend events for personal and professional development, ASK questions, and seek mentorship. I make mistakes, I learn from them, and move on. I read, I meditate, I pray, I journal, and I add time to my calendar for my own well-being.

I have made self-care non-negotiable. I am worth it and my little guy deserves the best version of me. It has taken me years to be able to say that I am worthy and ENOUGH, and not because someone else said so, but because I now finally am able to say it AND believe it.

ABOUT MICHELLE LEE

Michelle Lee is a multi-passionate mompreneur, author, Certified Jack Canfield Methodology Trainer in The Success Principles, business strategist, and intentional living coach who helps other entrepreneurs with scaling their businesses and their lives for more success, joy, and time to pursue their true inner purpose. Michelle started her passion for helping people at age seventeen, first becoming an EMT, and later furthering her emergency medical career. Michelle's passion for healthcare has led her down the path to gaining certifications in nutrition, fitness, and leading a higher frequency life.

Michelle's passion for helping people extends to guiding others to live cleaner lives through toxic-free products, from nutrition and performance enhancement to cleaning products. With her background in emergency medicine, finding her niche in the area of promoting health and wellness was an easy transition. Michelle also works with local domestic violence shelters and organizations that protect the identities of and help to rehabilitate survivors of domestic violence and human trafficking.

When she is not planning women's retreats or large events, coaching private clients, or growing her social marketing businesses, Michelle is spending time with her three-year-old son and family.

To learn more about Michelle, her coaching, books, or work with abuse survivors, you can find her at:

FB: www.facebook.com/michellekatherinelee
IG: www.insagram.com/michellekatherinelee
www.michellekatherine.com
michelle@michellekatherine.com

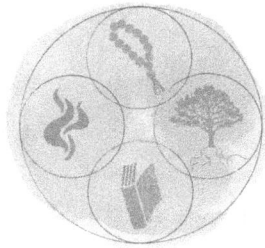

FROM SURVIVING TO THRIVING

Denise McCormick

Gone too soon! Why am I left behind?

A pristine summer's day golfing with friends.
Innocence intact, a life full of laughs.
Another friend appears; we all walk over to speak.
What takes place next shatters lives,
Our innocence no longer intact.
I race to the clubhouse, seek help for my friend.
Since Jeannie teed off, the ball hooking,
Then racing toward and hitting Kathy's head.
Confusion ensues; we all disembark,
An accident piercing a day now forever lost.
I leave for vacation, return the following week,
Not even aware of what havoc had ensued
During that passing week.
I lie down in disbelief after calling a friend;
Kathy died the next morning from that blow to her head.
Too many questions, no one to talk to for answers.
God, why did you leave me and take her instead?
I was standing right beside her;

Why am I left behind?
Her family so loving,
Her goals indeed lofty.
What can I do now? Choices must be positive.

—Denise McCormick

This golfing accident occurred when I was thirteen years old, and it had a tremendous impact on my life that I didn't fully realize until decades later. The realization occurred when I was the instructor for a graduate class with the Iowa Writing Project on teaching writing for K-12 teachers. We were writing the stories of our lives, and I decided to reflect on this experience, one I had never shared with anyone but my husband. It took the form of a poem, and after I read it to the class, the floodgates opened and tears of gratitude poured from my soul as I shared how that event had positively impacted my life.

FACING FEARS AND INSECURITIES

I have always challenged myself to face my fears and insecurities. Growing up with a very difficult family life does not usually give you the strength and confidence to face your fears. My mother tried to deal with my father and three brothers, but she seemed powerless to influence any of them in a positive direction. A book of quotes and being a voracious reader gave me the belief that I could survive the emotional abuse and trauma that I was subjected to in my very early years.

Following the golfing accident, I believed that God and the universe had a purpose for my life. From that day on, I put positive energy into my life and never used my dysfunctional family life as an excuse. I also found positive adult mentors who greatly impacted my life.

The first one was my grandmother. She was a marvelous piano player, and her house was an escape for me. From age seven on, my piano skills thrived through her love and attention. Her love of music was a passion that she passed on to me. Another great mentor for me was Betty Becker, a high school music teacher. She insisted that I try out for the first community theater musical, *Gypsy*, when I was a senior in high school. I remember walking into the university building for tryouts and wanting to turn around and walk out, but Betty's encouraging words echoed in my mind. Her belief in me helped me overcome my fear. I was chosen for the lead of *Gypsy*. This experience gave me the confidence and courage for a lifetime of choices that I would be making following my marriage three years later.

Our wedding took place on a hot, sunny Iowa day in June during the bicentennial year of 1976. The ceremony occurred in the same church where both of our parents and grandparents had been married. I was so happy to be marrying John, who has been my best friend and soulmate for forty-two years now. We met the previous summer before I returned to college at Iowa State University. It was my junior year, and by the end of the first quarter, I made the decision, with John's blessing, to return to our hometown and go to college at Iowa Wesleyan University.

Since I had experienced an unstable early childhood, I never expected I would meet anyone like John. He came from a large, loving family of twelve children. As I got to know him, his character was what I most admired. His father had died when John was a senior in high school. He had taken over the responsibilities of their fourth-generation farm with his older and younger brothers to help his mother support his siblings. We were engaged by that Christmas, and after the wedding, were on our way to Florida for a two-week honeymoon at my grandparents' condo. Little did I know that events beyond our control would make it impossible for us to take a two-week vacation again for twenty-five years.

We made the decision to start our family the next year, since I was a music major and had found the job market in our town limited. We both agreed that I would return to college when our children were in school. Our first daughter, Laura, was born in October 1977, and I was in love with her and becoming a mother. She was a beautiful, dark-haired, blue-eyed baby, and her sister, Michelle, blonde and blue-eyed, joined us in May 1979. Farming was good in the 1970s. John is five years older than I, and had been working. We felt our future was secure. We happily remodeled our farmhouse with the help of my grandfather. If we could've had a glimpse into what the next decade would bring for us, we would have made a different decision about my delaying finishing my college degree. But hindsight is always 20-20.

DOING WHAT YOU FEAR YOU CANNOT DO

The 1980s were a decade for Midwest farmers unlike any since the Great Depression. Surviving the 1980s Farm Crisis has been a story that's been riding around in my mind for more than thirty years. It's time for the story to come to light. By the grace of God, I can write this down. Eleanor Roosevelt said, "You gain strength, courage and confidence by every experience in which you really stop to look fear in the face. You are able to say to yourself, 'I have lived through this horror, I can take the next thing that comes along.' You must do the thing you think you cannot do."

This story is about what I didn't think I could do, but had to. I need to see it written down. I need my children and grandchildren to know, and I need John's family to understand. But most importantly, I want to inspire and impact others to know that they, too, can get through any situation with faith, determination, and perseverance. What follows is my story and how I know that people can survive and thrive despite adversity.

The crisis that struck the American farmer in the 1980s had tremendous human costs for so many people in the Midwest. Near our hometown in Hills, Iowa, a desperate farmer killed his banker, his neighbor, his wife, and then himself because he was extremely overextended.

Near Ruthton, Minnesota, a farmer and his son murdered two bank officials who had encouraged them to keep borrowing. In South Dakota's Union County, a Farmers Home Administration worker killed his wife, daughter, son, and dog before committing suicide. In the note he left behind, he shared that the pressures of his job had become too much for him to bear. Also during this time, cases of child abuse and neglect rose ten percent in the nine-county rural area in southern Iowa where we lived. Studies also showed an alarming divorce rate and alcohol abuse in farm families. Many individuals broke under the strain of the economic disaster, and many more who relied on agriculture faced financial ruin.

I share this because the hardest part for me during this time was the isolation we felt because most of the country didn't even know what was happening or what had caused it to happen.

Why did it happen? During the 1970s, the trade barriers were lowered, and there were record Soviet purchases. The farm prices and commodity prices soared. There was also a removal of restrictions on Federal Land Bank lending, coupled with increased lending by other entities for farmland purchases, which led to rising land values. The low interest rates persuaded farmers and would-be farmers to go deeply into debt because they assumed that prices would continue to rise. During these years, income was above the national average, unlike in the 1960s, when income was below the national average.

By the 1980s, this boom was over. Tight money and high interest rates (going from eight percent to twenty-one percent) burst the bubble enjoyed during the 1970s. Farmland values dropped by sixty percent between 1981 and 1985. Things were exacerbated by the grain embargo enacted as a means of punishing the Soviet Union for its invasion of Afghanistan. The loss of this market was felt deeply by farmers, and an oversupply of grain made prices plummet. The average farmer's income was once again below the national average.

We were devastated by these factors and suffered along with other farmers. We watched as many of our friends lost their farms and many others left their farms to get other jobs to support themselves. John's older brother, Phil, left the farm to go back to college. I remember the day I stood in front of John asking, "What do you want to do?" He emphatically stated, "I can make this work, but it will take a long time. I want my mother and siblings to be able to stay on the farm, and I want to ensure my mother's future. I promised my dad before he died that I would take care of everything."

From that moment on, I knew that our lives were going to drastically change. John's younger brother, Pat, was farming with him, and they hired some part-time help. Their Uncle Gene was able to help part-time, too, and John's cousin, Mark, merged his operation with ours for a couple of years to give confidence to the banks of our commitment to survive the crisis.

I knew that I would need to finish my education now instead of waiting. I volunteered at our daughters' school and then worked part-time as a teachers' associate. I loved working with elementary students, and my mother-in-law and mother encouraged me to finish my degree in education. I could only afford to go to school part-time and used my many part-time jobs to pay those expenses. I had been playing the organ at church every week since I was thirteen. I also played and sang for weddings and funerals. My mother-in-law and I took turns taking hot meals to the field. Other jobs included weeding bean fields, selling advertising for a farm magazine, teaching eight piano students on a weekly basis, and taking the maternity leave for a pharmacy assistant.

Our children had no idea what was going on at the time, as we believed that they shouldn't worry about our trials. They loved growing up on the farm with dogs, lots of cats, and pigs to keep them entertained. Dance lessons and lots of extracurricular activities were never denied. John and I did without anything that wasn't a necessity so the girls could continue to thrive. John knew what to do to make things work, and although he never complained, he struggled with alcohol abuse as did many other farmers during those years. I remember being on my knees in prayer many times. There were weeks when we had to go to the bank to borrow money before his Friday check would arrive. The pressure began to lift after the first two years when John and Pat began growing seed corn and beans for Pioneer, and they no longer farmed with his cousin. Their hard work from that time on was instrumental in helping pay down the debt, although it was complicated and time-consuming, requiring triple the effort to plant the fields in the spring. We also survived two extreme droughts in those years, one in 1983 and one in 1988.

John and I knew we would not have made it through all these trials without our faith. We attended a marriage encounter to strengthen our marriage, a retreat to develop individual spiritual growth, and a parish renewal weekend to bond with our faith community for support. These loving faith experiences sustained us while we persevered through the decade of despair that was now known as the 1980s Farm Crisis.

TEACH SO OTHERS SUCCEED

By the end of that decade, we borrowed the money needed for me to finally go full-time to college. I would get up at four o'clock in the morning to study, go to class during the day and then study at the university library until our daughters' school day was over. I then went home to help our daughters with schoolwork and all the other responsibilities that go along with community and school involvement. I was called an overachiever when in actuality it was survival and determination that propelled me to be a straight-A student. I needed to be an outstanding teaching candidate. I knew I could not be average and get a job, as teaching positions were few and applicants were many. Our family desperately needed the second income to survive. I graduated in 1989 from Iowa Wesleyan University with a 3.89 grade-point average. I was the first person in my family to graduate from college. I was extremely proud of this accomplishment, as were those who love me.

That fall, I interviewed for a teaching position in the town of West

Burlington, thirty miles from our home. I went into that interview with my favorite affirmation, "People don't care how much you know until they know how much you care." I was overjoyed when chosen for the position and distinctly remember the principal walking me to my room after the interview and saying, "Good luck," as he walked away. I was to start the following Monday. It was parent open house that next week. I stood there by myself in my new classroom with gratitude for securing the position over ninety other candidates. I prayed that I would survive my first year of teaching and that my students would thrive under my influence and direction. I had eighty fourth- and fifth-graders, and there were thirty fifth-graders in my language arts class. Though the school year was very successful, I never worked so hard in my life. I secured a first-grade teaching position the following year in the small town of Salem in our school district, but it was still sixteen miles away. Again, I worked seventeen-hour days to help our family survive, and ensure that my students would thrive under my direction.

I took thirty hours of graduate school during my first five years of teaching. I started my Master's degree twice, but both times felt that my time spent in class was taking away quality family time and made the conscious decision that my Master's degree would have to wait until our daughters were through high school and college. When they graduated, I returned to graduate school where I obtained my Master's degree and two specialist certifications with a 4.0, and then went on to enjoy teaching college and graduate courses for ten years.

FROM SURVIVING TO THRIVING

John and Pat were now enjoying a thriving farm business due to their sacrifices and good stewardship of the land. They continually won awards for the seed corn and beans yields. We have never forgotten the lessons we learned during those years of surviving the 1980s Farm Crisis. We learned that with faith, hard work, and perseverance, anyone can weather the storms of life to go from surviving to thriving.

WOMEN WHO IMPACT

When I think back to the hundreds of students whom I have impacted during my twenty-six years of teaching, I am humbled and grateful. The privilege of teaching children to read and learn to let their light shine out into the world is a rare and precious gift that they gave back to me. I conclude my story with a thank-you note that I keep in my gratitude journal. I received it two years ago from one of my former third-grade students upon her graduation from high school.

Dear Mrs. McCormick,

Thank you so much for coming to my party! You have no idea how much it meant to me that you took the time to come help me celebrate! I truly meant it when I told you that you were my favorite teacher. You taught me so many lessons I will never forget and many of them through music, which is why I enjoyed it so much! As I continue my education this fall, I will always remember to "be the best I can be." Thank you for all you have done for me and so many others!

Caitlyn

Thank you, Caitlyn, for reminding me why teachers are women who impact.

ABOUT DENISE McCORMICK

You gain strength, courage, and confidence by every experience in which you really stop to look fear in the face. You are able to say to yourself, 'I have lived through this horror. I can take the next thing that comes along.' You must do the thing you think you cannot do.
— Eleanor Roosevelt

This quote has inspired Denise to face her fears with a positive attitude of caring while navigating the ups and downs of family and career.

Denise is passionate about empowering women to live their best life, honor their roots, and achieve their goals through defining the actions necessary to move them forward. Her two daughters and fourth generation family farm in Iowa inspired Denise's courageous triumph over adversity in her personal stories captured in two books: *Women Who Impact* and *Ordinary Miracles: True Stories about Overcoming Obstacles and Surviving Catastrophes.*

Denise seeks to inspire and support female entrepreneurs in growing businesses that make a difference in the lives of others, and creating lives they truly love living. Her current work with the health and wellness industry affords Denise the opportunity to share her caring spirit with women seeking friendship and entrepreneurial endeavors. She aspires to mentor women in achieving their dreams of owning their own businesses and leading them through the process to success. As an active volunteer and chairperson of the 25th Anniversary Celebration of the Iowa Women's Foundation, Denise has made it her goal to help shatter the barriers to women's success that will then allow them to become economically self-sufficient. www.iawf.org

Denise's teaching career is highlighted by a Literacy Award for demonstrated contributions to language development and learning of literacy in the state of Iowa, awarded by the Iowa Council of Teachers of English Language Arts. She holds degrees in Elementary Education as well as an MAE in Education, K-12 Reading Specialist, and K-8 Reading Endorsement. She taught for twenty-six years, spending twenty-three years in elementary education and ten years teaching undergraduate and graduate level courses. For five years, Denise traveled as the Primary Delegation Leader with People to People Student Ambassadors to ten different countries with middle school students.

Denise is an inspirational speaker who also facilitates Jack Canfield's Success Principles Workshops as she completes her Train the Trainer certification. She assists others in discovering their unique gifts and potential through one-on-one coaching or in group sessions.

Denise and her husband John have been married for forty-two years. Together they have two daughters and five grandchildren. They travel often to Australia and Colorado, enjoying time with their families. When at home in their restored farmhouse, they enjoy reading, gardening, restoring antique tractors, and their two collies, Polly and JT. Denise is a singer, songwriter, and pianist who gives her time to many organizations and groups. She is currently compiling the memoirs of their fourth-generation family farm as a legacy to pass on to their daughters and grandchildren.

You can connect with Denise at: www.denisemccormick.com
Facebook: www.facebook.com/denisemccormickauthor
LinkedIn: www.linkedin.com/denisemccormick
Instagram: @deniseamccormick
Email: denise@denisemccormick.com

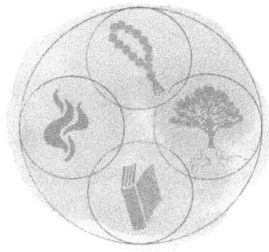

THE FINE LINE

Debbie Pettit

've lived many lifetimes in my sixty years. I realize now that God labeled me a caretaker; that was the job He gave me as my purpose here on earth.

As an only child, I had to take care of myself and felt I also needed to protect my weak and naïve mom, who never stood up to my father, not even to protect her child. The abuse in my childhood home was both mental and physical, and this is where my caretaker journey began.

As my childhood journey continued, I experienced bully after bully for being overweight. As the harsh words, and often times, harsh punches were being thrown my way, I often wondered, *Where were the teachers*? It became clear once again that I needed to step up and take care of myself.

As an adult my caretaker journey continued as God blessed us with a special-needs daughter who couldn't walk or talk. When she was born she was given only a year to live. However, she was also someone who beat the odds. For almost twenty-three years she taught us the true meaning of life until her passing in 2007 from Type B Flu.

I can see now it was those experiences that led me to my chosen career. I eventually lost weight and got into the health and fitness field for thirty-seven years, even opening a successful, award-winning women's health club where I helped many women lose weight, get healthier, gain confidence, and change their lives. It was important to me to create a place where women could go to feel supported, encouraged, and empowered.

Life continued to test my role as caretaker, as I was called to walk with my mother through the end of her journey as I watched her slowly die from cancer. Although I know my purpose is that of a caretaker, this particular experience had a different effect on me. As I nursed my mom through her passing, I was so close to every aspect of her illness. I watched as she walked the very fine line between the two worlds of life and death. This fine line shifted something inside of me, and after she passed I began experiencing PTSD.

In reflection, I realize my life has been a series of walking fine lines. It was these experiences that built up over the years that would bring me to my greatest challenge yet.

* * *

My earliest memories were scary and lonely. I never had the sense of security or love that a tight family unit shares. Both of my parents were hard workers and held full-time jobs, which left me with babysitters most of the time. My sitters were often people I did not know well and was not comfortable being around. My parents never took me anywhere or did things with me as they had busy lives and didn't get along with each other. When we were all home, the environment was one of anxiety and instability. I would retreat into my bedroom, and at times cover my ears so as not to hear my parents' loud arguing and fighting. Many times during my dad's fits of rage, he would hit my sweet, timid mother, push her, throw things at her, and a few times he ripped the phone off the wall so she couldn't call the police. I remember crying, scared he was going to come after me. I was a good child, but it seemed like it didn't take much to set him off into abusive rages. My mom was afraid to stand up to him, so there was no one to protect me from this man.

As I grew older, I was brave enough to sometimes step in on his attacks on my mom and try to diffuse the situation. Sometimes I was able to get to the phone and call the police. They would make my dad leave, but unfortunately, he came back. At night I would lay in bed, listening for his car as he pulled into the driveway. I dreaded him coming home. I was always in survival mode.

As I entered high school, the domestic turmoil drove me to stay active and out of the house. My parents were in a continuous cycle of separation and reconciliation. Why my mother ever took him back, I never could understand! Finally, after my high school graduation, they divorced. My mother told me that my father was gay and she knew it when they got married, but thought once married he would change. I was devastated and angry. I felt like a pawn, like they had me just to cover up the fact he was gay! Being gay was not accepted in those days as it is now. This explained some of his rage and abusiveness, especially towards me. It also explained why my parents would never let me have friends over, let me go over to other people's houses, or have birthday parties.

While in college, I met my husband. We were married in July of 1978, and eventually had three beautiful children, a perfect family! I began to feel a sense of security and comfort. My mother remarried a wonderful man who made her happy. It did my heart and soul such good to see her in a relationship where she was appreciated and loved. My father continued to be a problem, but I finally made the decision to end his negative influence in my life. It was no longer just about me. I knew that his scrutiny and controlling nature would be a very negative force in my children's lives. I ceased all contact with him. I forgave him for all the hell he put me through. He passed in April of 2010.

My mother and stepfather were both diagnosed with cancer in March of 2016. I never imagined they would come down with cancer at the same time, my mom a tumor on the head of her bile duct, and my stepfather, lung cancer that metastasized to his liver and eventually went to his brain.

My mother had smoked since high school and my stepfather was a heavy smoker as well. Their house, their clothes, and all of their belongings reeked of cigarette smoke all the time. No matter how much my kids and I tried to get my mom to stop smoking, her addiction prevented that from ever happening. She was in constant denial of the health hazards associated with smoking. In 2003, doctors discovered a carotid artery 100 percent clogged. Shortly after that she had to have surgery to replace a defective heart valve, and then she came down with COPD. Over time, her breathing became more and more labored, which required her constant use of an oxygen machine. She finally accumulated enough health issues that forced her to quit smoking.

My stepfather immediately started aggressive chemo treatments, which at the time worked well for him. My mom, however, was too thin, frail, and weak for doctors to even think about any type of treatment for her. Mom did not want to stand by and let the disease progress, so she opted for very low doses of chemo treatments. Getting chemo was detrimental to her, a clear case of the treatment being worse than the disease. A little over a year from when she was diagnosed, the doctors told her they could no longer do anything for her.

My mom was sent home to die; she wanted to be in her home, rather than a hospital, for her final days. From the time she was diagnosed with cancer to the point they could no longer help her was the most traumatic time in my life. Watching her deteriorate day by day, trying to get her to eat, to walk, making sure there was food in the house for both of them, making sure their house was cleaned, their clothes were washed, their bedding was changed, all while holding down my part-time job and taking care of my own family. She still felt she could recover, that this was just a bump in the road. At times she asked me, "Why am I not getting better?" She didn't understand her grave condition, which made it even harder for me to accept the inevitable.

Eventually, I had to get hospice involved because her condition required more than my stepdad or I could give her. The amount of time we were allowed to have the hospice caregiver was minimal. I tried to make them understand they needed more help than hospice was allowed to give and that they would have to pay for any extra help. They could afford the extra care, but were very private people, and didn't want more caregivers in their house.

A week before she passed, mom had a stroke, unbeknownst to my stepdad. When I walked into their house the Sunday before mom passed, he told me that she was still asleep. I went into her dark, gloomy, hot, bedroom to check on her; there was my mother, looking like a skeleton lying in her bed. As she turned to look at me, I knew something drastic had changed with her; she hadn't been that incoherent the day before. The look she gave me was terrifying; you could read in her eyes that she knew and finally accepted that she was dying. She couldn't move, she couldn't talk, and it was frightening. I wanted to run out of the room, but I couldn't leave my mom. I immediately called hospice. Then I called the rest of the family. I truly felt she would not be with us another twenty-four hours.

I realized at this point there was nothing more I could do to protect her. I had no control over her passing. When and how that would happen was out of my hands. I had spent a big part of my life trying to protect her and realized I could no longer do that. This was so far out of my control that it spiraled me into deep anxiety. This is when I began experiencing what eventually was diagnosed as Post-Traumatic Stress Disorder.

PTSD is a monster that lives deep in your soul and rears its ugly head when you are most vulnerable. It strips you of all the things you love and sucks the life right out of you. It preys on your mind and morphs you into a person you do not even know. It places such unexplainable fear in you and scares you to the point that you question your own existence. It takes over your body and mind like a snake slowly devouring its prey. It drains you of your strength, mentally and physically. Not only was I losing my mother, but I was losing control of my mind, my life, and my world!

Something was telling me not to go back into that house. I just couldn't do it. I felt as if something drastic would happen to me if I set one foot in their house anymore. It was as if I was a block of frozen ice, unable to move. I was scared out of my wits! Thank God people were coming to sit with her, because I couldn't.

Two days passed and mom was still with us. Just the not knowing when she would pass was so stressful. I couldn't sleep, I barely ate, and my mind was constantly racing. I fretted over knowing that I had to go back to her house at least one more time. The guilt of not being there was killing me, but my brain said, "NO, NO you can't go there!" I knew I couldn't go to my mom's house by myself, face this dreadful situation, and be in this dark, gloomy place another time. My husband and daughter persuaded me to go with them. At this point Mom was incoherent, just lying in bed in her dark room. I mustered up the courage to see her, tell her I loved her and that it was okay to let go, as my daughter, April, was waiting for her in heaven. My mom and April adored each other!

My brain, my mind, my inner child would not let me go see her any more after that. The guilt rode me the rest of the week, but my fear of being there was greater than the guilt. That was the last time I saw my mom alive. She eventually passed on Saturday morning. I am very thankful and forever indebted to my stepfather for his courage, strength, and dedication in caring for my mom during her final days, despite his own declining health.

My mom's wishes were to have a private viewing and service with just family and a few close friends. My job was to write her obituary; how could I do that? I could barely think straight, this was going to be torture for me, writing my own mother's death announcement! Then, I had to choose an outfit for her viewing. I didn't want to even look at her clothes or go into her closets; more reminders that she was not there! I still had a very hard time being in her house, I couldn't do it; my brain was not going to let that happen. At this point I had to get help from a dear friend, a therapist who also helped our family get through the passing of my daughter. I worried and fretted over going to mom's viewing and service. I didn't want the sight of my mom in a casket to be the last memory I had of her. I stayed in the waiting area of the funeral home until they shut the casket, and then sat with my family for the service.

I thought at that point I would start to get better mentally, but I didn't. My anxiety just kept getting worse. Through all of this I was still trying to work at the fitness center, teaching classes and personal training. I thought that would help bring me back to my old self, but the exact opposite happened. I was restless, I couldn't sleep, and I was having intrusive thoughts. My mind was making me think I couldn't breathe, especially when I worked out and taught classes. I would constantly shake and feel like I had no energy. I was so anxiety-ridden at that point that I couldn't grieve the passing of my mother.

When my daughter passed, I developed a fear of going to the doctor. I suppose it was from spending a total of eight months in the Children's Hospital of Philadelphia during her illness. She eventually had come home on a ventilator and we had home-care nursing around the clock. I was so scared of the ventilator, I hated having nurses intrude our privacy, and I was angry that God let this happen to our sweet daughter who didn't understand what was going on. Despite my fear of medical professionals, I knew I had to go to the doctor when my mind began telling me that the constant ringing in my ear was a tumor. The nurse practitioner told me I had earwax build-up. I told her what I had just been through with my mom and she prescribed anxiety meds to take as needed. I looked at that script and thought, *I will never take this! I am not a medicine person! Medicine is poison!* I did not want anything to do with this prescription.

I became anxious 24/7 and the anxiety would come in waves. It got to the point that I was afraid to be by myself. I couldn't drive and had to take a leave of absence from working at the gym. One morning, as I was lying in bed wide awake and extremely tired, I said to my husband, "I can't go into the gym this morning and teach class, I just can't, I am too exhausted, this is it, I need a break." My husband had become my safe zone. I was so scared I did not leave his side. He took off work for a few days to be with me. The day he had to return to work was so hard; I was afraid to be in my own home alone. I would pack up my blanket, pillow, and food for the day, as he was leaving for work at 7:30 am, and go across the street to my daughter's house to stay on her couch until my husband got home at 5 pm. Thank God she lived across the street; I don't know what I would have done if she didn't. There were many times I remember looking out of my daughter's front window at my house, crying and wondering, *Why can't I be in my own home? What am I afraid of?*

As time passed, I realized that my mind thought I was at my mom's house. The darkness in my house caused my brain to think I was still taking care of my mom in her dark, gloomy house. I couldn't sit in my recliner that faced the front door because my mind thought I was sitting in the recliner at my mom's house that faced her closed front door. I could not have our front door closed at all. In just over a year since my mom's death, I still am uncomfortable with the front door shut, as it makes my house darker. I am better at accepting it shut, but it still makes me uncomfortable.

My therapy sessions were once a week at first and my husband had to take me. I was afraid to drive. My therapist decided that taking the anxiety meds as needed was not working for me and suggested I go on a different type of anxiety medication. I was also doing cognitive behavioral therapy, which is trying to reframe your way of thinking, getting EMDR therapy, and reading about PTSD. I wanted to be as educated as possible, and do everything I could to recover quickly. Well, guess what? You don't recover from PTSD quickly, it takes months, even years!

Being under extreme stress, such as I was, changes your brain chemistry and that is exactly what happened to me. The new medication would help raise the serotonin in my brain so I could think normally and, hopefully, return to my regular routine. I was scared, though, of the medicine and its possible side effects. Reluctantly, I started taking the tiniest dosage possible. I was given a 10mg pill and broke it down into .25mg.

Four months after my mom passed, my stepfather left this earth. To relive a viewing and funeral, something that was so fresh in my mind, sent anxiety through my body once again.

I continued to take my meds, but only .25mg a day. My daughter and my therapist knew that dosage wasn't going to help me. I bravely upped it to .5mg for a while. It was during that time that I decided I wasn't going to waste my life sitting on my daughter's couch anymore. I started staying in my own home, driving my car, and going back to the gym. My mind was still telling me that if I exercised I wouldn't be able to breathe right; I would pass out, then what? But I plowed through that, too! I started going to the gym a couple days a week, worked up to taking my classes back, to training and being there and working five to six days a week. I eventually worked my way up to the 10mgs, but that was because my doctor got firm with me.

Many times I wondered, *Why me? Why did I come down with this?* Educating myself on this subject, I found that abused children are very susceptible to PTSD as adults.

So how did I get to where I am now? First of all, God. I realize He has written my story and given me the strength and favor to get through this, as He has a higher purpose for me. My faith in Him is the biggest thing that is helping me heal. Then, I think my strong will and survival mode kicked in from my childhood. I wasn't going to let this anxiety take things from me that I loved. It made me angry enough that something pushed me to get through. My husband and my daughter have been a huge help to me in coping with my anxiety. Next, cognitive behavioral therapy, prescribed anxiety meds, getting not only therapy but also coaching from a Visionary Mentor, my friends, my co-workers, exercise, and going to the gym have all played huge roles in my continued progress.

I am not completely healed yet, I wake up every day with morning anxiety that I have to talk my way out of; eventually as the day goes on, it subsides. I also have a problem with change, anything out of the normal schedule throws me off; I have to talk myself through it. I still get uncomfortable being in certain parts of my home, but each day I am better. I realize now that I have to accept everything that is happening to me and not be afraid of it. I cannot control this, just like I could not control my mom's suffering and passing away. I am to the point where I'm moving through, I'm on the other side, looking back with gratitude. I see things clearly, I know what to do, I know I'm being guided and soon I will be recovered.

These painful moments in my life have changed my entire world, but they have made me stronger, wiser, and more passionate about helping others to pick themselves up when things get tough. I am now able to help others have the confidence and motivation they need to keep moving on.

ABOUT DEBBIE PETTIT

Debbie Pettit is a certified personal trainer, group fitness instructor, and weight loss coach. During her 37-year fitness career, she was the owner of Lady Fitness Health Spa, an award-winning women's fitness and wellness center. She taught fitness classes, trained, mentored, and coached hundreds of women with their weight loss journey, teaching them how to deal with weight loss mentally, as well as changing eating and workout habits. She continues to work in the fitness industry, teaching classes, personal training, and doing weight loss coaching. Debbie has worked with seniors, children, teens, and adult men and women in individual and group fitness settings.

Debbie has been very active in local organizations and volunteering in her community, and was the first female to run as mayor in her town where she was narrowly defeated. She founded "April's Run", a 5K event designed to raise funds for families with financial hardships who have children with long term illnesses and hospital stays at The Children's Hospital of Philadelphia in honor of her daughter April, who passed away in 2007 in The Children's Hospital, forming the April Nicole Pettit Memorial Fund.

In 2003, Debbie received The Salem County Women of Achievement Award in recognition of her positive impact upon the quality of life of the citizens of Salem County through her remarkable record of community leadership and volunteerism, as well as her significant contributions to the community, which also commended her as a woman of remarkable character and exceptional determination.

Debbie's passion is to help others through promoting positivity and empowerment to achieve their personal best both physically and mentally. Her mantra throughout life has been, "Be strong, have gratitude, be the best, and stay focused."

Debbie is a lifelong resident of Salem County, New Jersey. She has been married to her biggest supporter and love of her life, Larry, for forty years. Debbie loves spending time with her husband, two children, Amber and Adam, daughter-in-law, Erin, and two beautiful grandchildren, Leah and Travis.

You can reach out to Debbie through:

email: ladyfitnesss00@hotmail.com
facebook: Debbie Pettit, Woodstown, NJ
instagram: @ladyfitness00

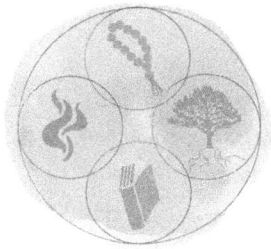

RECLAIMING ME

Violeta Potter

'm a light-skinned person of color, which means that I often have to face little challenging things when it comes to my identity. Like when I'm trying to find just the right emoji to capture what I'm trying to say on social media.

My go-to is the sassy woman one. You know, the one gesturing with her hand?

On an iPhone, you have to press and hold on the emoji to pick the color you want to use. I do that every time, because there's just no way I'll use the yellow one. And each time I do it results in a mini-identity crisis.

I see myself as the brown one. I was born in Mexico. I grew up listening to Juan Gabriel. When I got in trouble as a little girl my mother would call me by all four of my names—Violeta Alejandra Lerma Moreno, and growing up my father's nickname for me was "prieta" because I was the brownest of my siblings. I still am and he still calls me that.

But though the brown emoji makes the most sense for me, I often hesitate to use it. See, online, people don't know my history, and all they see is my light skin tone and make assumptions.

For me, a seemingly simple act like choosing the right emoji devolves into an intense inner dialogue that sounds something like: *Will people think I'm appropriating the wrong race emoji? Maybe I should use the one with black hair? But that one is waaaay too white and it seems like she's supposed to be Asian. What about the yellow one? Nooo, it's yellow and she has blonde hair! … and, aaaaah.*

I know it sounds ridiculous to have a mini-crisis over an emoji, but I actually got called out for using the brown one I identify with! I wrote a poignant post about racial tension on Facebook, and a woman responded with, "I guess I'll overlook that questionable emoji choice, since you make a good point."

She didn't know that I'm Mexican, and she definitely didn't know that her comment triggered the racial identity crisis I've had my entire life.

* * *

I grew up in Santa Ana, California, a city where seventy-six percent of the population is Mexican, though in my circles, ninety-nine percent is a more accurate number.

Amongst my peers, I was one of the few who was born in Mexico. A fact I would often brag about: that I'm a *real* Mexican.

When I would get in arguments with some of my peers, they would use my source of pride against me and throw it back in my face. Without fail, one of the kids would call me a wetback, or tell me to go back to Mexico. They would make fun of my name, too. While I have a very strong Spanish name, most of them had more assimilated American names like Michelle, Nancy, or Laura.

With them, I was too Mexican.

Yet when I visited family in Mexico, they would call me a Pocha, a whitewashed person who has left her Mexican culture. They would comment on my Americanized accent, or make fun of me when I didn't know the right word for something in Spanish.

With them, I wasn't Mexican enough.

What I understood was that no matter where I was, I wasn't enough of the right thing. I was "other," no matter where I was.

And though I was super proud of my Mexican heritage, I grew up in America, and learned early on that if I wanted to survive, I had to adopt traits, beliefs, and ways of being that went directly against my own culture and upbringing.

I had to negate my natural ways of expressing myself, make sure I didn't have an accent, value rationality over emotions, trust reason over spirituality, and adopt a work-hard-till-you-drop mentality. I had to do everything possible to mold myself into the white American standard.

And I molded myself to the point that I didn't even recognize who I was. I didn't know my true tastes, my true beliefs, my true desires, or my true dreams.

I never even let myself feel my disappointments or any of the confusing realities I had about my race and identity. I understood that fitting into the dominant narrative meant denying those setbacks, denying my emotions, and denying the injustices and racial trauma I had experienced. I learned that those things made me weak, and the last thing I wanted to do was be weak.

But at the end of the day, all that inner turmoil chipped away at my person, and no matter how hard I worked to create success by doing all the "right" and "acceptable" things according to the society I grew up in, it never generated the results I thought would come when I followed the rules.

Then in 2017, it hit me. I would never generate success by molding myself into a person I could never be. Because no matter how much I tried to fit into the white American standard, I would always be "other." I also realized that anything I created while trying to fit into someone else's mold would never be right. It would never be me.

It also became clear that if I wanted to generate the massive success I desired, I had to be wholly and completely me. I had to call back all the parts of my personality, my self-expression, my heritage, that for so long I had buried, sanitized, and tried to shave off in order to fit into a mold that I, a Mexican immigrant woman, could never thrive in.

It was time to reclaim me.

* * *

For the last year, I've been on a journey of reclaiming my magic. A journey of allowing myself to shine, to have a voice, to be healed, to love myself in my shortcomings, and even to be a wholly complex being with many facets.

I've been relearning who I truly am, and becoming more of the loving, spirited, and vulnerable person I've always been, but never felt safe to be.

It's been a beautiful journey of healing, growing, and blossoming.

I feel more confident, lovable, and true to myself—with all of those feelings coming from within instead of searching for validation and approval from without.

But the best part of this whole journey has been the utterly comforting feeling of grounding into my heritage, of grounding into my people's way of being.

I've detoxed from the idea that money and power validate my success and worthiness, and instead have returned to the belief that the impact I make and the quality and depths of the relationships I have are what provide true success in life.

I've removed the harmful belief that the individual is more valuable than the collective. Instead, I'm leaning into sisterhood, creating collective opportunities for success, and focusing my efforts on benefiting the greater good.

I've rejected the idea that there is only one truth (often based on what Western, and often white people, believe to be true), and instead reintegrated into the idea that there are many different realities based on individual experiences.

All of this grounding has strengthened me to be a voice for social justice. A voice that calls out the deep hurt, trauma, abuse, and violence that a society—in which whiteness and white ways of being reigns supreme—inflicts on Black, Indigenous, and People of Color (BIPOC).

I know I've been called to be one of the voices that change the tide for the future generations of BIPOC children.

For so long I wished that things could change for me, I wished that racial inequity would stop. I wished that American society as a whole would just one day wake up and create racial justice.

But now I know that a key component of making that a reality is when BIPOC stand up to radically reclaim themselves. When they reject all the insecurities that have been imposed on them by a society that looks down on them and undercuts their humanity at every turn.

The Black American historian and professor, John Henrik Clarke, commented that, "To control a people you must first control what they think about themselves and how they regard their history and culture. And when your conqueror makes you ashamed of your culture and your history, he needs no prison walls and no chains to hold you."

And he was right. That very strategy has worked for the last 300 years of American history.

But now we have a reached a time of awakening and reckoning. BIPOC everywhere are waking up. We are reclaiming our whole selves, allowing ourselves to shine, speak up, and demand justice.

And I am proud to say that putting out the call for BIPOC to radically reclaim themselves is what I was called to do. It's the impact that I was sent to make.

I know now that what I once considered my curse is one of my great gifts. My experience as a light-skinned woman of color who is simultaneously brown and American allows me to be a bridge.

A bridge who can create impact and highlight threads of commonality on two sides of the social justice divide, brown emojis included.

BIPOC, now we rise again.

ABOUT VIOLETA POTTER

Violeta Potter is a high-level business strategist, copywriter, mentor, author, writer, and speaker. Her highest vision is to create a more just world filled with opportunities and respect for future generations of Black, Indigenous, and children of color.

Violeta serves her vision by supporting business owners and brands with mindset and strategy consulting, and copywriting services to women of color and the allies who support this cause. She also serves her vision through high-level masterminds, local networking groups for people with minority identities, and by using her privilege to speak to diverse audiences on a mass scale.

Learn more about Violeta and her work by visiting https://www.violetapotter.com/impact.

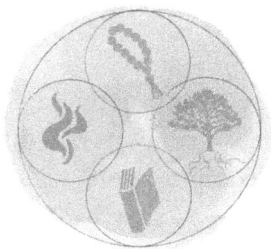

NURSING'S IMPACT ON MY LIFE AND THE LIVES OF OTHERS

Donna Wald

I was five years old looking through the Sears Roebuck Christmas catalogue with my six-year-old foster brother, Arvin. Of course he was looking at the trucks and tractors and anything that "moved", saying, "I hope Santa brings me this one! Oh look—this the one I want!" As we turned the page, I finally saw what I wanted. There was a doctor/nurse kit with a cap that had a big red cross on it, a gray plastic stethoscope, a plastic thermometer to check temperatures, a plastic syringe to give shots, a watch, a toy microscope, and some other "instruments" I had never seen. But best of all, many "candy" pills for different ailments, all of which were housed in a small suitcase with another big red cross on it! I almost wore the catalogue out going back to that page as the weeks went on.

Christmas morning came and there, among other gifts, was the doctor/nurse kit! I don't remember a single other gift I received that year. I was busy telling others that I needed to check their temperature or heart and then administering the "right" medicine for their ailment. By mid-afternoon I had treated so many "patients" that I was out of "pills." When another cousin came to me being very "sick," I had to give them imaginary medicine. But the seed had been planted and from that day on I knew that I would be a nurse.

I had been taken away from my parents, twin brother, and three sisters when I was two-and-a-half years old and placed in three different foster homes before I ended up at the Heinles at age four. It should have been the perfect placement, as I now had a brother one year older and another five years older than me, except that my foster mother was very abusive to me physically, mentally, and emotionally. My foster father was a passive, gentle man who did everything possible not to provoke his wife to anger, which was not an easy task. I quickly learned that my foster mother was jealous of any attention I received from others and especially from my foster father, so I tried to become as "invisible" and elusive as possible and not draw any attention to myself.

When I finally could go to school, I loved it. I learned to read quickly, loved arithmetic and was a straight-A student all through school. It was fun having recess and the noon hour to play with friends. In truth, I dreaded when the school year was done because then I was at home all day helping my foster mother in the house. I was never quite sure what mood she would be in and I was fearful of her anger. I quickly volunteered to feed the chickens, gather the eggs, weed the flower beds or garden, water the cows, sheep, and other animals, anything I could think of to get out of the house. I'm not sure that others knew how abusive she was to me, but my older foster brother did. He frequently confronted her about it even though she would then turn her wrath on him. He died in a car accident when I was fourteen, and I mourned the loss of his protection for a long time.

In high school, I enrolled in all the science and math classes because I knew they would be beneficial for me in nursing school. Many times I was the only girl in the class. I was in many extracurricular activities after school, drama club, school paper, pep band, Future Homemakers, class plays, church choir, Luther League, etc. Arvin had a car so he usually would take me home, but he graduated a year earlier than I and went into the National Guard. That left me afoot and without a way to get home more times than not. My foster mother said I couldn't get a driver's license until I was of legal age and I believed her. If I was lucky, one of the neighbor kids would give me a ride; if not, I would have to ask one of my friends if I could stay overnight. Either way I hated feeling like a "beggar."

The summer before I went to college I had two surprises. The first was that the Heinles took in another foster child, Richie. The second surprise united me with my youngest brother, Arvid, who had been born after I was taken away. He was placed as a foster child with neighbors two miles away. I felt bad that I would be leaving for college and would not be able to see much of either one.

Looking back, I realize how fortunate it was that I was allowed to go to college, as it must have been a financial burden for them. However, my foster mother had gone to Bible College in Minneapolis at a time when women were supposed to get married and raise a family, not get an education!

The drive to Minot, North Dakota, seemed forever. The college and the nursing program were expanding, so the first year nursing students had to find off-campus housing. I was placed in a home with two other nursing students in one of the upstairs bedrooms. The one bathroom was downstairs, which the owner's son seemed to always be in or would rush into when he saw us coming. I and my roommate were transferred to another home close by due to the many problems we encountered.

The first day of orientation at Trinity Hospital was a long walk. I noticed two other girls ahead of us and asked if they were going to Trinity. They answered, "Yes," and we introduced ourselves. That was how I met my dear life-long friend, Lois.

She and I ended up in Group A, our roommates in other groups. This meant that we would do all of our classes and department rotations together. Neither of us had the ten cents for a bus ride so we walked from our off-campus homes to the college, from the college to the hospital, and from the hospital home each day, a five mile trip. We were in great shape and usually beat the bus to the hospital!

Our second year we moved into the Nurses' Home, which had a creepy tunnel under the street that was connected to the hospital. We didn't have far to walk! We were allowed to work for pay, $10/shift, on our days off. Many parents wanted us as babysitters for $0.50-$1/hour. For spending money, I babysat, worked at the hospital, and took care of the Presbyterian Church nursery for $2/hour on Sundays. Classes, studying, and a mandatory scheduled work shift didn't leave much spare time, even though we had many chances to date as the Air Force Base was located nearby. If we would be gone later than 10 pm and weren't working, we had to check in and out of the Nurses' Home.

Our last year we were charge nurses for the various floors on the PM and Night shifts. We had a PM and Night supervisor we could call if we were uncertain or needed clarification, but otherwise we were expected to take care of the patients' needs, something a hospital's liability insurance would not cover today!

We were given two weeks' vacation in the summer and two weeks at Christmas each year. I met my husband-to-be, Ron, after I returned from my summer vacation before beginning my last year of nursing. We married the next summer, had a brief honeymoon, and then I stayed at the Nurses' Home during my work week and went "home" to the farm, where Ron worked with his dad, on my days off. I graduated in August and started work at a neighboring hospital. His dad couldn't understand why I wanted to work, didn't I have a husband to take care of me? I had to quit before Christmas however as I was pregnant with debilitating morning sickness.

Our daughter, Jami, was born on our first anniversary. I knew when I held her and nursed her that I wanted to be a stay-at-home mother to my children. I told Ron that when our kids were all in school I would like to go back to work and he agreed. We had three other children, Nathan, Matthew, and Zachary, in the span of seven years. I was kept busy cooking for hired men, driving silage equipment, summer fallowing, driving grain trucks, milking cows, feeding calves, raising chickens to eat and for eggs, and taking care of the yard and a large garden. Many times I had at least two little ones in the vehicles with me. I helped Ron as much as I could outside and he helped me when he could in the house and with the kids. We were a team and it worked.

I became a 4-H leader when the kids joined, taught catechism, was active on the church council, was president of two Homemaker's clubs, and very active in community affairs. I was very busy and loved my life, but I missed nursing.

We bought the home place and two quarters of land from Ron's folks, but they didn't want to sell us the rest. We knew we needed a bigger place for our family so we sold our land in North Dakota and moved to a ranch in Montana. That first year was very trying—sleepless nights and a worrisome time as the banker who owed us a large sum of money went bankrupt! The kids were all in school, so I went to work at Indian Health Service as an RN. We lived on my salary and borrowed only what we needed for running the ranch. I taught guitar lessons, sewed clothing for others, decorated cakes for special occasions, became the Nurse Supervisor for the Nursing Home in Hardin on my days off — doing everything possible for income. Ron was a good manager, which became evident to the bank, so instead of selling us out, they gave us a line of credit. We continued to work hard and own the ranch today.

I was offered a job as the Community Health Educator for the Little Big Horn College. I was Supervisor of Surgery at IHS, a part-time position I really enjoyed, but I also worked as Charge Nurse to be full-time. I agreed to continue my Surgery position and began the Educator position. I loved teaching the students. I would take them to IHS and supervise them as they practiced their skills. It was a win-win for all; IHS had extra help and the students had real patients to practice their skills on. My program was eliminated when funding to the college was drastically cut.

I volunteered to teach for the American Red Cross, a non-salary position. I taught First Aide, CPR, and Disaster Nursing to the community.

I thoroughly enjoyed this as well, but it usually had to be in the evening, which made my work days long.

The School Nurse position became available and I was chosen. This was an ideal job for a mother! I could watch my kids participate in school activities and sports, be a chaperone on a trip to Yosemite National Park, educate the wrestling coach on the pros and cons of weight loss, and develop and teach a comprehensive health curriculum K-12. And I had summers off! School personnel and students continue to tell me that I made a big impact while in that position.

I used those summers to get my Bachelor in Science, Chemical Dependency Counselor license, and Master's in Counseling. I was approached to apply for a counselor position for a Coal Grant in Big Horn County. Even though it would be a drastic reduction in pay, I chose the grant. I did family and individual counseling at the high school for three years and then the grant ended. I was hired by the school, but confidentiality became an issue when principals demanded I give them confidential information about students. I wouldn't compromise the students' confidentiality so I quit.

I did private counseling for some time and then began working for Big Horn County Memorial Hospital, eventually becoming Director of Nursing for seven years. During that time I earned my Nursing Home Administrator license and graduated with a Ph.D. in Health Services Administration. My published dissertation was *A Comparison Study of Registered Nurses and Business Students for Codependency Traits.*

The Director of Nursing position was very stressful and demanding, especially with the acute nursing shortage. I didn't realize how much responsibility rested on me until my last day of work. As I walked down the hall toward my car, I literally felt a heavy weight begin to lift from my shoulders!

I started teaching classes at Little Big Horn College, became the Department Head for Human Services and then was promoted to Academic Dean. We had the task of taking students who were deficient in math, science, reading, and writing skills to where they could successfully complete a four-year college degree. This made a very positive impact on the community. During that time I was also teaching online classes for the University of Phoenix.

I became (and still am) the Parish Nurse who presents educational programs about various health concerns to the entire community. I take blood pressures once a month. I also make and donate quilts to those who are baptized, ill, dying, or need comfort. I have received many grateful letters and calls from the recipients or families involved. Many who died are buried with the quilt I made for them.

My nursing journey took me to being Supervisor of Big Horn Hospice. Cindy Upchurch and Dr. Upchurch were influential in starting hospice in our community. Many people have asked, "Why would you want to take care of the dying. Isn't it depressing?" When I answer that hospice nursing has been the most satisfying type of nursing I have ever done, they look at me in disbelief. But it truly has been. To provide palliative comfort measures with the patient in his own home, with family around, is rewarding in itself. Most family members are more than willing to learn how to operate unfamiliar equipment, bathe, dress, transfer, move, and make the person more comfortable, give medications properly, and know when to call for help. It's the nurse's duty to teach all these and more to the family and patient so that everyone understands and is knowledgeable about the patient's care.

I found many times that the family members were playing a game of denial: I knew that I must break through that denial so family members could close any unfinished business they had with the dying. I oftentimes was the first to say that "so and so" was dying, did they have anything they needed to discuss? Most of the time, the word "dying" had never been vocalized. This gave the family the impetus to talk to the dying person in a meaningful manner. I remember well when the wife of a dying patient kept telling me they were planning a trip for the summer. I tactfully reminded her that her husband was dying and that he didn't want to let her down and was playing along with her "game." She looked at me in shock when she realized what she had been doing. We went into her husband's room and discussed the situation. He looked lovingly at her and said, "I can't do this any longer, honey, I am dying." She broke into tears and finally they could talk about what needed to happen when he died. Whenever I see her today she gives me a big hug and says, "Thank God you were there for us!"

Dying is a part of life, but most of us do not want to accept that premise. I am thankful that I was able to help others understand and accept that their loved ones were dying so that they could enjoy those last days or hours together in a meaningful way. Yes, I did become close to these people and I felt a loss when they died, but I had been enriched 100-fold in the interactions with them and their families, and that counteracted the loss. I was there fully to help them during a difficult time, and that made an impact and lasting bond for all of us. To me, Hospice Nursing is truly nursing at its very best.

ABOUT DONNA WALD

Donna and Ron live on a beautiful ranch in Montana. They have four children, ten grandchildren, and four great-grandchildren. Two sons also live on the ranch and have taken over raising the cattle and horses and other ranch activities. Ron and Donna continue to run a B&B at the ranch.

As a Registered Nurse, Donna did private duty nursing, was Supervisor of Surgery, taught Community Health, First Aide, CPR, and disaster training; was a School Nurse, Health Educator, Nurse Consultant, Chemical Dependency/Family Counselor, Director of Nurses, Professor and Academic Dean at Little Big Horn College, Parish Nurse, Hospice Supervisor, 4-H leader, Cancer Crusade Chairman, Secretary Church Council, Lay Minister; president of: Jailhouse Gallery's Board, Homemakers Club, Sew & So, and Civic Club.

Donna received a Bachelor's in Psychology and Sociology, Master's in Counseling, and Ph.D. in Health Services Administration. She is a Reiki Master, HBL Master, Life Coach, and Energy Healer. She is also a published, best-selling author.

Donna enjoys assisting people to utilize their unique gifts and potential to the world. She is a speaker on health issues, inner voice, spirituality, and consciousness, as well as related topics. She does private and group sessions on life coaching and can be reached at waldranch@nemont.net, Facebook and http://waldranch.com.

DAILY LIVING AS AN EMPATH

Katherine Wolff

With the current upshift of energies over the last few years, there is an emergence of people awakening to their empathic sense. Many who know they have this ability are becoming quite sensitive at an extremely rapid pace. While perusing the Internet, I noticed that while there are thousands of articles describing an empath, they have very little information on how to cope with and manage this ability. Plus, what is available is shallow and does not give in-depth instructions as to how to manage daily living as an empath.

Most of the time, those who are gifted with these abilities (though at times it feels more like a curse) are left to figure it out themselves. The things we sense and feel are practically indescribable. And when we try to explain what we can do, it is dismissed, rationalized, or chastised by others. To add to the confusion, it changes as we mature. The older we get, the more complex it becomes.

We apply feelings to every single experience. I call this the subtle energy vocabulary. Almost every molecule has a feeling attached to it. The more experience we have, the more our emotional vocabulary broadens. Think of it as an energetic association game. Everything has a meaning, and we translate the information based on what we know physically, mentally, emotionally, and psychically. Abstract information filters through the physical vehicle, making the intangible tangible.

In order to learn how to manage and use this gift, we must understand how it works. When I asked my guides to show me how this ability works, I kept sensing a dark blankness. It's similar to being in a room devoid of light. I asked for detailed clarity and the first words spoken were "Null Space." Then I had a vision of having a life of vision and then becoming blind.

Imagine being in a darkened room, wandering around with your arms outstretched, trying to identify what may be in your path. You bump into a table. You run your hand over it to feel the texture and shape and dimensions. Your mind produces images of a table that feels similar from your vision. As you explore the table, you happen upon a vase with a flower. Again, your mind produces a conceptual image of what you feel. Suddenly a fly lands on your face. You're startled; you couldn't avoid the fly because you couldn't see it. You knew it was in the room, but had no idea how it got there or where it was going.

Our gifts work very similarly, but on a much more complex basis, depending on an individual's sensitivity.

A part of our consciousness resides in null or negative space, floating around in silence and peace. As we move through time and space this part of the consciousness moves with us, always reaching out to detect what is in front of it. When any energy comes across our path, the consciousness sends back the information for the physical to filter and process. When an energy or other consciousness directs their energy in our direction, we do not see it coming and it smacks us in the face. This is when we feel someone is attacking us or sending us bad juju. It is startling to our whole being because we didn't see it or know it was coming.

Our reaction and how we deal with it is determined by a database created through life experiences. The negative experiences, perceptions, and beliefs we have of ourselves and others hinder the body from translating information cleanly and clearly. The information being filtered through an individual's physical reality will be distorted. I call this having a dirty filter. This is the number one reason why those with the empathic ability struggle. It is time to clean the filter.

My life was heading down this path. I was an extremely toxic person, because my childhood sucked. Like every other gifted child, I was a little different. My mother was an undiagnosed bi-polar alcoholic with narcissistic traits. My father was a beautiful spirit, but passive. He drank to numb himself from my mother's negativity. I am the youngest of four children. My siblings are fourteen, twelve, and nine years older than I. By the time I arrived on the scene, Mom was in her worst stages of alcoholism. Because I was the late-life surprise, she never physically abused me like she did my siblings; by then she was extremely overweight and riddled with health issues. Luckily for me, her reflexes were slower and she was too broken to chase me to beat me. What amazes me to this day is, no matter how drunk she was, she always had her A-game when it came to verbal and emotional abuse.

I was known as the over-sensitive weird kid with poor social skills. I hated reading because I couldn't focus. Arguments and conflicts caused me to become very upset and cry. This is why my mother never needed to physically punish me; the projection of her toxic words was physically painful. I played with imaginary friends. I was scared of various places on the property I grew up on, because I knew there were bad people waiting to get me. People were oddly drawn to or repulsed by me. I had the ability to piss people off without trying. I still do, but now I can do it with calculating intent. I truly picked the life I needed to be groomed for what I do today. I was so sensitive and pure, my mother's negativity was repulsive to the point that I hated her touching me. The more I rejected her, the more I stirred up her emotional crap to be thrown back at me in some form of punishment.

Adding to my torture—I mean life-lessons—I was the bullied kid in school. What I didn't get in physical abuse at home, I got in school. Being the odd kid made me the target for every other kid, physically and emotionally. There was never a moment of solace. I dreaded going to school and I dreaded coming home. The few times I told my parents of what was happening in school, they assumed I did something to provoke the other kids. Their other response was to just ignore the bullies and they would eventually leave me alone. It didn't matter if I kept to myself or not, I was constantly on the receiving end of someone's abuse. My life was nothing but survival.

Unfortunately, I was tagged as being lazy and not very intelligent. Most things were a challenge. In my forties, I found out I should've been diagnosed with Asperger, but autism wasn't even known during that time. As a child I had A.D.D., poor social skills, impulsive thoughts and actions, inappropriate or unfiltered comments, was easily frustrated and overwhelmed, and emotionally sensitive with a lack of empathy. I am extremely intelligent, with amazing problem-solving skills, but couldn't focus and concentrate for shit, which added another layer of misery. Plus, I was alone through most of it. My siblings had each other growing up, but by the time I was in fifth grade, I was home alone. The older ones moved out and I was left to deal with the insanity alone. Except for one friend.

In the fourth grade, a new kid moved in from Ireland. The first time I met her was in church. She had a funny accent and weird clothes and we instantly clicked. We accepted each other unconditionally. Like Dr. Seuss said, "We are all a little weird and life's a little weird, and when we find someone whose weirdness is compatible with ours, we join up with them and fall in mutual weirdness and call it love."

The girl was my sanity as I was hers. Her life was a different type of hell. We just accepted and understood each other. We had so much fun with belching contests, cheese puffs, and whoopee cushions. We had and still have warped senses of humor. We would talk for hours over the stupidest, most in-depth and intense things. I was lost when she moved to Maine, during our high school years. When things sucked most, it quickly became worse. I was now completely alone and it was time to implement all my survival skills I had learned to date.

The biggest thing I learned was to toughen up and suck it up. I found a method of control. Show no emotion and don't bring attention to myself. Sit back and watch and sense if danger approaches. Trust what you feel about people, because no one can be trusted. Watch for open opportunities to hide from the stress, chaos, and abuse. Use negative situations to my advantage.

My soul signed up for some crazy life lessons. I swear I was lured in to this life. Just like the as-seen-on-TV infomercials: If you call within the next 10 minutes, we will add not one, but TWO bonus seminars, "How to Feel Like a Loser Before the Age of 10," and "How to Hate Myself and the Universe to Extreme Depths." These two seminars usually retail for $1 million, but for a limited time we offer these courses for just $1! WAIT! There's more … We're excited to extend an additional offer, "How to Believe You are a Fat, Disgustingly Ugly Person and Will Never Amount to Anything." This highly-sought-after class usually retails for thousands of dollars, but if you call within the next ten minutes, we will give it to you FREE! WAIT! There's more … when you call to order your life-lesson package, with the additional bonus seminars and free gift, by mentioning this ad and using the promo code, "I SUCK 4EVER," we will ship you to your living hell of learning at no additional charge. Now for the part we always seem to miss at the end of the commercial. The Universe does not guarantee the use of this product. No returns, exchanges, transfers, or breach of contract after the first nanosecond. What part of this did my soul think was a stellar offer? Ugh!

This is where I was; an anxious mess, trying to keep my ship afloat. I lived in constant irritation, sarcasm, and exhaustion. I was—and can still be—extremely hard on myself, always striving to be and do better. I wanted more, but was too busy controlling and making sure everything was perfect before I could proceed. I never could proceed because it was never good enough. I was overwhelmed all the time and had no idea why. I needed to stay within the confines of routine and rules, because I couldn't cope outside of my self-imposed structure. Inside my structure,

I was anxiously calm and felt I had everything under control. If any deviation occurred, I would become hysterically enraged because of my inflexible mindset. When there was a plan, it flung me into fear of failure. I believed if I didn't do it all myself I was a complete loser. I had to prove to everyone my capability. I spent my life being told of all the things I did not do well. The negative overshadowed all the wonderful accomplishments.

I remember when report cards were mailed home. I wasn't a great student; my grades made that apparent. I did well in the subjects I loved, but failed horribly at the ones I despised. Report cards were a time of dread. Rarely, if ever, was I praised for a good grade. That was an unquestionable expectation. I was interrogated about grades that were not good. Even if there was an improvement in my grade from a C to a B, it was followed with, "Then why was it not an A?"

No matter what I did it was never good enough, so I gave up and completely failed the ninth grade; slept through the whole year. My parents felt that holding me back would be better than making up the classes in Summer School. What it did was teach me to do just get enough to get by, because why kill myself; I would never be good enough. This threw me into complete defeat. I lost another layer of trust towards my parents. They never helped, just criticized. I even pointed out the big improvements I made one time, only for them to say, "So you did that, why could you not do it for the rest of your classes? You keep this up you will never be able to go far in life. You will never get a good job to live on your own." That comment gave me a deep-seated fear of failure and the perception that no matter how much I accomplish, it will never be enough. I will never be enough.

Asking for help wasn't taught in my family. I rarely had help with learning and studying. If I asked for help, I felt ashamed because I wasn't smart enough to understand it myself. So, I did what I could, but knew it would never be good enough. Constant fear and constant disappointment fed on each other. The internal struggle intensified as

I got older. I worked to constantly be successful, to prove to everyone how intelligent and capable I truly was. My emotions were filled with depression, agitation, self-loathing, defeat, and rage. The only way I could control all of this was to control my environment. Everything had a specific process. My views and problem-solving skills became very rigid. Anxiety and depression was a way of life. Change is torturous for a control freak.

What does the Universe do best and predictably? Change. Just when you think you have it all together, the Universe steps in and says it's time for you to face your crap. When this happened, I became hyper-vigilant. I would devise a course of action and start to move forward, following each step. Then something or someone would create a roadblock. I was so rigid, I couldn't see a way around the obstruction. I would become angry and blame everything and everyone. I was wrapped in such personal negativity, I could never trust. I used my empathic gifts to sniff out potential danger. No one was to be trusted, especially not happy, cheery, giving, positive people. I always felt they had a hidden agenda. Nobody can be that happy and nice and not have ulterior motives.

I started to become aware of my clair-sentient gifts around my mid-to-late twenties, but had no idea my unusual ability had a real name. I tried to understand it, but the Internet was relatively new and not much information was available. To talk openly made me the weird kid again. Little did I know I wasn't weird, rather gifted, with a ton of emotional bullshit layered on top. I wanted to open and expand my clair-sentient abilities, but I hit roadblock after roadblock. I realized I was getting frustrated and angry at myself. Little did I know that developing my gift of clair-sentience required cleaning out my inner emotional sewer. Denial could no longer be my best friend. Denial had to be served a restraining order and forcibly removed from my personal residence, kicking and screaming every step of the way.

I learned about the strength and sensitivity of my empathic sense. I had been using my gift to avoid potential physical and emotional harm. I had an unconscious habit of "scanning" a person even before they spoke. It was my way of surviving a lifetime of toxicity. I could sense truth and lies and when to cut a relationship early, so as not to be hurt and let down. I was judged harshly for this, but I knew to my core when a person was going to betray or take advantage of me. I learned that part of my trust issue was sensing the negative emotions people hid about themselves. I was a bit happy to understand what I was feeling was spot on, but I was reading the information through my own dirty filter. Every person hides their personal shame and shortcomings, but it was my personal judgements that warped my perceptions.

I beat myself up over this for years, and not a single person could help me understand. When I would try and explain what I was sensing to other spiritual people, I was told to be spiritual and be in service, to give of myself and love all unconditionally. I was surrounded by so many "sensitives" who preached about how you must protect yourself from the negative energies. Shield, protect, and only live in the light. Every negative feeling or thought will lower your vibration and you could succumb to the darkness. If you feel negative towards yourself or others, change it to a positive so you do not lower your vibration. Judgement of another is wrong. If you judge someone, you are not judging them, you are only judging yourself.

I tried so hard to fit into that role, but it felt all wrong. What I was being told and what I felt were completely opposite. This is when it started to make sense. This is why I didn't trust and understand the overly positive and giving people. This is why I had a hard time fitting in with many of the spiritual concepts. Though their outward intentions were wonderful, all their actions and beliefs of what it is to be spiritual and a good person were based on the same emotional shit storm I had: fear.

My clair-sentient gift has an incredibly strong empathic sense. My ears were hearing the words, my eyes were seeing their actions, but my gift was picking up on their emotional sewer. My childhood forged my empathic sense to be an early detection for danger. Because of that,

I only knew how to detect negative emotions. I was picking up their emotional sludge and reacting based on my emotional sewage. Then I realized the person who does everything for everyone has a broken emotional platform and is misinterpreting their empathic sense. If this person had a need to be accepted and valued, they would go to the ends of the earth for anyone just to be accepted and valued. Where I lived in fear of being abused, this individual may have had a life of neglect. They still were living in fear, but their circumstances created a different coping mechanism.

My head just about exploded with this concept. In my healing practice, I started paying closer attention to the commonalities, diversities, and adversities within the individuals and their gifts. Then I started to pay attention to different online forums, and realized the number one commonality is, nobody understands how they feel. Empaths and clair-sentients have a hard time explaining their needs and emotions for themselves. We spend our lives using our gift for survival. We learn to read other people to navigate through traumatic events and difficult situations. Those born into abusive situations are constantly monitoring what the abuser is feeling so as to avoid being abused. Those who grow up with a narcissist constantly scan to anticipate the needs of the narcissist to validate their own self-worth. Empaths spend their whole lives attached to what others feel so that we never learned how to feel for ourselves. This creates a feeling of isolation.

As a teenager, my best friend, Sandra, wrote a poem when I was at one of my lowest points. At the time I understood it from the perspective of living within my personal hell. I have forgotten much of the poem over the past thirty years, but the first part is still embedded in my memory. I now see it with a whole new meaning.

Alone you stand atop this hill,
Loved by one and hurt by all
As I see you sitting small
A smothered cry, a choked remark

I wish I could remember the second verse. When I read this as a teen I bawled my eyes out, because she captured what I was feeling from my physical experience. However, I was unable to describe the feelings I carried deep within. Over the years this part of the poem has drifted in and out of my awareness. During my writing, it floated in again and the deepest part of my soul stirred. It was time to bring words to give to all the clair-sentients and empaths the comfort in knowing we are not alone and what you feel deep within is legitimate.

An Empath's Cry of the Soul

We are in a sea of people, yet feel utterly alone. All we want is for someone to understand us. We sense and know things on levels we are not yet aware. The constant influx of information comes in from all directions. The energetic borage exhausts our souls. Yet, through exhaustion, pain and misery, we are able to rise above to give a little extra to those in need.

All we want is to be left alone and at peace. We crave for rest, but souls do not know the meaning. We know we have a mission, but what can that be? The constant questioning of Who am I? What am I? What is my purpose? The non-stop circle of asking the same thing, with no answer. We search for things and others to fill our voids. We search for those who give to us what we give to all. Still, we are tired, lost, and confused.

Many look to us to be their strength, but who will be ours? When the pillar starts to crumble, those who do not understand are paralyzed in shock. Those who understand watch in fear that they may be the next to fall. We are the strongest, yet we feel we are the weakest. We see purity within the murkiest of souls. We are the balance of light and dark. Many of us have survived darkness so we can give to others who are fighting their darkness. Yet we guard our purity like no other.

We are a prize to be won, but the prize is unobtainable. Though we give so much to others, there is a part that will always be locked away. We know to our core the piece we withhold is the purest bit of our soul. We know to never entrust this piece to another. If this last piece is given and mishandled, it will not be broken, it will be shattered, with no hope of repair. This would be worse than hell, it is what death would be for us.

We feel incomplete, yet feel we are not worthy of completion. We fight to keep the peace, because we feel the pain. No one understands who we are. We are tired. We are achy and sore. Yet we continue for the sake of the whole. We, too, want to be loved as deeply as we love, but again we do not feel it will be enough. We are caught between worlds. We want to go home though we need to stay. Our souls remember God's love, but our bodies no longer remember this love.

As this channeled through me, tears flooded from a place I was feeling for the very first time. The tears were first of grief and sadness, for being lost and imprisoned for so many decades. Then the tears turned to joy and a huge feeling of openness and peace followed. Writing the feelings of what could not be identified opened my self-imposed prison. The fear of always being different and isolated left. This identification allowed my soul to reach beyond the shadows. The peace of absolute purity finally emerged after being buried for decades. The purest part of the soul will emerge when you know, trust, and honor yourself on the deepest of levels. This soul peace will come forward when it knows you will defend and protect it, but never place it back into imprisonment. This is why we do not entrust another with this purity. It is too much of a responsibility for another person to defend and protect.

Almost every empath I showed this to has an emotional response. We spend our whole lives with this gaping hole within ourselves, but it is indescribable. Every person wants to be understood, but how can that happen if it cannot be described. I was gifted with the opportunity to finally give words so the healing of the internal void can begin. For sensitives, the goal in life is to learn to live through neutral objectivity. Most of us with this gift have had some crazy and harsh lives. As you begin to clean your filters layer by layer, not only do you learn about yourself, you begin to understand others and humanity as a whole through a compassionate perspective. Too many needlessly struggle and suffer, and that can be changed. What I offer is not a cure, but maybe the first steps to better mastery of your self and your gifts. Time to understand some of the whats, whens, and hows about yourself, and many of the whys will be answered.

ABOUT KATHERINE WOLFF

Katherine Wolff is a Psycho-Therapeutic Intuitive, Reiki Master Teacher, Cranio Sacral Therapist and massage therapist. After being in a science-based career for twenty years, she decided to take a new direction in life. Always interested in holistic healing and with a background in science and athletics, massage therapy was a perfect match. Shortly after graduating massage therapy school, more than fourteen years ago, she was invited to be a massage therapy instructor. For many years, she enjoyed imparting her knowledge to future massage therapists, while developing her own business and expanding her education of the mind, body, and spirit.

Through the years, her quest for knowledge has led her in many directions. She has been trained or certified in more than twelve different massage modalities. Her knowledge also spans into the esoteric practices. She has been a Reiki Master Teacher for more than ten years. She is educated in Somato-emotional techniques (releasing emotional memory from the body), Emotional Freedom Technique (EFT tapping), Chakra Balancing, Sound Therapy, and Crystal Therapy.

The combination of Katherine's healing journey, innate gifts, educational background, and professional experience allow her to guide an individual to heal from past negative experiences and traumas which perpetuate unhealthy, self-sabotaging thoughts and behaviors. These negative experiences create blocks for an individual from their greatest potential of living in peace, harmony, and having a genuine love for life. Her goal is to be a guide and a support for an individual to discover, understand, and come at peace with these past experiences and uncover an authentic, peaceful, healthy, and loving self.

Visit www.MoveOutofYourWay.com to learn more.

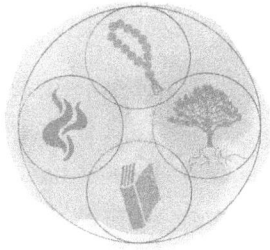

LIFE IS A MERRY-GO-ROUND

Carole B. Young

believe it's safe to say that I didn't have the typical childhood most kids do. When I think about the perfect family dynamic, my mind immediately shifts to the American television sitcom "Leave it to Beaver." If you aren't familiar with "Leave it to Beaver," the show debuted and filmed in 1953, and ended its run mid-year 1963. It was about an ideal suburban family who exemplified the perfect picture of what family life should look like. June was a stay-at-home mom raising two sons, and Ward worked a nine-to-five job, the two sharing one car for the family. Dinner was served at the family dinner table by June while wearing a conservative dress with mid-to-high heels and a soft strand of white pearls. The boys, always involved in an unfortunate incident, received an uplifting and moral lecture given by Ward, the father, to teach them, and the young TV viewers, life lessons. Following dinner, Ward and June Cleaver relaxed on the couch while he read the daily newspaper and drank his coffee.

I grew up watching the reruns of "Leave it to Beaver" in black and white and wondered if all families lived that way. Please come with me as I take you through the journey of my childhood, my life transitions, triumphs, and definitions of the many successes that sometimes we tend to overlook.

I was born and raised in Fort Worth, Texas, by two loving parents, but with a unique and diverse lifestyle. My childhood experiences varied due to the fact that my parents did not have the ordinary nine-to-five jobs, and most of the time their work was performed out of town. My father's name was Buster Brown. I know what you're thinking, the same thing everyone else thought when I was growing up; my dad was a shoemaker. No, my father was not a shoemaker. My father contracted polio when he was four, around the year of 1940. Back then, poliomyelitis, a debilitating virus, also known as Heine-Medin disease, was a mystery to doctors. One of the first medical reports released defined the outcome of the virus to be "paralysis of the lower extremities." How far the disease crept up the spine determined the outcome for each patient. For some patients, it could even affect the respiratory system, but in my father's case only the lower extremities. After multiple surgeries, he lost the use of his legs. One leg shorter than the other, he was dependent on walking with crutches for the rest of his life.

Growing up as a paraplegic, he didn't play sports, but loved baseball and coached a team of his own. He led a normal life that included graduating high school, marrying my mother, and fathering my sister and me. Although he had this adversity of a disability, he was so genuine and authentic that people hardly noticed. He was well-respected, an exceptional and successful businessman. He co-owned and ran the family business, founded by his grandfather in 1910, that was passed down to him from his mother and grandfather. My mother was and still is an awesome mom, although she isn't as present in the mind as she used to be. She's a devout Christian, has always made sure that God was in my heart, and we attended church most Sundays when we were home in Fort Worth. Due to my father's disability, he needed assistance and she stood by him proudly. She was the "June Cleaver" without the high heels and the pearls, taking care of his needs and being a good wife and mom, as well.

She and my father both instilled important ethics, morals, and values in my life. She was a stay-at-home mom for three months out of the year. The other nine months, she was an "out-of-town" stay-at-home mom until I was ten years old and finishing up fifth grade. While being homeschooled through the fifth grade, I traveled with my parents for nine months out of the year. They made sure I had a solid education, which was of great importance to them. After the first few years of homeschooling, my mom found a school that offered the option of homeschool and in-classroom participation, which meant that I physically went to school and participated in class during the winter months of November, December, and January. The new school did the A.C.E. program (Accelerated Christian Education), which is still offered today. There were no thick school books, but small packets ranging from twenty-five to forty-five pages each. These packets were called Paces. Twelve Paces in each subject were to be completed to move to the next grade. There were no desks in the middle of the room, but instead rows of side-by-side cubicles with no distractions. Located at the top of the cubicle was a small hole in which you would place a stick flag when you had a question about your school work. The teachers would then come to answer your questions one-on-one. This was very different from a regular classroom setting that I later experienced in high school. The curriculum allowed me to attend school for the three months of winter that my parents were in town during the off-season. Then it was time to pack up, load the RV, collect the school work for the next nine months and head out of town. We left around the first week of February, not to return until early November.

I was fairly nervous about attending my first day and already felt that I stood out like a sore thumb coming in to school in the middle of the year. The day always began with pledges and then prayer. When we did the pledges, we pledged allegiance to the American Flag, the Christian Flag, and to the Bible. Still today I remember the pledge to the Christian Flag and the Bible:

I pledge allegiance to the Christian Flag, and to the Savior for whose

Kingdom it stands, one Savior, crucified, risen, and coming again, with life and liberty for all who believe.

I pledge allegiance to the Bible, God's Holy Word. I will make it a lamp unto my feet, and a light unto my path. I will hide its words in my heart that I might not sin against God.

By the time we had free time, it was even more awkward to explain to my new friends why I was only attending until February and I wouldn't be around to play and have fun with them during the summer.

"Why are you only here for three months?" my friends asked. "Where do you go in the summer?"

"My parents work out of town and they take us with them," I responded.

"Oh, what do your parents do?" they asked.

"My parents own a carnival," I said with a smile.

"A carnival!" they exclaimed.

I can't remember my exact thought or reaction back then, but what I do remember is how they looked at me after that. I don't believe I ever thought anything about what my parents did for a living up until that moment. The other kids would make fun of me and ask if I cleaned up the elephant poop in the circus. Looking at them, bewildered, I would tell them that it's not a circus, it's a carnival! I knew the exact difference between the two. This is when I started to feel a little different than the other kids, although I excelled in my schoolwork and really enjoyed making friends during the months that I attended. The only thing I didn't look forward to was that every new school year, upon my return for the winter months, there were always new kids, and my friends from the previous year would eventually share what my parents did for work with the other kids. The cycle of the circus questions continued. As I got older, I kind of got used to it, but I found myself avoiding the question of "What do your parents do?" altogether.

For the record, there has always been a stigma about being a "Carny" in our society. The majority associate it with lower class people who have missing teeth and no aspirations about bettering themselves. This is unfortunate. Although there were some people when I was growing up who fit that description, that was not the case for me and my family.

Let's go briefly into "Carnival 101." A company comprised of rides, games, and food that has put in a proposal for bid to provide fun and entertainment for a Fair, Festival, or event for that specific city, county, or state. FYI: no circus animals, clowns, or trapeze acts. It is a business just like any other. On my father's carnival, the games and food were owned by independent owners. These families were long-time participants. I tell you this because some of my closest friends to this day are the kids I grew up around in the carnival business. These other kids and I shared a commonality in that we were raised the same way when it came to school and lifestyle.

While on the road, my mother tried to keep things as normal as possible and because we were always working on the weekends, we did not have the opportunity to attend church. She still found a way to bring God into the mix. In the summer months, she would hold a Sunday school class for the kids, teaching her favorite Bible stories. Considering the other children were from different cities in Texas, I did not see them in the winter months. It was like I led two different lives. My life and friends on the road and then my life and friends at home. I really felt like I didn't fit in with my friends at home. Sort of like an outsider looking in.

By the time I reached middle school, my parents realized that I was missing out on school functions, sports, and other opportunities. So, the decision was made that I go to school full-time. My mom wasn't able to stay home with us due to my dad's handicap, so I stayed with a sweet lady who was the wife of one of the managers who worked for my father. She had two sons of her own and always came home to Fort Worth to put her boys in school. When the show (carnival) was within 300 miles or less she would drive to the city where the carnival was to see her husband and I got to see my mom and dad for the weekend. Before all of the kids were of school age, she was the designated babysitter on the road, so I was very familiar with her already. If I'm honest, I remember it being difficult emotionally being away from my mom. As a child, I was totally a mama's girl. I remember crying when saying goodbye to my mom, squeezing her tightly as she leaned in the car window when it was time to drive back to Fort Worth. Being a mom now, I realize how difficult that had to be for her, but at the time, in that moment, I was very sad for a day or so, then tried to focus on school, counting the days until I got to see my parents and my carnival friends again. I always looked forward to the summers on the road. My dad had secured a route of fairs and festivals up in the northern states where the temperatures were cooler and there were always new things to see on the fairgrounds. All of my carnival friends were there and we would explore all of the destinations and just have fun.

My dad always encouraged entrepreneurship when I was a kid, although it wasn't a popular word back then, as it is today. My first actual job was blowing up balloons for the dart toss when I was around ten years old. As the players threw the darts at the board to pop the balloons for a prize, the boards would have to be restocked with fresh "blown up" balloons and I was the young girl on the other side attaching the balloons to the boards as they rotated. I did this during peak times on the weekends during the day when the games were very busy. "Bust one and you win" was what the workers would say as they called the people in to play the game. I made $5 per day doing this for several hours.

By the age of thirteen, during the summer, in order to stay out on the fairgrounds during open hours after dark, my parents had a rule that we had to be in a stand or working, otherwise back to the RV to watch TV. I didn't always get paid, just volunteered to help in any stand or game to be out and about. Being the owners' daughter had its pros and cons. I was taught to lead by example, and of course everyone was always so nice because they knew that my dad had the final say! My first time working in a food stand, I was trained by a special lady who

I still deeply respect today. (If you are reading this you know who you are.) She taught me how to spin cotton candy in an airtight bag, twirl candy and caramel apples, work the popcorn and sno-cone machines, and how to work the windows.

Standing there, wearing a uniform shirt I said, "May I help you?" Working the windows meant you were responsible for taking the order, gathering the items, totaling up the amount owed, all with a smile. We didn't use registers back then so this was done manually. I became really good at working the math in my head on the spot and making change for the big bills and coins! My dad would tell me, "The customer is always right," and it was our job to make sure their experience at the fair was outstanding. By age sixteen, during the summer, I was in charge of the food stand and making a nice percentage of the revenue. My dad was big on money management. He insisted I save the majority and budget a bit of spending money from week to week. I learned so much from my father!

During the years of high school, I stayed with "My Mimi," my paternal grandmother. She was the best grandmother anyone could ever ask for. She went every day to the nursing home where her mother was bedridden and lived her last ten years. I watched her care deeply for her mother. As my grandmother was aging, I found myself helping her around the house and taking care of tasks she was no longer able to do. She passed in 1998, and I believe I inherited many great qualities from my grandmother and gained a compassion for others from watching her on a daily basis.

As a freshman in high school, I applied for my driver's license at fifteen, and my parents bought me a car so that I could drive myself to school. By now, I was in a different private Christian school with more opportunities. In high school, I played volleyball, basketball, and was a cheerleader. If I had to return to a past life, it would be the 9th, 10th, and 11th grades because I had so much fun! I was independent, responsible, and self-sufficient as a teenager.

Graduating from high school one semester early, from public school, I went straight into college. Completing nearly two years, I decided to take a break from college, go out on the road, travel, and work with my parents. I worked every aspect of the amusement business, working for others at first, then eventually going into business for myself with the help of my father. This was one of the turning points of my life, realizing that I actually owned my own business at age twenty-two. I bought my first amusement kiddie ride, financing and everything. It was called a Berry-Go-Round. Four huge strawberries with seating inside the berry and a wheel inside to turn with your hands that would spin the strawberry around and around. I was so happy and proud. My father co-signed for the loan and made it very clear that this was all my responsibility. "Keep all receipts, make payroll deposits, take out taxes on employees and prepare your return for the CPA," he said. This was much to learn and I was over the moon to be mentored by my dad! He guided me through with advice and tips to make sure all legalities were taken care of properly.

I learned so much during this time. Most of all, how to be a great boss to my employees. I had learned from the best while growing up, watching my father interact and show respect to all of the workers, encouraging them along the way no matter what their circumstance. The Kiddie ride was brand new in the industry and it was a big hit!! All of the children wanted to ride and I was making a great income while paying off the loan. I felt fortunate to have the opportunity.

During this time, my grandmother voiced her feelings of wanting my father off the road. She felt that he worked too hard. She wanted him to sell the operation and retire. Later, my father did actually sell interest of the company, with the stipulation of remaining in the position of management to ensure the future success of the company while changing hands. Without divulging the details, he was in the process of buying part interest back when a tragedy happened.

It was on a Thursday, August 2nd of 1990. A beautiful summer day at the Central Wyoming Fair in Casper, Wyoming. The sky was blue, the air was crisp, and it was just two days before my mother's birthday. My father wanted to do something special for her. We had decided to throw her a surprise birthday party up in the Casper Mountains with a picnic setting. My sister, brother-in-law, and I went ahead early to get things set up. I will never forget how beautiful it was as we drove up the mountain, climbing in elevation, leaning into the winding curves and admiring the stunning scenery and soaring green trees. It was breathtaking!

My father told my mother that he wanted to have lunch away from the fairgrounds and she thought that they were just going to grab a quick bite at a restaurant. Not knowing the time that my father and mother left the fairgrounds, we waited. As time passed, we wondered what was keeping our parents, and then suddenly a strange car pulled into our picnic site. A young lady driving a red car steered into our area and asked if we were waiting on someone. We replied that we were waiting for our parents. The woman said that there had been an accident, to follow her and she would lead us there. As we drove around the winding road, we came upon the accident. For the first few seconds when I saw my dad's pickup truck, I wasn't sure what I was looking at. Then I realized that the truck had turned upside down and landed on its top. The cab of the truck looked nearly flattened on the rocky dirt road. I couldn't believe what I was seeing! As I got closer, I saw my dad's lower body inside and that is all I could see. I wondered why the emergency team wasn't trying to pull my dad out. Feeling lost for words, I could tell by the looks on their faces that he wasn't alive. I felt a warmth come over my body. I remember this feeling so vividly as if it was just yesterday. For a brief moment I believed that I had lost both of my parents.

The emergency workers told us not to get too close and were keeping everyone back. As I looked around, my eyes following them until someone pointed upward away from the accident. My heart pounding out of my chest and the fear practically numbing my body, I turned my head to the left and saw my mother up on a hill with the EMTs. The ambulance took my mom to the hospital. She had a mild concussion and just a few bruises and scratches. It was a miracle that she survived. The next couple of days were a blur and I realize now that I was in a state of shock. Days later, my mom told us the story of their ride up the mountain. She said, "I had no idea where we were going, just that it was a pleasant ride until the truck went into a skid towards a big boulder, which the truck hit and turned over."

She believes my father died instantly. Still to this day, if I had only known that earlier that day was the last time I was going to be able to see or talk to my dad, I would have told him many things, most of all how much I love him. I know in my heart that he knew. Sometimes we don't understand why God will allow bad things to happen to good people, but we have to move forward with our lives and heal. From that day on, moving forward, my life totally changed as I had known it.

The family atmosphere was not the same, as I had mentioned earlier, my dad had sold interest of the company and the dynamics of doing business without the presence of my father were not in my favor. So that next season, my boyfriend and I took our rides on an independent tour of fairs, booking mostly the good ones. Shortly after turning twenty-three, I married my boyfriend and was a stepmom to a beautiful young girl. We continued to work in the carnival business and spent the following two winters in Florida. My mom, sister, and brother-in-law stayed with what remained of the family business in spirit only, to make sure that all of the current fair contracts remained in place and the reputation of our family business stayed intact. Two years later, I divorced. Deciding to get out of the amusement business altogether, I sold the amusement equipment and moved back to Texas. Healing from my divorce, I moved in with my mother and took some time to do some soul-searching and get my bearings.

The feelings of not belonging, feeling inferior and a sense of unworthiness came rushing back, though I was an adult. I felt that my background, lack of knowledge and inexperience in the regular workforce would be challenging. How do I go out into the workforce without a resume? I did attempt to make one, but no matter how you spin it, the carnival business wasn't the best past job experience. The stigma still remained. No one wanted to hire a "Carny." The interviews for management positions did not go well, though I felt I had much to offer being a previous business owner and knowing how to deal with people. So, I figured out that I needed to go into business for myself, once again.

I enrolled in school to become a Licensed Massage Therapist. While interning there, I met my daughter's father. Our personalities clicked. Nearly a year later, in 1997, we married and I became stepmom to his boys who were five and six. While leasing a space and working my massage business, I started helping my husband in his business, as well. My husband, also self-employed, was in sales and was really good at working with people, so he taught me everything I came to know about the Merchant Service Business. Merchant Services is financial services that allows businesses to accept credit and debit card transactions using point of sale equipment or software. This was my first experience with residual income. I was now working in a world that had felt so awkward to me before. I was the June Cleaver with two stepsons. This was one of the first times that I felt victory in making changes in my life and overcoming the adversity I had faced.

Five years later, I got pregnant and was so overjoyed that I was going to be a mom. Her name is Payton and she is the "Pop in my Tart" and the "light of my life." After eleven years of marriage, being self-employed, and having my four-year-old daughter, I divorced again in 2006. I knew that I wanted to raise my daughter on my own for a while. Deciding to make her my top priority and be present in every aspect of her upbringing, I ran my business, volunteered at her school often and turned my focus to how I was going to make her feel normal in a divorced family. I use techniques in raising her that provide stability, a solid foundation, a pure heart of kindness, generosity and compassion for others, and a very consistent structure that I didn't have as a child. Most importantly,

I kept God in the center of our world. Single-parenting isn't easy. After much discussion, her father and I worked together in making her feel loved and cherished.

My goal was to re-frame the idea of the feelings a young child goes through in a divorced family. That she's not any different than the other kids in school. Words are so powerful! The power of the tongue can be a blessing or a curse. I chose to use a Godly approach in telling her how she is fearfully and wonderfully made and is God's divine creation, as it states in Psalm 139:14. Here's the funny thing: in teaching her these things, I was having to practice what I preached and receive the positive words of encouragement for myself.

Several years later, I felt that life had more to offer, I just couldn't put my finger on it. Sometime around June of 2014, I remember getting an email for a FREE 10-Day Transformation mini-course from Jack Canfield, and I thought, *What the heck*. I signed up. I received another email talking about a Breakthrough To Success 2014 event that was due to take place in August. I watched the informational video, which talked about discovering life passions, eliminating limiting beliefs and that it would take me to the next level, even though I didn't have any idea of what that looked like. Realizing that it was in Arizona and a four-to-five day event, I immediately shot it down, thinking that it was too much of an expense, and I had never done anything like that before. I had never spent any money on myself for personal development and actually never really paid much attention to the concept before that email. The hassle of finding childcare, the flight, hotel expenses, food and so on, I just decided to pass. As the days went on, I kept getting the emails talking about registration ending soon and how amazing it was going to be. On a whim, I decided to call the phone number and ask some questions. I remember talking to someone in the Canfield group and they made it sound so amazing. I just felt a little voice inside saying, "Make the arrangements, clear your schedule and just do it." I had daydreamed how it would be, again not feeling up to the standards of other attendees who

I didn't even know. I look back now and feel silly about that.

The good news is that I went and it was truly amazing. I was confronted with some painful memories from my past. One of them being losing my father in my early twenties. I realized then that I never had allowed myself to grieve his passing, I just went on with business as usual. I realized the sense of feeling unworthy or less than had been amplified by events in my marriages leaving me with a feeling of distrust and a hardened heart. Even though I had found success in business outside of the carnival industry and knew I was a great mom, I still heard the voice in the back of my mind saying 'you are less than.' I had carried it with me all that time. I came back refreshed, with a signed copy of *The Success Principles* by Jack Canfield. Thanks to saying yes to that event, I had opened up a whole new world to be explored.

After that event, I prayed passionately that God show me my true purpose. In the meantime, go back about a year before in February 2013, I noticed my mom not wanting to get out of the house as she used to. She became very independent when my dad passed away. She was seventy-two years old and I had noticed some changes. She always attended my daughter's sporting events, but I noticed over time she would decline the invitation, saying she was just tired and would stay home. I remember her going to the doctor and I asked her what the doctor had to report. She could not give me the whole story, so I started going to the doctor with her regularly to make sure she was ok. I found out that she was seeing a neurologist and was taking a small dose of Aricept. The doctor was in and out so quickly, he said this was for memory, nothing to worry about, just something to enhance normal memory with aging. I didn't worry about it. He made it sound like normal aging. I had noticed that she was losing weight as well. So the next visit to her primary care physician, I asked him to go back twelve months and tell me what her weight was. I was stunned to find out she had lost seventeen pounds in twelve months.

I have a friend in the field of Social Work who caters to seniors who I would see occasionally in the hallway at my daughter's school. I mentioned to her my concerns over my mom. I suggested a meeting. I told my mom that I wanted my Social Worker friend to come over and talk with her. She was not having any of that. So, a month or so later, I arranged a lunch for the three of us; my mom was guarded. A few months later, she agreed to an in-home meeting with my friend. My friend said she seemed to be fine, but again she was on her toes! I expressed that I was not convinced that my mother's neurologist knew what he was doing and I wanted her to see a specialist in neurology. She mentioned a place downtown that specialized in memory and worked with a team of doctors, but you couldn't get in without a referral. The good news is that we were able to get an appointment, but due to the popularity of this facility, we had to wait eight months for an opening.

Fast forward to summer of 2014, my mom was calling me more and more often expressing her loneliness and needing my assistance around her house. Out of concern for her, I offered to move her in with me. Restoration is one of my spiritual strengths and I was trying to remedy the situation. She said no at first, but finally, she agreed to move in. She moved in on October 20th, 2014. Things were going great after she moved in. She would come and go, running her errands, and I was doing my thing and we would see each other in the evenings. She was much happier, but it was an adjustment for my daughter and I since it had just been us in our house for the last eight years. The eight month wait for the doctor's appointment finally arrived and she had two-and-a-half hours of testing to make sure her memory was good and she was healthy. This was a slow moving process and we did not get the results until December. They called and wanted to have a family results appointment.

My mother and I drove together and my sister and my friend, the social worker, met us at the doctor's office. They called us in to a nice room with a wooden table and several chairs. We waited patiently for the neuropsychologist to join us. He arrived and explained the testing that she had and was very thorough in the details. He told us that she had

Early Onset Alzheimer's. We all just looked at each other in disbelief. How can this be? She's only seventy-two years old. I don't remember the medical terms about amyloid plaques and the frontal cortex of the brain; we were all in shock. My mom told him he was wrong, that she was fine, that she did not have Alzheimer's. Next was his recommendation that she no longer drive anymore. I don't think she comprehended that the first time, not because she didn't understand, but because she knew that she had to be able to drive, otherwise how would she get around; this was unacceptable to her. He went on to explain the processes involved in driving a car and that her testing showed that these multi-step processes were becoming a bit more difficult for her. My mother has a strong personality, so she was not giving up her car keys. This changed everything for her.

The months immediately following were difficult. I believe everything happens as it's supposed to and that God's plan was in motion with the fact that she was already living with me. It had never occurred to me that she was going to be diagnosed with early onset Alzheimer's. I knew that she might have had mild memory issues, but never thought about Alzheimer's. I had to keep a close eye on her, as she did not want to accept not being allowed to drive. She was very demanding of me and my time when she wanted something. After several months I thought I was going to lose my mind. With her strong personality, used to getting what she wanted and doing things in her own time, I finally realized that there was no way I could be at her beck and call, run a business, and take care of my daughter. We had a long discussion about hiring someone to be her driver. She agreed. As the months passed, I noticed more changes in her memory and behavior, living in the same house. She went through a depression, expressing that her life might as well be over since she was not allowed to drive anymore.

My heart was breaking for her and there was nothing I could do to change her diagnosis. To all of the family caregivers who are reading this, my heart is with you right now. The emotional toll it takes on one's mental state creates stress to our physical body. It's very important to take time to breath, be still with your thoughts and feed your mind. One will not understand the responsibility until he or she is in it. When the parent becomes 100 percent dependent on you, it's a role reversal. My mom was my confidante, my rock, and my best friend. We would laugh, cry, and just be there for each other. I remember about a year and a half after she moved in, I realized that I was slowly losing my mother as I remembered her. This was the first time I actually felt alone. We take our parents for granted thinking that everything will always be okay. Take time out and make the most of your time left with them. I'm grateful she is still here, that I can go to her, hug her, and tell her how much I love her. After four years, I believe taking care of someone with Alzheimer's is a learned skill that takes ample time, smart psychology, and extreme patience. There are many responsibilities when you are taking over someone's life. It's like having another child who cannot be left alone. To be quite honest, it has made me stronger than I ever thought possible, and I'm grateful for yet another gift that God has allowed me to experience through this adversity. The gift of strength and patience.

I believe that God has a plan for all of us. I know now in my heart that he allowed the previous challenges in my life to teach and grow me as a woman of God so that I could reveal His glory to others.

I would like to extend my heartfelt gratitude to Jack Canfield and the BTS event of 2014. It opened my eyes to realize that I absolutely do have the potential of living out my dreams. The event allowed me to discover that even though I grew up in an extremely unique and distinct paradigm, I was able to experience life in a way that not many children did and not very many people understood. The barrier of understanding between the public and the carnival industry caused me judgement at a young age. Although this was difficult at times, I see it differently now. BTS gave me the tools to break out of my old story and start creating a new one. I now perceive the diversity of my formative years as a gift of life lessons that has given me a clear perspective in how to live out my passion of helping others.

One of these gifts and freedoms is that I am someone who has never worked for anyone else. The life training that I received in the carnival business and being mentored by my father was priceless. I was more independent as a teenager in high school, working the summers in the carnival business, taking on more responsibility. These gifts of lessons and knowledge allowed me to make the transition later on in life to the Merchant Service Industry with confidence, freedom, and independence. This freedom and self-determination are what gave me the courage and self-assurance to raise my daughter as a single parent, the way I wanted her to be raised and to set her up for success. I absolutely love personal development and the way it makes me feel. I wanted to help others feel this way in knowing they can realize their dreams. All of this time I have wondered what my passion and purpose was and it's been right in front of me the whole time. I am my happiest and most fulfilled when I'm helping others.

My daughter is now seventeen years old, a senior in private Christian school, and just received her letter of acceptance into the University of North Texas to study psychology. At fifty-one, I am over the moon excited about the next chapter of my life, sharing the wisdom and the tools to help others take the appropriate steps to change their direction in life. To create the mindset to know, regardless of the challenges, you can still move forward to live out your dreams, no matter your age, and discover your full potential.

ABOUT CAROLE B. YOUNG

Who is Carole B. Young? Carole is someone who lives life gracefully with intentional purpose. Today, she stands firm on the God-given spiritual strengths of belief, responsibility, deliberation, restoration, and adaptability that He has instilled throughout her life.

Belief - Having intentional core values, high ethics, being altruistic, and having a consistent set of priorities allowing the ability of acquiring trust.
Responsibility - Following through to completion, having a strong word, dependable, committed and finishing what is started with care.
Deliberation - Planning ahead, identifying and assessing the risk/reward. Careful, vigilant, approaching with reserve, observant.
Restoration - To fix or problem solve, research/analyze with energy and enthusiasm. Studying the symptoms and offering solutions, restoring others to fullness.
Adaptability - Able to accomplish various tasks or demands in the moment. Welcomes unforeseen detours, spontaneous, creative, and flexible.

Carole experienced entrepreneurship at a young age. Utilizing these strengths has allowed her success in working with a community of business owners in the Financial Payment Services industry for more than twenty years. Carole takes great pride, present and past, in her choice of raising her now 17-year-old daughter, as a single parent for the last twelve years. This choice has allowed her to deliver a style of "Purposeful Parenting" that includes teachings of open communication, planting seeds, allowing choices, and praising the efforts, not just the outcomes, just to name a few.

A Certified Canfield Trainer in The Success Principles, her gift of intuitiveness and diverse experiences gives her a unique skillset. Carole's desire and altruistic compassion for helping others and professional training will allow you to break out of "Old Stories" of sabotaging beliefs, increase your confidence, empower you to live out your dreams, desires, and ambitions, getting you from where you are to where you want to be in achieving your full potential.

Carole enjoys working with Small Business and Corporations, teaching The Success Principles, and the importance of team building. She teaches "Purposeful Parenting" to single parents and families. She offers a four-to-six week workshop, "My Game Plan," for high school seniors, providing them the tools that build belief, self-assurance, and fearless confidence for transitioning into adulthood.

Lastly, holding a special place in her heart is working with families of aging parents, preparing them for "The Next Stage" in their parents' lives. Carole is currently working on a Dementia Care training program to achieve her Alzheimer's Association EssentiALZ Certification.

Visit with Carole at: www.carolebyoung.com
Facebook: @carolebrownyoung
Instagram: @carolebyoung
Twitter: @carolebyoung
Linkedin: @carolebyoung

A VERY SPECIAL PROM

Jessica Amaro

The promenade dance, an end of the school year event that high school juniors and seniors look forward to, especially the young ladies. Yes, it's that time of year again! The windows of every department store and boutique's "theme" is prom. The array of dresses that glitter and sparkle captures the attention of all.

I felt Christine's tiny hand gently slipping away as she was drawn to a red dress so eloquently showcased; this became her focal point. I followed her in silence, without uttering a word, so as to not disturb her thoughts. The look on her face was illuminating, and for a moment her gait was no longer a drag of her right foot. As Christine led the way into the department store to get a closer look, her attention was immediately refocused on two teenage girls as they admired themselves in the mirror. Their dresses were gorgeous, their attitudes were infectious, causing all spectators to smile.

After this encounter, Christine and I had a conversation that would begin and end the exact same way. "Jessie, I want to go to the prom."

As a big sister I wanted to accommodate my younger sibling's request; however, this was not a reasonable request (so I thought). I asked, "Christine, do you remember going to the prom?"

She replied, "Yes."

"Did you have fun?"

"Yes," she repeated, "and I had a red dress! Do you remember, Jessie?"

All I could do was nod yes and smile. I began to explain that proms are for students who are still in high school. She then said she wanted to go back to school. I looked into her eyes and knew she was not giving up.

"Yes, but Jessie, I want to go to the prom again," she protested, as if I could just make it happen.

I have always watched over my younger sister, Christine. Not just out of the need to protect her. Not just because she is my world, but because she is special. Christine was diagnosed with William's Syndrome at birth. This meant she would most likely never drive a car, get married, or be able to live on her own, but she didn't want to discuss those things, she just wanted to talk about prom.

The more she talked about prom, the more I felt compelled to do something. I deeply wanted to create a prom experience for my sister, but there were so many reasons why I couldn't. I couldn't because I was unemployed. I couldn't because I had a four-year-old and I was pregnant again. I couldn't because I was struggling to finish graduate school. I couldn't because I didn't know how.

Almost two months after giving birth to my son, I decided I was going to create an opportunity for my sister to go to prom again. It would take a great deal of work, but more than anything it was going to take faith, believing that I could even if I didn't know where to start.

I promised myself that I would make it happen no matter what. In the beginning, no matter what meant that I would have to ask for help. No matter what meant that I would make mistakes along the way. No matter what meant I was going to create a special prom for my sister. A Very Special Prom.

Every day, I would begin with a list of tasks and every day the universe would provide. It's still amazing to me now, as I look back; I didn't realize that every time I asked, I received. I remember the day that I negotiated the price of the venue down from $1500 to $500; that was the same day that I received a check in the mail from my mom for $500 in support of my vision. The next task on the list was food for the event. I had decided that I would try to get all the food donated from local restaurants by asking for one or two items from their menu.

I remember my first meeting with the general manager of a local restaurant. His exact words were, "So, you expect us to just donate two items from our menu to set alongside the food from our competitors … we can't do that." As I began to thank him for his time, he interrupted me, "I am not willing to share the catering, however, would you being willing to allow us to do it all?" I exhaled. Could I allow them to do it all? He used the word "allow," as if I was doing him a favor, but even then I still didn't see how so many things were working in my favor.

I created a registration form and a flyer that read, "A Very Special Prom, an opportunity for special-needs individuals to create their own memories." I distributed these packets throughout the city specifical- ly targeting organizations that served special-needs individuals and neighboring schools. I spent countless days sharing my vision at local schools. On one of those days, after a long conversation with a school administrator and leaving my keys on the counter, I ran back inside and a young man stopped me. He explained how glad he was that I had returned because he was listening to my plan and wanted to be a part of the vision; he wanted to know if I had a DJ for the event. It was the very next thing on my list. We exchanged information and he promised that he would send me over an affordable invoice. Later that evening I received his invoice for $0.

As momentum was building and my anxiety began to set in, I received an unexpected invitation to speak on a local radio station. I really don't remember what I said, but I remember my voice shaking and when it was over, beating myself up over all of the things I should have said. But little did I know just how many people would hear my voice on the radio that day. I received my first call from Presley, who would become my first volunteer because she heard the broadcast. That would also be the week that I connected with Kim, a community advocate who would connect me to so many people because she heard me on the air waves. That would be the month that city officials would contact me to support my vision because someone heard me on the radio.

"Hello, we are trying to reach someone in regards to supporting A Very Special Prom."

"Well, you've reached the right person …"

"Great, what is the name of your organization?"

Without hesitation the words came out as if I had said them a thousand times: "For the Exceptional."

That conversation was the first time I ever thought of what I was doing as more than an event, and like that a seed was planted. For the Exceptional, an organization geared towards creating social outlets for special-needs young adults. All I had to do was show up. Nervous, unsure, voice shaking, uncomfortable, no plan, but I showed up and as a result, what I was seeking found me.

One of the many memories that I will always keep close was created that night. "I didn't know he could dance," she said, cupping my face with her hands as I watched the tears stream down her face and we stood there crying. "I didn't know if he would even try … thank you for doing this." She went on to explain that her 29-year-old son had begun to regress since graduating high school and seemed to not be interested in anything over the last few years. She smiled through the tears. "I didn't know what to expect but we can't wait to do this again."

A total of thirty-two special-needs young adults, seven volunteers, eight teachers, 300 balloons, four hours of non-stop dancing and it was over.

Looking back, what I did not understand is that I wasn't just hosting a prom for my sister. I had created an opportunity for special-needs individuals to be surrounded by other exceptional individuals. I had created an opportunity for parents to sit and exchange resources. I had created an opportunity that allowed exceptional individuals to connect in an environment that was created just for them.

The truth is, I ended that night with an overdrawn bank account, a messy house, an "F" in one of my graduate classes and a feeling that I will spend the rest of my life chasing. My soul was full, my spirit was on fire because I had done something that meant something.

For almost a decade and counting I have been impacting the lives of special-needs individuals, and currently "For the Exceptional" has served more than 250 special-needs young adult attendees annually, and is 100 percent community funded. Under the For The Exceptional umbrella I have been able to impact so many lives. I ran day programs for several years and it was a wonderful experience that allowed me to work hand-in-hand on a daily basis with special-needs individuals and their families.

A few years ago I had the honor of being one of Charleston, South Carolina's 40 under 40 recognized by *The Business Journal*. During this event I remember listening to a speaker explain how we are grown by people and projects. A Very Special Prom was my first project and it has connected me to so many people who have led me to countless opportunities. That night, while sitting on that stage amongst Charleston's emerging leaders, I realized that growth is not about perfection, but about the things that you learned along the way.

I have grown to believe that all struggles are just growing pains that must be endured to become the person that you were purposed to become. I was being prepared far before the seed was planted and I am thankful for every experience and what it has instilled in me. I am driven because I am the oldest of three girls who were raised by a single teen mother. I am strong because I am the daughter of a man who was sentenced to life in prison on her sixteenth birthday. I am courageous because I accepted my sister's challenge to do the impossible. Each year I continue to grow the prom experience and every day I am dedicated to following where my passion leads me.

ABOUT JESSICA AMARO

Jessica Amaro is the Founder and Executive Director of For The Exceptional, located in Charleston, South Carolina. For The Exceptional is a non-profit organization that provides interactive social outlets to young adults with disabilities while providing their parents and the community with information, support, and resources. Since 2010, Jessica has been responsible for bringing together hundreds of special-needs young adults and their families, using A Very Special Prom as the tool of connection.

Jessica has become a vital part of the special-needs community through aligning herself with local businesses. Equipped with a Master's Degree in Management and Leadership she has also been able to utilize strong business principles to build a non-profit organization that is 100 percent community funded. She has dedicated herself to creating a city of opportunity that requires her to work hand-in-hand with local businesses to fund services needed for the Tri-County special-needs populations. Jessica is a loving wife, proud mother of two, and the sibling of a special-needs adult.

www.ForTheExceptional.com
Email: Jessica@ForTheExceptional.com
Instagram: I Am Jessica Amaro

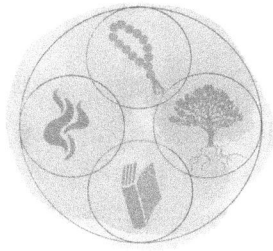

DISCOVERING GIFTS THROUGH TRANSFORMATION

Sagoo Arora

As I entered the building, I was struck by the starkness and immense size of the waiting room. Nervously waiting for my appointment, I observed young women entering in wheelchairs, too weak to walk unattended, and bald from side effects of chemotherapy. I became suddenly overwhelmed by fear and sadness and started crying, which turned into uncontrollable bawling. I realized I did not want to die at the age of forty-one.

This was God's wake up call to GET OUT. Get out of my unhappy marriage as soon as possible, or I knew my health would continue to deteriorate and I would be one of those women in the waiting room of the cancer center. The chronic stress from walking on eggshells was slowly killing me. I had suffered with insomnia, reflux, extreme anxiety, panic attacks, frequent vomiting, and for the last six months, unexplained daily fevers. I went from specialist to specialist and none of them could diagnose what was causing the fevers except for high cortisol levels indicative of severe adrenal fatigue and chronic stress.

I knew I needed to make a drastic change in my life and soon. This was the second time since I had been married that I had suffered from chronic low-grade fevers. The first time in 1994 (only a year into the marriage), I developed hypothyroidism after having fevers for more than a month. I knew my immune system was again about to collapse.

Unresolved emotional issues continue to build up in our energy centers (chakras) and eventually become physical ailments that we can no longer ignore. At the time, I did not realize that my hypothyroidism was a result of not speaking my truth. When your throat chakra is closed and the energy is blocked, your thyroid function can be directly impacted. My experience had been that if I did speak my truth, it was received with silent treatment for days, sometimes for weeks by my partner. I did not feel that I could express myself fully or openly. I felt very isolated and alone even though I was married. Our bodies signal us to pay attention, and when we ignore them, the issues continue to compound and escalate until we hear them loud and clear!

A few months after this wakeup call, I asked for a separation from my husband once I mustered up enough courage to follow through with it. The first night I was alone in my home was the first night I slept for eight straight hours peacefully in almost two decades. I could breathe freely again. I began a daily meditation practice that I continue to use religiously. Quieting my mind centers me in such a profound way. I honestly do not know how I lived without it. It has shifted me in ways I had not imagined. It has made me more mindful and calmer. I now can appreciate the simple beauties of nature: an amber sunset, the pattern of the clouds, the luminous full moon, the grandeur of the trees. I enjoy each moment and can be fully present to all life has to offer. I am calmer, sleep well, and react to stress with a totally different outlook. I feel grounded, centered, and rarely get flustered.

After my separation, I was searching for my spirituality and embarked on what I call my "Journey of Faith." I felt lost and wanted to reconnect to Spirit and the Universe. Over a period of a year and half, I visited several houses of worship to find the best fit: churches, synagogues, satsangs, Buddhist and Hindu temples. After reading many books, researching the history of religions, and discussing my thoughts and questions with several clergyman, I realized at the end of my journey that my divine connection with Spirit or God was a personal one with unconditional support, love, and guidance. I loved different aspects of each religion and house of worship and the feeling of community they offered, but none of them fully aligned with my soul. In order for me to commit to a particular path it had to fully resonate with my being, therefore, I created my own! Yes, I am a bit of a rebel. I suppose I am still a Jersey girl at heart!

I was introduced to energy healing through friends who had training in shamanism and other energy healing modalities soon after I was divorced. They gave me firsthand experience how energy healing could help me. I was astounded and excited to have discovered an alternative way of healing. I started regularly seeing an energy healer while simultaneously seeing my therapist. I read many self-help books, took group therapy classes, and listened to thought leaders. After a few months, I realized that the energy healing sessions were helping more than psychotherapy and I stopped seeing the therapist. I could feel the layers of limiting beliefs slowly being released from past lives and past generations. I had limiting beliefs surrounding the abundance of money, my capabilities, and self-worth. As I healed my self-worth, I learned to speak my truth and stand in my own power. This allowed me to express myself to others with authenticity, compassion, and openness. I created healthy boundaries in my life with my time, energy, and commitments. I released unhealthy patterns around being a caretaker, rescuer, and people pleaser that had created codependent relationships. These unhealthy survivor traits made me feel that I had to be needed and always accepted to be loved.

As I felt my vibration elevate, my relationships with my daughters and my parents shifted in a positive way as well. My divorce was very challenging for my parents, especially my mom. She wasn't supportive at first and felt devastated by the loss of my marriage. As time went on and I healed, however, she did as well. I came back to my old self and childhood friends stated they were happy to see the "old me" resurface. My joyful, energetic, and humorous self resurfaced. I was also able to decrease my dose of Synthroid to half for my hypothyroidism and am in the process of healing it completely. Stress can create emotional issues that long term can affect our physical bodies and present as issues in our immune system, gastrointestinal, chronic pain, or even cancer.

In my first session, the spiritual healer I was seeing told me I could be a healer, too. I didn't believe her. I felt so broken that I could not imagine being able to heal anyone else. After a few years of healing sessions, meditation, and mindfulness, I started to feel more empowered and became interested in possibly learning an energy healing modality. I attended a Reiki share where the participants took turns performing Reiki on each other. Reiki is a safe, natural therapeutic technique that reduces stress, pain, anxiety, and provides relaxation, thus promoting the body's own ability to heal. Universal life force energy (Reiki) flows through the practitioner to the recipient. I was excited to be a part of the Reiki share and meet other like-minded spiritual souls. When it was my teacher's turn to receive Reiki, I stood above her head (crown) and placed my hands over her ears. After we were done, she turned to me and asked me if I had taken Reiki classes before. I told her I had not taken any classes and really didn't know what I was doing. She told me I had a natural ability for Reiki and was a powerful healer. I had always been an intuitive person, a nurturer, and a confidante. People would feel at ease with me quickly, and share their life stories when first meeting me. But knowing that I had the capability to be a healer took me by surprise; I was thrilled!

After I completed my Reiki Master, I realized I wanted to help free others from old unhealthy patterns. I had found my path and purpose in life. This was a whole new, fascinating world for me. I was so grateful to have found energy healing and the incredible impact it had on my life. I was the lotus flower blossoming from beneath the thick mud and water, and had begun a new, beautiful chapter of my life. Being able to give back to the world the divine gift that had been bestowed upon me was now my life's work. I began my own healing practice with the support of my parents and close friends. This has been incredibly rewarding and with each session I am amazed and grateful to offer healing in a loving and compassionate way. It fills my heart with such joy and peace to see another soul be released from the chains that are holding them back from living their life with intention, self-love, and open-heartedness.

I continued exploring energy healing modalities such as Archangel Light and Shamanic classes and added them to my tool belt. Archangel Light is a profound spiritual energy. The energy goes directly to the root cause to promote healing. The love of the Divine Feminine Energy as well as the Archangels are experienced when receiving this energy. Archangel Light allowed me to shine and bring forth my feminine energy that had been hidden for years. I had spent so much time being codependent and a caretaker, causing that part of me to diminish. Shamanism is the oldest and most enduring human spiritual tradition. It offers a holistic view of healing that embraces the body, the psyche, the soul, and the spiritual dimension of well-being through practices such as chakra clearing, soul retrieval, and releasing limiting beliefs. With Shamanic healing I was able to uncover my inner child and playful joy in my life. I released unconscious beliefs that I was not worthy of an authentic and loving relationship or abundance.

A recent session with a client revealed that she was struggling with feeling stuck in her love life and with a close friend. We were able to clear her limiting belief surrounding love and relationships rooted in a lack of self-worth during the powerful healing session. We also performed a cord cutting that released any unhealthy energy cords with this friend and requested to maintain only healthy and vibrant ties. When I spoke to her after a few weeks, she was much happier and in a loving relationship. She had released herself from the unhealthy codependent friendship that was causing her angst and strife. After just one session, she manifested large shifts in her life.

Other aspects of energy work that I incorporate in my business are house clearings and blessings. I clear heavy energies from homes and properties along with any spirits that have not crossed over to the light. These spirits often feel like heavy energy and can present themselves as flickering lights or sounding smoke alarms. During one of these house clearings, I discovered a restless soul, a young boy of ten years. He had been a slave who was fitfully roaming this realm for more than 100 years, searching for his parents. I could see his grave below the home with my mind's eye. His soul was put to rest after this clearing and the homeowner could feel the lightness in the home immediately. I received guidance that the land the home was currently on was previously a graveyard. The homeowner researched the public records and confirmed that the land beneath the homes on her street were previously used for graves. These graves had been moved across the street to build their homes.

Energy work, meditation, and mindfulness have transformed my life. I am thankful I was given a second chance to build a new and fulfilling chapter to my life's story. I have observed that each day brings a gift and a lesson. How we reframe these lessons and use them moving forward in our lives is in our hands alone. I know that the energy I put out in the universe is what I will attract into my life, and my goal is to keep my vibrational energy high. I no longer allow unhealthy codependent relationships in my life. I stand in my power and speak my truth no matter how scared I feel inside. I speak with kindness and compassion, always factoring in the other person's perspective. When I have expressed myself from an authentic open-hearted space, the results have always been positive.

By removing unconscious blocks and unhealthy patterns, I have created a blessed and joyful life.

It has also been important for me to remember to have self-compassion. I used to be my own worst critic and put undue stress on myself. My inner critic said things to me that I would never say out loud to anyone else. I wanted to be perfect all the time and constantly beat myself down. My wise nurturer is a part of me that gives accolades and self-compassion.

For example, if I failed a test the inner critic would say, "You are so stupid, you couldn't even pass this test," whereas the wise nurturer would say, "You did your best. Now you are aware of how to study for the next test and do well." What a big difference in how that makes you feel. Accepting myself wholeheartedly and embracing the light and shadow parts has been infinitely healing for my heart and soul.

The more I show up in the universe as who I really am, sharing my story with truth and vulnerability, no matter how fearful I may feel, the more deeply I connect to others, which gives me great joy. My journey was necessary for me to create the wonderful life I currently have.

It is vital to cultivate courage, compassion, and connection from a place of authenticity to have a wholehearted life. It is time to show up and be seen. We are ALL worthy of true belonging and unconditional love.

ABOUT SAGOO ARORA

Sagoo is an intuitive coach, energy healer, and holistic practitioner. She combines intuitive coaching along with energy healing including modalities of Reiki, Archangel Light, and Shamanism. Energy work in synergy with intuitive coaching provides the path to uncover the root of the problem and promotes healing emotionally, mentally, physically, and spiritually. Sagoo is certified as a Reiki Master, Archangel Master, and a Shaman.

Sagoo has always known that her soul's purpose was to help others to manifest the best version of themselves. She has earned a Bachelor of Science and Doctor of Pharmacy degrees. As a healthcare professional she has improved patient care with her extensive clinical knowledge base.

After practicing pharmacy for several years, it was evident that traditional medications and psychotherapy were not the ideal answers for all issues that she encountered with her family and for herself. She researched alternative healing modalities and was introduced to energy work. Having found energy healing to be integral in her own healing, she proceeded in taking classes for herself and found it to be her passion.

Meditation, Mindfulness, and Energy work have transformed her life. Her passion has shifted to healing other souls through the power of energy work, intuitive coaching, and motivational speaking. She is the founder of Love Light Lotus.

She lives an inspired and grateful life through her energy healing work and hopes to help you manifest the life you desire. Her passion permeates her being and radiates in an aura of joy and compassion.

You can find Sagoo for energy healing sessions, house clearings, and motivational speaking on the following:

Facebook : Love Light Lotus with Sagoo Arora
Instagram : love_light_lotus
Website: lovelightlotus.com
Email: lovelightlotussagoo@gmail.com

Love Light Lotus

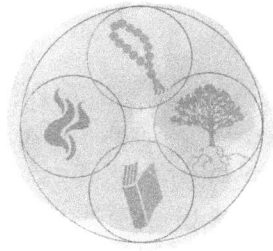

ESSENCE OF LIFE

Jodie Baudek

We get complacent with life, thinking, it is what it is. Take your hands off the steering wheel and let God help you. You are absolutely capable of accomplishing anything. I came into this mindset early in my life, thinking that people can accomplish anything.

My parents were married when my mom was nineteen. My dad had signed up for the Navy, and when he came back, he realized he didn't love my mom the way a husband should love his wife. I think this is really big. My parents chose to be the greatest of friends working through whatever they needed to work through so that we could operate as a family unit. I could not be more grateful for that.

My mom remarried a gentleman named Doug, who can't keep his hands off of her, constantly saying how much he's in love with her. Together, they had my wonderful sister Kyrsten, who is sixteen years younger than I. When Doug married my mom, it was the understanding that I am his daughter, that there is no difference between biological, stepchild, extended family. Family is family. I couldn't ask for three more amazing parents. I have tears running down my face telling you this, how blessed I really am.

If you can make the choice to get out of your own way, a lot of things can change for you. I thank my family for setting aside their own feelings, seeing the big family picture and getting the mindset that everything is going to be okay. When my parents divorced it was never a Tuesday/Thursday, every other weekend thing; my parents equally co-parented, 100 percent. There was never an argument about that. My dad was very visible in the neighborhood and in my life. Being a child of divorce in the '70s wasn't a real common thing, yet there was another family across the street from us who were also getting divorced.

I started getting bullied a lot and couldn't figure out why. We aren't talking about name-calling bullying, we are talking about being pushed down sewers. I would climb trees, they would step on my hands, kick me in the face, and I would fall out of trees. At a picnic, a girl sliced my face with the plastic knife she had in her hand. There was an older female babysitter who was supposed to be watching out for me. She was exhibiting some unhealthy behaviors toward me. It was tough getting physically and verbally abused.

When I was young, I was tiny, with long blonde hair, a fair complexion, and this huge inner light. With the bullying, my light started dimming. I was spending time in my room, not going outside, hiding in my closet and having nightmares. My dad could see something was really bothering me. He would take me to Karate class, throw me on the mat and say, "Teach this kid." My parents sat me down to talk about what was going on. In the '70s, therapy, webinars, and coaching weren't available. My mom's philosophy was to be super nice. My dad's philosophy was kick their ass once and you will be done with it.

The day came when my mom had it after several conversations and nothing was changing. It came time to finally confront the problem. I took my dad's route. I confidently stood up to the bullies. I told them there was no way this was going to happen anymore. I spoke up, allowing things to go my direction. If there was something said, rather than just leave it alone, I would confront it. I would tell them, this isn't right, this doesn't feel good. This changed a lot of things in my life—long term.

When I was twelve years old, we moved away. At that point, my dad did Jazzercise, where I met Judi Missett. I liked Jazzercise, it was cool and fun, and I loved watching from the stage as people changed during their routines. When I was sixteen, Judi asked me if I would be interested in teaching. I said no. I wanted to make money and be creative in my own way. I did a few things, didn't feel like I was making my mark in the world, so I opened the studio, my light brightened, and something changed.

I had worked at gyms prior to opening the studio and noticed that people are intimidated to work out; they don't feel good about themselves. I wanted to do a boutique style studio, still reaching the masses, but in smaller amounts.

We all have gifts to share with each other. Some people have the gift of money, some of love, some of coaching, whatever that gift may be. I get presents a lot from clients which I used to struggle with until I realized that is their love language. I don't give a lot of presents. I would rather give you experiences. Everyone has their own love language. I am in a really good vibration with a lot of amazing people and my parents taught me that we are all equal. When you come from a place of love, beautiful things can happen.

One of my companies is called Essence of Life. I own several yoga studios, which are really nothing more than a front to get you in the door to live your absolute best life. Because of these studios, I get to interview some of the most amazing people in the world. I've gotten to interview Miguel Ruiz, Jr., Dr. Demartina and Lisa Nichols. These people, Kate Butler included—I can actually just pick up the phone and call her. I call them my friends. I can reach out to them because I put myself in this great vibration. I had a lot of coaching for me to be able to say, "You have a gift, share that gift."

When I opened the studio, it wasn't cool to teach meditation or yoga. I guarantee you that any class I teach, whether it be spin, dance, self-defense, you are going to get meditation. People come to spin class. I say, "Close your eyes, let's visualize this." They would come to me after class saying, "Wow, I feel so different, letting things go and seeing what is right with life."

On my journey, in high school, one of the girls who bullied me asked if she could tell me her story. When her parents divorced, her dad just left. My dad was a part of my life, and she thought that if I was out of the way, my dad would become her dad. I said, "Wow, that is absolutely amazing to have enough strength to go to therapy and then apologize to me, letting me know why you did what you did." I think that's why I started watching people's patterns, studying the things I study now. I'm trying to learn how to empower and inspire people.

I recently sold my home to pursue my dreams. I moved to the city and live in a condo. It's easy to get tunnel vision as I work. I have to set my alarm and go outside. There is a beautiful garden at my studio where I put my feet in the grass, connect with the earth and breathe.

I teach one breath work/meditation class and certify people to teach yoga, Pilates, and reformer. I am adamant about meditation and breath work. We need to take time for ourselves every day. That might mean you have to set your alarm to put your feet in the grass, connect with the earth, and breathe. You want your intuition to click in, you want some clarity in your life, you want to learn how to let things go—breathe and meditate. I promise you, it will change your life. I took a step back from my personal life and started growing my professional life. It has been a lot of learning and beautiful opportunities. In doing that, I forgot to have fun.

I know this is a book called *Women Who Impact*. When you are the boss babes that you are and you walk around the world doing all these great things, remember to be the beautiful, sexy, feminine woman that you are. Remember to laugh and dance. I want you to remember that vulnerability is not a sign of weakness, it's a catalyst for your growth in so many ways. Allow everyone around you to help you and allow other people in your life to do things for you and with you. Especially your significant other.

Recently, I met a man named Brian. He has been an inspiration to my growth. That kind of in-your-soul growth. Don't get me wrong, there are warm fuzzies but we all need to let our trust, our intuition work and our guard down, just asking and trusting. He has reminded me about femininity, vulnerability, and letting the masculine energy stay at work, allowing me to be feminine when I'm at home, on a date, etc. Ladies, I know you hear me and see yourself here. We don't have to take care of, control, or know it all. Just allow and prepare to be delighted and surprised.

Remember, it is important to take time out for you. Often times we get in our "women who impact" mindset, we are going to change the world, take care of our kids, our aging parents, our businesses, our home, and we forget to take care of ourselves.

Meditation, breath work, movement, yoga, just taking a moment to walk outside and breathe. If you drive your car and never put gas in your car, it is going to die out and then you won't get anywhere or do anything for anyone else. Take that analogy and refill your soul. Visualize your energy and vibration in alignment, you're feeling great, have a balance of feminine and masculine energy in your life, you are allowing yourself to give and receive. I promise everything around you is going to change for the better. Your energy changes, because you choose to take time for you.

You will find yourself in alignment, this beautiful love source where people in your life are so incredible. Don't stop your growth, don't stop moving forward. You matter, you are loved, you are appreciated, and you can accomplish anything standing in your confidence, shining your light.

Move forward on your path. Say you had a situation in your life and it was negative, a bad relationship. Look at that relationship, sift through it and say, this is where I showed up. I'm not going to beat myself up about it, I'm going to see where I can be different in my next relationship. I'm going to choose to see how I can be better, what I learned, how I can grow and allow myself to move forward so I can constantly be shedding the layers of what is not right and moving into my best self.

If I could gift something to every single person in the world, I would gift confidence. If you want to give light to others, you have to glow yourself. I appreciate you for allowing me to share my story and journey with you. Namaste.

ABOUT JODIE BAUDEK

Jodie is an international speaker, author, and coach. She is the Host of Empowered Life and the Dr. Jim and Jodie shows. You can find her a few days a week at one of her Essence of Life yoga, pilates, breath work and meditation studios, which are located in the Chicagoland area. When she is not in her studios, she is traveling, or she is in another one of her favorite places, Los Angeles, working on projects. She spends most of her time teaching 360 degrees of coaching. Her unique approach to shifting your mindset, by using the blend of mind, body, and physical movement with a spirituality connection, has been known to have her clients completely change their lives to achieve things they never even dreamed of.

She fell in love with yoga because she sees life as a beautiful dance and is known for busting a move anywhere she is. Another reason she loves yoga is because, as she explains, you can see people's souls dance when they practice it. Letting go and coming from a place of love will bring you so much peace and allow life to shift in beautiful ways. Forgiveness is the key to unlock any door. Live a life in gratitude. Waking up every morning and saying thank you God/universe/source for the beyond blessed life you have given me, and continue to give me, are a few of her mantras.

If you would like to connect with Jodie, she is in social media as Jodie Baudek. Her websites are:

jodiebaudek.com

essenceoflifechicago.com

Essenceol.com

BECOMING H.E.R. (HUMBLE, EMPATHETIC & RELENTLESS)

Natalie Citarelli

The phone rang. "Natalie, are you sitting down?"

"Yes, I am. Why?"

"I have something to tell you," she said.

As we hung up I sat in silence. I started to cry and couldn't catch my breath.

It all started while I was on vacation in Florida visiting my grandma. The night was cool, my cousin and I got dressed and headed out to the club to do my favorite thing, which was dancing. As I was swaying across the floor a man grabbed my hand to dance with me. I pulled away at first, then decided, what the heck, I'm here to have fun. One dance turned into spending the entire evening together, leading to an exchange of phone numbers. I had been single for three years and enjoying my independence. I was not really thinking of dating, particularly since this guy was a Floridian; I lived in New York. However, the remainder of my vacation, he spent all of his free time showing me around Orlando. The vacation came to an end and I went back to New York.

After a year of being courted by him, both of us flying back and forth, I decided that after I graduated nursing school I'd move to Florida. We eventually moved in together and became your ideal "power couple." We both were successful entrepreneurs and enjoying the best things life had to offer. I was more of a risk taker, but he trusted my vision. This relationship lasted eight years. They were some of the best years of my life. I had no complaints; we were engaged and planning to be married.

Good news came, I was about to be a mom! This meant we were going to become a family. We held off on our wedding plans and awaited the arrival of our son. As the months went by, I started to feel a disconnect between us.

One morning I woke up and asked, "Are you ok?"

He said, "I don't want to be with you anymore."

My heart sank and I wanted to vomit. Here I was, six months pregnant, envisioning what my home with my son and husband would look like, and then I was crushed by a few simple words.

The next few months were torture. He would stay at our friend's house until the early morning hours. Our friend was going through a break-up after a long relationship. His daughter was living with him. I assumed the time he was spending at our friend's home was because he was having his own issues. Perhaps a midlife crisis, and wanted to hang out with his friend since he was now single. The daughter and I would talk, she would ask how I was and what was going on with us. She would visit me and rub my stomach and talk to my baby. It was also comforting to confide in her.

We slept in the same bed, but without any physical contact. He would kiss me on my forehead in the morning when he left for work. I could see he cared, but he didn't care enough. I was crying every day. I was pregnant and alone. My house felt so empty, our life together didn't exist anymore. Unable to sleep, I walked around during the day like a zombie. I would wear new lingerie and purchase new perfume hoping he would notice me. Maybe when he came to bed he would touch me like he use to; this was not so. Months went by and nothing changed. Every time he walked in the door I hoped that was the day he would say, "I'm sorry, I am just feeling nervous about the pregnancy." That never happened.

The time arrived; I was in labor. I had an emergency C-section. My son was born healthy and strong. In the operating room he kissed me on my lips. I felt a big sigh of relief, thinking "It's all going to be ok. It was the pregnancy; he wants to be back together," I thought. We stayed at the hospital the next couple of days until it was time for discharge. The evening of my discharge he was dressed to go out. The room became cold and silent. I knew we weren't getting back together; something was going on. At home he asked me for a hug. I hugged him. He then turned to me and said, "See? I hugged you and felt nothing." I fell to my knees crying in pain. Now what? Who lives in our house we built? Do I go or do you go? What about our new baby? What about our new family? What will I do without him?

I became severely depressed. Thankfully, I had help from my family with my son. I was just sobbing day after day. My family decided it was best to get me out of the house so they moved my things into a vacant room in my sister's home. Subsequently, Mom came to get me to bring my son and me back to New York. My sisters could see that I was not doing well and were concerned for my mental well-being. So my three-week-old baby had his first car ride to New York. I was going back to where I came from, the home I grew up in—love was there.

I was not quite two weeks in New York, at my mother's house, my son almost 1-½ months old, when the phone call came. This call answered all of my questions as to what happened to our relationship. I was betrayed in a way I could never have imagined. I felt so stupid, duped, and weakened, I wondered if I would ever make it through this horrific ordeal. It was more than I could handle. Here I was, a new baby, not in my home anymore, staying at my mother's in New York. My life as I had known it for the past eight years was never ever going to be the same. The hopes and dreams I had for our new family gone. A new normal had begun. The caller stated that my friend's daughter was living in my home now, and that my son's dad and she were together. She was in my home, my bed. How could she rub my stomach and talk to our baby while I was pregnant? She got close to me to keep an eye on him. The nights I was up crying he was with her and everyone knew. The questions she posed to me in creative ways were to see what was going on in my home. I inadvertently gave her the answer. No, he wasn't intimate with me.

After I found out what really happened to my relationship, I went back to Florida. My son was now three months old; he needed to have his father in his life. Even though New York is where I originate from, I had built a life in Florida. My career, my friends, my business associates, my sisters and dad's family were all there. Florida was home. I had to face the pain I had avoided for so long. When it came to visitation, I would drop my baby off to his dad. She opened the door to the home I built, took my son from my arms, and closed my door on me. My senses told me she was cooking in the kitchen that was once mine, the one with the double-wall oven and the island overlooking the family room. I didn't have to see it to visualize what was really going on. She had her clothes in my closet and her toothbrush on my sink. Eventually my son was even calling her mom.

The pain was unbearable. I compared myself to her. I began to belittle myself. I told myself he left me because my butt and chest weren't big enough. My stomach wasn't flat enough, or my hair wasn't long enough. I compared myself to her every physical characteristic. I got a belly ring because I knew she had one. She was Spanish with tan skin and I was white with pale skin and blue eyes. I focused so much on her looks, I forgot to focus on the things that were good about myself. She had no job, no career, and no goals. Yet the things I prided myself on didn't matter in this moment.

I got a letter in the mail from an attorney asking me to sign over the full deed to our house. We had a few properties together, but this was our dream home we had built together. He was willing to give up his rights to our other properties if I gave up any legal rights to this one. I wanted to fight, I wanted her out of my home. My goal was to get her out of that house. Instead I got tired. I was tired of fighting, tired of planning revenge. I went to my attorney and signed the deed solely over to him. I got in my car and cried, but it was at that moment I realized I needed a game plan. I needed to get back to the woman who had had it all. My credit was destroyed. I had one property left that was rented to his parents. I was living in a rented townhouse with a female roommate.

I spoke with an attorney and concluded filing bankruptcy was in order. I was hitting the restart button emotionally and financially. I kept three credit lines open, modified the only home I had left and decided I would only live off my nursing income, not the commissions from real estate sales. My commissions would go straight into my savings account. My goal was to have three more properties over the next three years. I tried doing things that made me smile; different foods, weekend getaways once a month, and dancing; primarily my favorite, to Latin and reggae music. Groupon became my best friend for deals and new adventures. I would read one inspirational book a month. I started networking with people who took me out of my comfort zone. People I would not have met while in my previous relationship. I got to a point where I could work twetnty-four hours a week and enjoy an income of $100,000 plus. All the while enjoying time with my son, friends, family, and just as important, with myself.

I was finally transitioning back to the core of who I was and even a better version of me that I didn't know existed. I decided to reconcile the relationships with my son's father and my friend's daughter. I was choosing to forgive them for what they had done. I started focusing on how great she was with my son. She had potty-trained him, picked him up from school, and most importantly, I felt she really loved him. I was a business woman and she stayed home, so it worked out well. When I needed to run to meetings or show houses, she took care of him. If I had to go away or just needed to get away, it was never an issue, his dad would get to enjoy him. We all did such a great job co-parenting we didn't need a court order for visitation. We did what we felt was best for our son. My son has a great relationship with his dad. They go fishing, camping, and have conversations about spirituality. Even though on some things we don't see eye-to-eye, the majority of the time we agree on what's best for him. I was finally feeling more at peace. You never FORGET what happened, but you can FORGIVE what happened.

Today I achieved those three additional properties that were part of my goal. My real estate career is successful. I have opened my company, Citarelli Realty Group, as a boutique real estate brokerage; helping people create financial stability and security. I find fulfillment in helping others find what can be the biggest investment of their lifetime, a home for themselves or a good investment that will secure their future with passive income. I mentor others on how to build meaningful relationships instead of transactional ones. I take pride in guiding people in a direction where they can make the best decision for themselves. This is not limited to a career in real estate. It is learning how to work less and have enough time for the ones they love, enjoy life's adventures, and have less debt. This can all be done working part-time.

I have spoken to people who felt emotionally broken when their relationship ended, regardless of the reasons. I tell them my story with the hope that they can see when you allow the anguish and the pain to subside there is a phoenix rising inside of you. You can learn how to forgive and become HUMBLE. How to take a negative experience and become EMPOWERED. Lastly how to focus on their goals and become RELENTLESS.

ABOUT NATALIE CITARELLI

Natalie Citarelli is an author, entrepreneur, and investor hailing from New York. She is a dedicated mom and has a heart to help and empower others. Although she is an established and successful entrepreneur, Natalie has had her fair share of challenges and betrayals. The gems from her experiences have helped to make her who she is today. After thirteen years of selling homes in Central Florida, she opened her own real estate company called Citarelli Realty Group. She has a solid team of expert real estate agents, focused on meeting and exceeding all of their clients' needs. Natalie deeply desires to share her story to empower others to overcome, chase their dreams, and achieve success. Her ultimate hope is to empower women and teens globally by providing the powerful keys and action shifts she used to break through the most impossible circumstances. Below are Natalie's social media links:

Facebook: Natalie Citarelli and Citarelli Realty Group
Instagram: @natalieyourbroker
Website: CitarelliRealty.com
Email: Natalieisyourrealtor@gmail.com

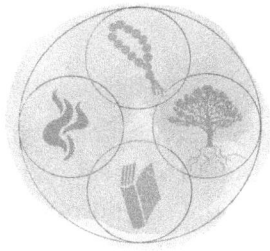

THE BUTTERFLY EFFECT

Megan Datz

Words don't come easily to me. I'm not one of those people who can just write some lengthy, great sounding paragraph on Facebook. I don't like to get up in front of people and talk. I try to avoid it as much as possible. So, to be writing my story here for you to read isn't something I would normally choose to do, but it's a story I feel is important. If you have a passion for something, no matter how difficult it is for you, you can get past the hard parts and channel that passion to take your dream to a reality.

I grew up in a small town in southern New Jersey with my parents, brother, and sister. I'm the oldest of my siblings and we always got along well, still do to this day. We had a very happy childhood and always were encouraged to find a passion or activity that we loved. My brother found his passion as an ice hockey goalie and my sister and I both danced multiple days a week. My mom is one of eleven children and we would get together with her side of the family once a month for holidays or birthdays, considering there was at least one birthday every month. All of her family lives in Pennsylvania, so each month we would drive the hour and a half to my grandparents' house to celebrate. All my aunts, uncles, and cousins would be there. However, it wasn't because of the birthday or holiday that I loved to get together, but because of the cousins I would get to see.

I have nine sister-cousins (a term I have affectionately coined for my female cousins who are more than just cousins in my book) who are older than me. Sheena was the second oldest and five years older than me. I always looked up to her, as I did most of the sister-cousins. Sheena was the first one to take dance classes and because of her, we all did. I looked forward to her dance recital every year. I can still remember sitting as a small, wide-eyed child in the bucket seats of the theatre, so excited to see the costumes, lights, and dances. Every time one of her dances came on I knew it was her. Sheena was very talented, graceful and made dance look easy. She was always front, center, and stood out in such a positive way. She had such an elegance and you could see her love for dance every time she stepped on the stage.

When we were at every family get together, all the sister-cousins would perform a show. Now, I'm not talking about a show that we would throw together and laugh through. Every detail was thought out and we did a different show each month. Sometimes it was a play that incorporated dance moves. We once did an entire nativity show for Christmas. We made up our own lines and songs. I was the angel and sat on my cousins' shoulders with a blanket around my waist, so I looked like I was floating. Sometimes it was just dance after dance. We would make up dances to the newest songs, Disney songs or our parent's favorite songs. We had every part of these shows choreographed and every line memorized. We would spend hours making up the show and at the end of the night would get all twenty-two parents to sit down to watch it. They would all pile in my grandparent's family room, sitting on the couches, chairs, floor, or each other. Our little performances united our entire family together in one single room, even if it was just for a few minutes.

One of my favorite memories was when Sheena came to stay with my family for a week. It was in the '90s, so we videotaped the entire weekend with a big bulky video camera. I tried to wear the same outfit as her every day and my hair the same way, with two pieces falling on either side of my face and the rest pulled back into a tight flipped under ponytail. We made up movies, acted like we were on a talk show, asking everyone in the house questions such as, "What is your most prized possession?" and "What is it like to have such an awesome family?" We made up dances to songs from *The Lion King* and *Ace of Base*. We picked out costumes and would do changes between each dance piece. It was because of her and her love for dance that I started dancing and loved it so much. She encouraged me to make up dances of my own, so I started doing shows at home with my sister, neighbors, dance friends, and school friends. Sheena taught me how to choreograph a show and turned my love of dance into my passion. As I grew up, everyone would tell me I even looked just like Sheena, and I absolutely loved that. We both had small frames, light hair, light eyes, and freckles. Yes, freckles, and as much as I hated them growing up, I learned to love them because I looked like her! Sheena grew up to be a dance teacher at multiple studios in Pennsylvania, and I followed right in her footsteps, but in New Jersey.

When I was twenty years old I was attending Rowan University and had gone out to celebrate my birthday with my college dance friends. My birthday falls in the same week in March as Sheena's. It was Sheena's 25th birthday and that night she had also gone out to celebrate. It was also the night that she was killed by a drunk driver. When I got home the next morning, barely awake, I walked into my parents' kitchen. My mom was standing there and said, "Sheena was in a car accident." I remember feeling like I was punched in the stomach, and I started sobbing. I cried for a long time as my mom held me. Looking back and hearing the words my mom said, it was the first time my intuition really took over. I had a feeling in my gut and heart that she wasn't going to make it. Have you ever felt like that? You didn't need to hear another word, but you just had a feeling that you knew what happened but weren't sure exactly why?

I was in Rowan University's dance company at that time and two weeks after Sheena passed we had a big four-day performance scheduled with multiple departments. It was one of the biggest performances Rowan has ever had. It included the music, theatre and dance departments, and we all came together to work on this huge piece to be performed in Phleeger Concert Hall. It was so exciting, and I was looking forward to it for months. My dance friends and I would practice the show everywhere we could, in the hallways, in the park, in apartments, and of course in the studio. Emotionally, when the day of the show came, it was hard to get into character and even smile when all I wanted to do was cry. I knew I was already committed to the performance and that the show must go on. I trusted my intuition again, feeling like this was part of a bigger picture in my life, and arrived at the Hall to dance my best. Before the first show I stood in a circle with my best friends and they said, "This is for Sheena," and that got me through. Every time I felt the lights on my face all I could think about was her. No matter how many years pass I still think of her when I dance, which is basically every day, and I still wear the same butterfly-shaped necklace every single day for her. The necklace was the same one that she wore every day and all the girls in my family have since bought one, too. If she couldn't keep dancing, then I would for her.

As I make choices in life, I decided to really follow my dream and love for dance. I still teach at a master class for Sheena every year at the studio she grew up in, and they put proceeds towards a scholarship fund in her name. I tried to work in different offices after I graduated college during the day, but ultimately, I knew that wasn't for me. I also taught dance after my different day jobs for five years. I was always happiest in the studio and knew that was where I belonged. If I had a bad day, I would always feel better after dancing. All the stress releases and I free my mind of anything else going on. The feeling of being confident, beautiful, knowledgeable, and free. I never imagined what would happen next, though. I opened a dance studio of my own in 2011 with my sister-in-law.

I am a shy and quiet person. Anyone who knows me knows I

don't like to talk in front of people, be the first to make a decision, or ever be a leader. I absolutely love to be front and center while I dance, but never in a room. As much as I love to perform, I feel like a completely different person on the stage than off.

I married my husband, Brent, in May of 2010. We bought a house with a pool and enjoyed swimming all summer. The following year I was relaxing by the pool with Brent's sister, Kara. It was a cloudy day, but we were making the best of it trying to float on rafts without touching the water because the water was cool and so was the air, but we were determined to enjoy the day. Kara has always been outgoing and has the ability to talk to anyone. She always had a dream of owning her own business. Kara and I are very opposite personalities, but that is why we work as business partners. She didn't grow up dancing, but did have a business and marketing background.

While we were together that day she said, "I have an idea. Why don't we open a dance and fitness studio?"

My first reaction was, "No way, that is completely out of my comfort zone."

I didn't want to talk to parents, make big decisions, or be in charge, but I did know I wanted to honor my cousin.

We told our families and they thought we were crazy.

"What if you don't want to eat Sunday dinner together anymore?"

"You are going to constantly be working."

Those were just some of the rebuttals. They wanted us to think about the big picture because it would be the rest of our lives. We got everyone on board and started planning. Found a little spot in the center of our little town and opened. There was a lot of blood, sweat, and tears those first few years as we moved three times to our now much larger space, still in town. We used the butterfly as a symbol in our logo and around the studio. Just like my necklace, when I look at the butterflies around the studio, they make me think of Sheena. It makes me happy that I have the opportunity to honor my cousin through every dance I choreograph, every competition and recital.

As I opened the studio, it was amazing to be a part of the community that I grew up in. Since we opened, I have come out of my shell and learned to talk to people a lot better. I feel more comfortable making decisions and stepping into a leadership role. I am still a work in progress, as we all are, but I feel like this is definitely what I was meant to do

We started a dance company called F2D Elite, which was my ultimate goal, and I love to see the growth of the dancers every year. Spending so many years dancing, my sister and I found a group who we are still able to call our best friends. Our families also continue to get together and remain close after all of these years. It warms my heart to see the close friendships my dancers are making and I hope they continue to make such positive impacts on each others' lives. My head spins with ideas for what comes next for all my dancers. It is beautiful to see the dancers bring joy to others when they are onstage or as we participate in events throughout the town. I wasn't just making my dream or Sheena's dream a reality, but also so many dancers who walk through my door can have dreams of their own and find their passion, and that really is an honor.

ABOUT MEGAN DATZ

Megan grew up in Sewell, New Jersey, and started dancing at the age of seven. Not long after, she was asked to be a member of the Dance Company. Throughout her young career she was in countless competitions, workshops, and performances where she earned her way as a top performer and lead dancer in roles like Cinderella in *Cinderella* and the Scarecrow in *The Wizard of Oz*.

Megan attended Rowan University and graduated in 2008 with a BA in Child Drama and a Minor in Dance. While attending Rowan University, she was a member of the Rowan Dance Team and Dance Extensions, holding the office of President of Dance Extensions. She was the only performer in her class to be asked to perform solos in every show each year. She was recognized with several awards and Honors, including the award for Best Choreographer and the recipient of the Bryna G. Goldhaft Dance Medallion Award and Scholarship, the highest honor a graduating senior can receive to acknowledge superior performance in her field.

Megan has taught at various dance schools in New Jersey, which led her to open Fit to Dance Studio with her sister-in-law, Kara, in Mullica Hill, New Jersey in 2011. The Studio has grown steadily every year. The Elite dancers at the studio compete at many levels in competitions, where Megan has won top choreography awards. Megan hopes to instill the love of dance and inspire young dancers to be the best they can be! Megan resides in Mullica Hill with her husband, Brent, and two children, Austin and Skyler, who are now her inspiration.

To learn more, please visit: www.fit2dancestudio.com

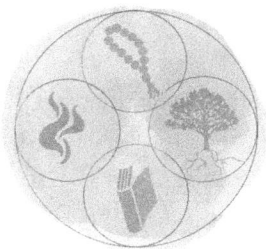

BREAKING THE MONEY CODE: ABUNDANCE FOR BUSINESS AND LIFE

Cameo Gore

When I was thirteen, I watched my hopes and dreams for my class dream trip dissolve into pieces as my father told me that he would not pay for me to go. My heart ached. And the truth is that my 13-year-old self couldn't comprehend the rationale behind what seemed to be a careless decision on the part of a well-meaning parent.

Can you relate? The bitter disappointment of being told no, ugh. And often in life we are trained to turn away from a deep desire and tell ourselves, "It's okay, it will work out next time," or "Maybe it wasn't meant to be after all," where we (once again) place our big hope and big dream into a file cabinet, never be seen again.

I want you to know that my "little self" at that tender age made a decision that changed my life. What I decided that day was that my desires were simply not worthy of actually coming true, and even worse, I began to believe that I should not ask for so much from life and people in general.

My life drastically changed when I began to question these beliefs and in the life I am now living (full, free, and abundant) what I know for sure is:

1) Nobody will tell me what I can or can't have/say/do, and

2) Nobody will stand in the way of what I desire to create in my life.

I invite you to step into your own BRAND NEW beliefs with me to unlock what's truly possible for you. To be completely transparent, looking back, it was a long and winding road to get where I am today. There were dark nights and it wasn't always easy. This is why without a doubt it's one of my life goals to shorten the trajectory for you into greater abundance and prosperity so that you can have all the things you most desire. Once I learned to shift into alignment to call in my desires (I even manifested my husband in twenty-four hours, literally after stepping off a plane in Las Vegas), I have always known I was a rapid manifestor. I realized then that life definitely didn't need to be as hard as I was making it. And it doesn't need to be hard for you, either.

The rapid manifestations that I have witnessed when we step in fully and make "the shift" are simply astounding. Over the years, within my events and programs, I have witnessed extreme abundance manifest overnight for clients, including the exact amount of money for a down-payment on a dream home, calling in soulmate love, being fully booked with clients in rapid time, and doubling and tripling incomes, which I know you may be destined for as well … because you wouldn't be reading this otherwise!

And over the years, by stepping into my own truth and finding my way in life, I have developed a code to activate abundance and prosperity within my life and the lives of my clients. This code has brought all of my desires into my physical sphere, and it can for you as well! When you activate this code within your consciousness, mindset, and your physical vibration (which is key), it will unlock a new level of abundance to your life and make all things possible and flowing to you!

YOU ARE MORE POWERFUL THAN YOU KNOW

After thousands of hours uncovering patterns, and helping women step into their greatness, it's amazing to witness how incredibly powerful we are. We are truly the only beings on the planet who can manifest the future by shaping our thoughts into realities. How cool is that? Your thoughts definitely become things, love. And at the root of all of this is that your thoughts, good or bad, carry a powerful vibration that speaks a universal language, telling the universe what you want to receive. So if you are lamenting over, "I would love to (whatever you desire), but I cannot afford (whatever you desire)," please consider that the universe is actually checking that box for you and will NOT, in fact, be sending you whatever you desire to your doorstep because you are not saying it's possible. Make sense?

So, what are you telling yourself? That you are unstoppable and a magnet for abundance and prosperity? Or that you can't afford whatever you want that your heart desires, yet again? The endless mind chatter running rampant and unchecked in your sweet head and what it is telling you is a key factor in determining the trajectory of how quickly you can break your own money code and step into bigger abundance. I recommend that you stop here now and write out what your mind chatter is saying, as big changes can happen quickly once you elevate your thoughts.

IMPLEMENT ONE WORD INTO YOUR LIFE TODAY TO MANIFEST ABUNDANCE

There is one word that wants to be your ally and can help you shift into abundance quickly. Sounds so simple, right? It's the word YES. Thinking back, how often have you told yourself NO when what you really wanted to say was "YES!" The word YES carries an expansive energy, which is an actual frequency that opens new doorways. These new doorways can lead you to the potential of the unlimited abundance for all that you desire. I have seen the frequency of YES transform countless lives and bring into existence seemingly impossible things, quickly. Can you feel the energetic difference of YES and NO when you say them out loud? When you feel a deep desire, say YES to it, even if you don't know the how and are not sure exactly how to make it happen. If you want to go on a luxury vacation, but it doesn't seem possible how can you still say yes? There are a million ways; just a few would be creating a vision board, creating small luxurious moments in your life right now that feel like a vacation, and going ahead to actually the plan the vacation as if you are going!

When you say YES to life and the desires you have, it creates an energetic vortex for you filled with opportunity and possibility. It allows the universe to know you are receptive and immediately begins delivering more of what you want. Doors will begin to appear out of nowhere and it is then your requirement (and your exciting duty) to push on them to simply see which ones will swing open for you. Yes … or YES?!

YOU ARE NOT YOUR PAST OR PRESENT, AND THE FUTURE IS NOW

There is complete freedom in truly knowing that you are not indebted to the chains of the past. If your background, upbringing, or history have been pulling you backward from stepping in fully to claim what you want so that you can move forward in a bigger way, then this is your time (and a clear sign) to finally break free! It's powerful to make decisions for your future completely free from the limitations of your past. And it's the only way to quantum leap into a new reality around all things money. It truly does not matter what happened to you in your past as long as you know where you want to go. It's time to release what's holding you back.

Create a vision of what you want for your life and business. Where are you living? What are you driving? How much money would you love to make? Get crystal clear on this and then take it one step further by visualizing what you would do once it's already here and in your hands.

Can you feel this? Go even bigger with this until you are excited and can really feel this! This is the future that is already there and waiting for you!

THE UNIVERSE PROVIDES MORE WHEN YOU ARE ALIGNED WITH THE INFINITE ENERGY OF ABUNDANCE

Quantum physics has proven that like energy attracts like energy. This is the basis of how the law of attraction works throughout the Universal Law and is the basis for how you are (right now) co-creating your own reality. What I want you to know is that you must be aligned with abundance NOW in order for you to create it (or to create more of it). Everything here so far has helped you to uncover your personal truth to prepare you for greater prosperity; however, to manifest this into your physical reality, you must commit to feeling abundant, grateful, and in sheer and utter wonderment of your life and business, even when it may not always feel that way. I know what you're thinking, this can sometimes be hard, but the key to all of this is knowing that when you align with what you want and the way that it feels consistently, you send a strong message to the universe about who you already are right now (hello, quantum leaps). You can then begin to attract more of your desires in rapid succession. This is where we also begin to create momentum, which is super powerful, and I will touch on next.

GET INTO THE JET STREAM: MOMENTUM EQUALS MOMENTUM

There is incredible value to having a support system of mentors and leaders (like you) moving in the same direction. Energy builds on energy, and if you are here to create a massive financial breakthrough in your life and business, consider that doing it alone may not work. The support of others lifting you into a more expansive space (which as mighty as you are, you simply cannot do for yourself), is uber powerful. Having a network supporting you and helping you expand into your greatness is a gamechanger for the momentum and breakthroughs that you can and will create. The truth is that most people want to quit right before their big breakthrough. And the even bigger truth is that you will have bigger breakthroughs when you are supported with forward momentum in your life and business.

For the next level of growth to happen, you must build on your wins and celebrate your breakthroughs. Momentum equals more momentum, which is positive energy and positive energy is abundance. Following? You need to be abundantly supported if you want to go bigger. The universe can feel momentum and wants to support those who are committed to staying in the #jetstream.

Hey, love, what I most want you to know (and feel deeply) is that any and all things are possible for you. I have created a seven-figure business by breaking my own money code and by tapping into these principles, and it is now my complete joy to witness and support smart women just like you riding the magic carpet into their greatness. By doing the work you love and living an aligned life that is freedom-filled, rich, and abundant, you are already breaking the code and calling in your desires. I truly believe that if I can do this, anyone can. It's my heartfelt mission to support and empower those who are ready. What are the shifts that you are willing to make TODAY and that are within your reach so that your reality is different thirty days from now? The time is always now, love. And you are definitely ready.

ABOUT CAMEO GORE

Cameo Gore is a Transformational Speaker and Success Coach who is awakening heart-based entrepreneurs to lead on a global scale. Having made millions in her executive career in healthcare, she now helps women tap into their unlimited potential in business while having the freedom and flexibility to do more of what they love. Cameo has recently been featured on TV on FOX news, and has been featured in media outlets such as *The Huffington Post*, Thrive Global, and I Heart Radio.

Cameo is co-founder of The Ignite and Expand Movement, a global platform hosting events, programs, and retreats around the world. Ignite and Expand empowers women by teaching how to tap into your purpose, infinite potential, and abundance. More than a decade ago, Cameo manifested her husband in twenty-four hours through her five-step manifesting process, which she shares through her programs, events, and workshops. She is now on a mission to empower women to reach their highest potential by helping them honor and ignite their power, the truth of who they are, and what they are meant to create in the world.

When Cameo isn't with clients or hosting beautiful retreats around the globe, you can find her soaking up the sun on the beach, booking a midday massage, hiking the trails, or hanging with her husband and kids.

For further connection with Cameo, visit www.cameogore.com.

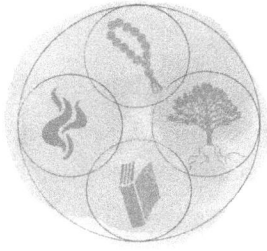

IMPACT AFRICA: A CALL FROM KENTUCKY TO KENYA

Amy Hehre

Tonight, I am sitting in my fifth-story apartment snuggling with my children. A typical night for most moms, except that my apartment is in a hospital and two of the children are my patients. Let me explain: the little ones nestled around me are my adopted daughter, Lily, my foster son, Moses, and two of my patients, Luka and Winnie, who prefer our living room couches over their hospital beds. Another fifty orphans, who are critically and chronically ill, are asleep in the units below us. Each child finds refuge here in their own unique way. Some of them will stay with us for less than a day, some for months, some for years, and some for the rest of their lives. Every day when I look at these children, I see the embodiment of my largest dream, but to them I am simply "Mommy."

At age twenty-three, I founded and became CEO of our non-profit Ovi & Violet International. By twenty-five, I began living and practicing medicine full-time here at our OVI Children's Hospital, a sixty-bed inpatient medical facility that exists to bring free, life-saving treatments to the orphaned and abandoned children of Sub-Saharan Africa. When laid out in such a brief description, you might imagine that I was particularly privileged, gifted, or anointed with a natural-born passion for impacting the world. However, that is far from my story. My life journey has been cluttered with trials and brokenness that, by God's mercy, He has redeemed for His glory. It is only because of His grace, goodness, and heart for the unworthy that He would entrust me with the life I lead today.

* * *

"I'll name him 'Cancer'!" I announced. Proudly, I pushed the tiny toy mouse against my face. I smiled up at the matching yellow balloon that was tied to my wrist, watching as it circled in the air with "Get Well Soon" bannered across both sides. Only days had passed since I learned my mother's diagnosis. At age five, the word "cancer" meant nothing more to me than any other noun. But a realization was on the horizon. And that realization would change my world.

As we pulled around the corner of Cedar Lane, I could see my mother in our driveway. I hopped out of the car and ran to the rusty, blue Buick that we affectionately called "the mommy mobile." She was seated in the passenger seat, modestly packed for a short trip to a hospital far from our little Kentucky home. My heart leapt as I gave her the balloon and extended my hand with the plush mouse. I remember her smile as she looked at me and said, "You keep him, Amy." I happily agreed, placing him in my backpack and searching for the painted fireworks I had made for her that day in my art class. She accepted the artwork with accolades as she kissed me goodbye.

Before this day, I had never spent one night without my mother. She was our chief executive parent who dedicated every moment of the day to raising her girls. In the beginning, the nights away were not so bad. My grandparents would make us popcorn mixed with full bags of M&Ms, and we would watch Nick at Night for about two hours past our usual bedtime. But soon these days would become a week, and a week would become several weeks. I missed my mom, and my young heart was quickly learning the pain this sickness would bring.

I never went back to being the carefree little girl with the balloon. Reality crashed around me and the circumstances aged my soul rapidly. Things as simple as a hug, kiss, or even holding my mother's hand were robbed from me by the recurrent radiation treatments. Even more were the whispers of careless children who would gossip about her condition. "Don't you know she's going to die?" one girl sneered. That day, I rushed home and told my mother what my classmate had said, only to find that she could not fully reassure me. "Anything could happen to any of us at any time, Amy." Even at such a young age, I could see that my mother would not tell me the whole story. That feeling of uncertainty would have been unlivable if not for the peace that I found in my faith in Christ. This faith was instilled in me at an early age and that peace has never left me.

* * *

As a teenager, I was able to celebrate my mother's miraculous remission, but this joy could not make me forget the emotional toll that twelve years of her oscillating health reports had taken on me. At eighteen years old, I was ready for a new beginning. My high school years had simply been burdensome, and I was ready for a clean slate. More specifically, I was ready for a new place far from the small town that knew my every flaw and insecurity. My heart was set on Ball State University in Illinois. This university was among the highest-ranking programs for broadcasting, the field that I had always imagined myself pursuing.

While my confidence at this time was subpar at best, I knew that others had applauded me for my physical beauty and for being well-spoken. With that, I decided to go after a career that could showcase those qualities. Beauty pageants and attempts at modeling and acting became my sports. I enjoyed the positive attention and the glitter of it all. The final month of my senior year in high school, I had just finished months of personal training. I had practically spent every penny of my waitressing tips to achieve what I then thought to be the most perfect version of myself. I had stars in my eyes as I pictured the years ahead and the newness they would bring.

However, the glimmer and magic of that new beginning would quickly come to an end. On a rainy Monday morning, my tiny convertible slid across some flood debris on a bridge just a mile from my home. Glass shattered as I crashed into the trees and off the embankment and with it went every plan I had set for my future. I had fractured my neck. The next few months, I laid in a hospital bed in my parents' basement. I ate frozen dinners and watched my newly toned body diminish before my eyes. My dignity plummeted as I depended on others to bathe and transport me from room-to-room. That summer, the medical bills and trauma from the accident convinced me to decline acceptance into my dream school. I settled to attend a university that could offer in-state tuition instead.

Attending university would, in fact, offer new beginnings. I joined the honors college, campus ministry, rented my first apartment, took every paying job I could manage, adopted a puppy, and fell in love for the first time. Still, my heart had a major void. The car accident had shaken me. It changed my perspective and multiplied my life-long battle with anxiety one-hundred-fold. I tried counseling, medicine, and constant life changes, but nothing seemed to lessen the sleepless nights and physical pain of my body. That is, until one day, when I reached into a hat and found the question that would change my life forever.

"If you could have any life, what would it be and why?" My response was immediate, "If I could live any life, I'd love to be a medical missionary who could bring life-changing treatment across the world."

What grounds did I have for this dream? Frankly, I don't know. Maybe it was because I had sponsored a cleft palate surgery for a child a few weeks prior. Perhaps the passion was hidden deep within me all along. But at that time, it was nothing more than a theoretical answer to this question.

Without any coincidence, this audience of ice-breaker activity participants heard my answer, but failed to hear the question. They thought this was my actual life! Throughout the entire event people would repeatedly come and applaud me for my charitable work. Time after time, I had to explain the misunderstanding. I would tell them that this wasn't my life, or even a life I was a pursuing, but just a far-fetched dream that I blurted out when put on the spot. I continued repeating this until one man, whose name and face I cannot remember, challenged me with one question that would transform every aspect of my future. "If that is the life you want to live, then why aren't you living it?"

* * *

So, I did. In that moment I was overcome with conviction. I dropped everything I knew and loved and ran towards this life I knew nothing about. My relationship, my major, and every other dream became former. From that reckless faith came a Google search for medical opportunities in Africa. Three weeks later, those findings would lead me to defy all logic and opinions of my family, to embark on a solo journey to a little-known place called Suna Migori, Kenya.

My time in Migori was spent volunteering in a small mission hospital. When I walked into the wards for the first time, the blistering heat combined with the most putrid smells caused me to physically collapse. When I resurfaced, I could see all the doctors crowded around. I remember thinking, "Really, God? Surely this cannot be what you have for me." From being a 4.0 honor student and life-long perfectionist, to failing my first chemistry class and now collapsing in the very place I believed I was called to serve. How on earth could this ever be my purpose? Wasn't I supposed to use the talents and skills He had already instilled in me? The answer was a firm "no." All the years of striving to be beautiful, accepted, and among the elite were over. God had placed me in a space where I would be counted a failure, unworthy, and be among the devastation of the unseen.

In that place of brokenness, I ultimately found restoration. All it took was seeing their faces—gazing into the eyes of children dying from a lack of access to medical care. Many were being detained because of outstanding medical bills and even denied treatment because resources were not available. It was then that I became burdened with a conviction I had never had before. "If children with parents are struggling so much to get the care they need, then how much more could the suffering be for a child who has no one at all?" From there, I set out to find the answer to that question. As I moved from orphanages and homes of vulnerable children in the community, the tragedies were evident. I witnessed infants who were malnourished and dying in their first weeks of life. I saw a young boy who had seized for nearly two hours because of a fever that could have been managed with Tylenol. I witnessed children with disabilities, withering away in institutions that could not support their critical medical needs.

Immediately, I raced to my notebook. My heart and mind were overflowing with visions of hope for these children. I saw a multi-story hospital with open air verandas for rocking the babies on every floor. I saw doctors that answered to "mommy" and "daddy." I pictured a beautiful refuge that could treat advanced diseases like cancer and AIDS. A staff that could empathize with tragedy. I saw myself holding and kissing the heads of these children who were bedridden. From these visions, I sketched a blue-ink drawing of the exact structure God had shown me. All together it was a messy, detailed plan for a hospital ministry that would provide the life-saving treatment and restoration I wished to see for the weak, orphaned, and abandoned.

* * *

Three years later, I became a new bride to my life-long friend from summer camp, Rob. We fell in love over our shared dream of using medicine to bring healing and the love of Jesus to the sick and dying. Rob began joining me on my journeys to Kenya and we would dream of the life we would have "one day." We did not realize how quickly that "one day" would come upon us. Just four months into marriage, God fulfilled my first vision of the blue building with verandas with undeniable exactness. What we imagined would take a lifetime to build was standing before us with even the smallest details shaped in brick and mortar.

The timing was laughable. I was in over my head in my first year of Physician Assistant school, Rob was struggling to find his first job as a PA, and we collectively had less than nothing financially. There was no worldly justification for our decision to embark on this mission, to attempt to raise half a million dollars for an orphan hospital. But the Holy Spirit continued to insist "now," and we chose to be obedient. This decision was not met with support. No matter the evidence of God's hand, it seemed as though no one could justify contributing to the impossible dream of these twenty-nothing-year-olds. After seven months of constant tears, rejection, confusion, and missed deadlines, the skies opened and out fell the exact finances needed for our hospital from a short list of heroes and one complete stranger. In that moment, the goodness of our Savior deeply intensified our faith. This would only be the first of the thousands of miracles that we would see and live by today.

For me, the most beautiful part of this journey has been the redemption of every pain and loss that I have endured. When a child like Emmanuel comes to our hospital without any mother to hold his hand, I hold it remembering how it felt to have that same void. When I listen to the rigid remarks of three-year-old Luka, I respond with empathy, because I know what it is like to have your understanding aged by suffering. When Winnie's cancer report reads Stage IV, I beg God to heal her as I saw Him heal my mother and praise Him on the day that the tumor disappears. When I bathe and feed eight-year-old Charity, I protect her dignity and thank God for my experience that I once counted agony. I have reclaimed the perception of my anxiety and depression. I now see gifts of empathy and endurance. These experiences drive me to give the best life to these precious children.

Every day I am able to heal and hold the broken and dying. I use my professional training to administer chemotherapy, suture wounds, dress burns, and diagnose disease. I use my motherly nature to let my patients know that it's ok to be scared, and to rock them to sleep in my own home. I get to read stories, change diapers, feed, sing songs, celebrate first steps, console through nightmares, and pray over each child by name. All this, pointing to my gracious God who enables the unable, who restores the destitute, a Savior whose plan for your life will far surpass your most impossible dream if only you take heart.

ABOUT AMY HEHRE

Amy Hehre is a US Certified Physician Assistant, Kenyan Clinical Officer, CEO, and Founder at OVI Children's Hospital—a 24/7 advanced medical facility offering free, life-saving treatment to critically ill orphans and abandoned children across Sub-Saharan Africa.

She currently serves full-time in Migori, Kenya with her husband and co-founder Rob, and their two children, Moses and Lily. Apart from her time in Kenya, Amy has traveled to nearly forty countries to serve, share, and simply indulge in the diversity of culture and experience.

Amy is a pediatric oncology enthusiast, orphan advocate, and global visionary with a passion for helping others achieve their largest goals. Her favorite name is "Mommy," and she assumes that role for every child she finds in need of that love.

In less than one year of operation, Amy's five-story hospital has been consistently booked to capacity. She plans to soon expand with a cancer institute, operating room, and additional international campuses.

Above all else, Amy is committed to investing in the lives of the orphaned and destitute. To offer the hope of health, love, and purpose to children who would otherwise have no access to the care they desperately need.

Website: www.OVInternational.org

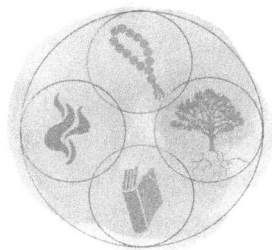

I AM ENOUGH

Stacey Kirkpatrick

Thirty-six hours sitting in ICU by his bedside. He was so young, but his life was ending right before my eyes. He was my fresh start, my next chapter. I was twenty-four and, yet again, my world was crumbling around me.

Kevin looked like he was sleeping peacefully, except for the sound of the machines monitoring his every breath, his every heartbeat. I ran my fingers through his blonde hair, but there was no movement. We should have been celebrating our one-year anniversary and planning his move in with me.

It was 1997, and he was in his first year of college. The semester had just ended, with last exams written, and it was a night of celebration. He left my house, saying he was going out with friends that night, but would call me the next day. With a mischievous smile, he said that he would take me dancing. I waited all day for him to call, not thinking much of it, as I knew he was out late the night before. The phone finally rang, but it was a family member who was coming to pick me up. Everything sort of stopped. The sound of the voice on the phone became muffled and incomprehensible. Someone came and drove me to the hospital. I don't know who; I don't remember much. It was like there was a thickness to the air, slowing my movements, rendering voices distant and muddled.

221

At some point I was told he went to sleep the night before and never woke up. The paramedics had been and his heart was restarted, but he remained unconscious. I sat by him in the ICU, willing him to wake up, but the minutes stretched to hours and doctors spoke with his parents, telling them there was no hope.

My world stopped. I felt like I was inside a bubble as people moved around me. How could life go on while something so tragic had happened? I wanted to yell, "Don't you know something awful has happened? How can you smile, laugh, and just go about your day?" Of course, they had no idea. They had no idea that the machines were turned off and this man who took his last breath while I held his hand was the only person who ever made me feel good about myself. I was pretty enough. I was smart enough. I was just enough.

When you sit awake in a hospital just waiting, you have plenty of time to think about, well … everything. My childhood was difficult. My mom divorced my dad when I was only two years old and as a single mom with health issues, she struggled, but somehow, I didn't realize how poor we were. She created many special moments, like drives in the country, exploring little dirt roads and adventures hiking through wooded areas or pasture lands. The problem was, she didn't know about some of the other moments that would colour my childhood. Starting at about the age of four until I was in my teens, I would endure sexual abuse from different men. The male role models in my life were either absent or abusive, and I had no image of a healthy relationship with a man. Like so many, I felt maybe I had done something wrong. I spent my childhood perfecting the art of lying to hide the abuse. Why did I hide it? I thought that I had done something wrong, something to cause it to happen, but I think, even more, it was the fear of destroying my family, and that I would no longer be welcome or loved.

Sexual behaviour was so intertwined with love and acceptance that in later years, I would mistake one for the other far too often. When I met the father of my first two children, he was caring and showed me respect, but I was too young and had such a warped perspective of relationships that it ended a year after my second child was born. It was like I had been playing house for four years, but I wasn't enough to make the illusion a reality. I was just twenty-two and the edges of my world were crumbling. After this, meeting Kevin had given me a glimmer of hope.

Months passed after Kevin's death and everyone else moved on. I went to work, and it was like life was just supposed to resume. It was like Kevin's death and funeral were just a commercial break and then you went back to your TV show. My children spent more and more time with their father and their grandparents, and I allowed it. I thought they would be better off without me around. I was never going to be enough; everything I did fell apart. One night, I sat sobbing, thinking everyone would be better off without me. I had a bottle of pills, but something stopped me that day. I called a friend and talked for what seemed like hours. I made it through that night, but I still had a long journey ahead.

It was a year after Kevin's death when I finally went back to the cemetery. In the dark, after any visitors would be gone, I sat leaning against the gravestone and thought about my life and his. The tears turned to sobs as everything that had happened rushed through my mind. I grasped at the memories, trying to hold onto his life. I clenched my hands when I thought of the abuse, but sitting there, I soon felt a calm came over me. Kevin knew life was precious and always said to live life to its fullest. Why was I sitting here stuck in my past?

I knew forgiveness was a part of moving on. One of my abusers had himself been abused as a child, and while not an excuse, in that moment I saw the reason why he did what he did, and it had nothing to do with me. I had spent so much time focused on my past, allowing myself to be defined by the actions of others. I had spent so much time facing backwards, but in that moment, I turned and allowed myself to see a future. I began to see that my self-worth didn't come from others but from within. Despite everything that had happened, there had to be more for me.

In the years that followed I got a job, met and married my husband, also named Kevin, got an even better job with the government, had my third child, and took a few classes at the local university. I was slowly taking control of my life, one class at a time, one day at a time until 2006.

Looking back, I realize 2006 was a pivotal year, the year of many gentle, little nudges that changed my life. I had fallen in love with psychology and figuring out why humans behave and think the way they do. I read every book, watched videos and completely immersed myself. I learned about gratitude and began a gratitude journal a few months before my fourth child was born. I felt the shift in my view of the world. I'd like to say I lived each day full of gratitude, but it's a process, an evolution that is ongoing. It was, however, a little nudge that started me on a journey. My son was born by natural childbirth at home. It was a difficult birth with moments where my husband thought we should go to the hospital. I had no such thoughts. Immediately after, I felt stronger than I ever had. Sure, some of it was hormones and nature's way of helping a mother get through childbirth, but I felt like I could conquer the world. I realized then, that when I set my mind on something, I would follow through. It was another little nudge. When I went back to work after my maternity leave, I met with a woman in upper management. She said that now was the time to finish school if I wanted to progress in my career. She saw something in me that she nurtured and encouraged. Again, a little nudge.

One evening, as my husband and I were getting ready for bed, he said, "You know, I admire you." Never had I felt worthy of someone's admiration. Never would I have thought that someone as smart and hard working as my husband could see something in me to admire. I knew in that moment that it wasn't just that I was pretty enough or smart enough. I was so much more and maybe, in some way I could share my experience, so others could know they, too, were enough. His words touched me and nudged me even further on my journey.

All those nudges added together and became the monumental push

I needed. After I went back to work that year I began doubling up on courses, often against other's advice. "Don't take on too much or you'll burn out." I had played it safe, but now I was on a mission to finish. From the first course, so many years before, to that final graduation day, thirteen years had passed, but I had done it. Just after graduation, my husband planted a seed when he said, "You're good at this school thing, maybe you should go back and get a Master's degree." I laughed it off, too exhausted to imagine ever going back to school.

Of course, those little nudges that turned into a huge push meant I had this desire for more. I became a certified coach and began helping others with gentle nudges, so they could believe in their dreams. I did finally apply for a Master's program in Counselling Psychology. I figured it was a long shot, but I was accepted. I began to visualize my life, my career, my family, and my contribution. I wanted to give back to others and I wanted to bring meaning to my life.

Apparently, I still like to take things slow and so I took the full five years allowed to complete the program, still working full-time through all but the last year, while raising a family and trying to maintain my sanity. But you know, it doesn't matter how long it takes. You just need to keep taking those small steps and surrounding yourself with people who will give you those gentle nudges. Today, I am a psychotherapist and a coach. I have dedicated myself to helping others overcome abuse, depression, and grief. I help people realize that you can take small steps and as long as you keep moving forward, you can achieve your dreams.

It didn't matter that I started out poor. It didn't matter that I suffered abuse. It didn't matter that I had failed relationships, loss and grief so deep that I didn't think there was anything left for me. I just kept getting up each day and when I fell, I got up again. I believed in myself, and while I can still turn and look at my past, I no longer spend precious time focused on it. I would never wish my experiences on anyone, but I wouldn't change them. Everything that has happened has brought me to the place I am today, and I like who I am. I am more than enough.

ABOUT STACEY KIRKPATRICK

Stacey Kirkpatrick is a Registered Psychotherapist with the College of Registered Psychotherapists of Ontario and certified coach in Ottawa, Canada. She spent seventeen years in government with various roles, including work in quality management and business development around intellectual property management. She completed a BA in geography, graduating with distinction from Carleton University and graduated from Yorkville University with a Master's in Counselling Psychology.

Stacey has been coaching for eleven years and uses her breadth of experience to help businesses with coaching programs for employees, around team work, customer service and sales while helping the individuals find fulfillment within their work. Stacey has a private psychotherapy and coaching practice, and sees individuals dealing with depression, anxiety, grief, and abuse. She works with individuals going through life transitions such as divorce, retirement, job loss and those looking for help achieving goals. She hosts workshops to bring people together, while working through everyday life struggles. Stacey has volunteered with many local agencies including most recently, a violence against women program.

Stacey's passion for writing has brought her back to working on several writing projects. She is an optimist who sees the best in people and helps them discover their strengths.

When Stacey isn't busy working, she spends most of her time with her family, including her amazingly supportive husband and her four beautiful children.

Stacey can be contacted through StaceyKirkpatrick.com

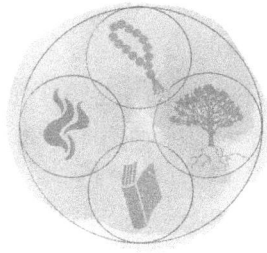

A MOTHER'S JOURNEY BACK TO LOVE AGAIN

Tina Raffa

On September 11, 2008, at around 4 pm, I was working on my homework for grad school and my life changed forever. There was a knock at my door by two police officers, and I was served with a move out order/restraining order. I was ordered to move out of my home, and I lost physical custody of the most precious person in the world to me, my son, Luke. He was eight at the time and I was thirty-eight years old, working on my master's degree in clinical counseling. Although I may have appeared successful on the outside, my marriage was hanging by a thread and it completely crumbled that day. I was almost four years sober, well-educated, and had a successful career, however my home life was in shambles. I was advised that I could not see my son or my husband at the time until after my court date which was approximately thirty days later. If I were to contact them in any way I was advised that I would be arrested.

I could not understand why this was so drastic. I had gotten into an argument the day before with my son's dad, but I had no idea that he was marching down to the courthouse to remove me from our home. (Today as I write this it is ten years later and we have reached a place of forgiveness for each other. It took a long time and a lot of hard work to get to this place.) I wasn't able to say goodbye, as they were not home at

227

the time. The police watched me pack my things, and as I drove away, the looks from neighbors were deeply painful. I didn't know where I was going or who to turn to. And I had to be to class in less than two hours!

I had so many fears, but the worst was that my little boy would think I chose this and that I abandoned him. That was my first fear and that is exactly what he thought for a very long time. Not getting to kiss my son every day and spend time with him was the most horrible experience of my life. I am also a survivor of childhood sexual abuse and not even that comes close to the pain of losing my child. Missing holidays and birthdays and not getting to tuck him in at night and read him bedtime stories anymore was the absolute worst. I truly wanted to die. I often wanted to give up because life without my son just felt like it wasn't worth living. My parents reminded me that I had to fight for him. My closest friends reminded me that my son needed me to fight for him. My friends, my parents, and my fiancé stood by me through it all.

The next few years were a horrific struggle to get close to my son again. I spent countless nights crying, missing him, wanting to comfort him in a way that I know only a mother can. As a means to cope I started a journal just for him with letters to him expressing my feelings. It is still my hope that maybe one day this journal will provide even more proof of how much he is loved now and he always has been. I often felt as if my heart was being ripped out of my chest from having to spend so many hours separated from my favorite little human on the planet. As a correctional officer I was required to notify my work, and I was not allowed to work an armed post until I could prove my innocence at the upcoming court date (more humiliation).

My sponsor told me to wrap my son in a blanket and give him to God. It was here that I began to do the inner work to find my part in this and find out what I did to create this. I put my trust in a woman who had a story as tragic as mine and had achieved great success with her child. She gave me a hope that I could not find on my own. People in my support group showed me a love I truly never felt before. They had an uncanny ability to understand me and loved me no matter what. They gave me the strength to love myself enough to figure this out and get back to the life that God intended for me. Besides God himself, my sponsor, Bear West, is the greatest reason I am here today to share my story of how I overcame Parent Alienation and Parent Alienation Syndrome. I had no idea that such things existed. Parent Alienation is the specific acts or words of one parent that are aimed at brainwashing a child to hate the other parent. This most often occurs during a divorce or a separation. Parent Alienation Syndrome is the specific behaviors exhibited by the child as a result of these acts.

At the first court date I was placed on supervised visitation (more humiliation). Some of my first supervised visits were done by a friend in my AA program, however the majority and remainder of my many supervised visits were at a professional center. I had to pay for my visits and I had to bring food and fun activities for Luke and myself. We sat at a table for our visit the entire time while my supervisor sat at her desk and looked on or did her own work. There were strict rules and we were only allowed to focus on the visit and enjoying ourselves. This was extremely difficult as we both had major issues going on, and I was not allowed to discuss anything regarding our case.

Luke was angry and hurt and was exhibiting symptoms of what I now know was Parent Alienation Syndrome. He made strange comments that were extremely painful to hear. My supervisor, Sherry Webb, went beyond the call of duty and taught me how to respond to my son's anger and pain. She taught me what he needed. She taught me in a firm and loving way to stop reacting to my child's pain and choose the responses that my son needed to hear and see from his mother. She showed me what those chosen responses needed to look like so that my child could feel the love I had for him. She taught me to put my child's feelings before my own. She taught me to communicate with my child at his appropriate age level.

I am embarrassed to say that I did not know these things. My love could be deeper than the ocean for him, however it meant nothing if I didn't have the skills to convey it. Our children need to "feel" our love for them and I learned how to communicate with my son at his age level from there on out. I learned to respect my child no matter what. It was extremely difficult because he was saying that he hated me, and he never wanted to see me again. He was very hurt, but I'm proud to say that he and I have a deep love for each other today, and our times together are my favorite.

After quite a few supervised visits, and many expensive therapy sessions, I was finally allowed to have visits with my son for two hours a week unsupervised at a park that was located directly in the middle of both of our neighborhoods. I purposely moved and strategically chose the home I live in today because it is directly across the street from his neighborhood. A part of getting close to your child is to physically put yourself there, and although it was difficult to find the perfect home at the perfectly safe and respectful distance, I finally found it after six months of searching with a real estate agent. The home was out of our budget, but my fiancée, knowing how much it meant to me to be near to my son, found a way to make that house our home and it still is today.

During all these visits, therapy sessions, reading books, and working the 12 Steps with my sponsor, I was frantically looking for answers. I dove into my support groups and spent many hours with my sponsor in person and on the phone. During all this I was struggling not to argue with my ex-husband. I was reeling with hurt feelings and wanted desperately to hurt him back. I learned that hurting him only hurt the most important person in the world to me, and that was my little boy. Every single action I took and every word I said reflected upon my little boy whether he was present or not. I had to really know and accept this, especially when I was having difficult conversations with his father.

I made a ton of mistakes. I had to learn how not to participate in the anger. If I had a dollar for every time my sponsor said, "Do not engage!" I would be rich. My ex-husband and I had fallen into this habit of arguing and I had to learn how to detach from that in a loving way. Learning not to engage in the fights and learning to forgive was a severely difficult lesson. There were many times that I had to excuse myself as politely as I could and say, "I just feel sick right now," and simply hang up so that I did not say something out of anger. I asked for help every single time I wasn't sure of my next move, or especially how to communicate something. I still turn to my sponsor to this day if I'm not completely sure how to handle a situation with someone I love.

Although I was fighting against manipulation and untruths being said about me, I had to learn to fight back with positive actions. The more I learned to respond in a loving, respectful manner, and the more I dove into the written work given to me by my sponsor and my therapist, the quicker I got better and so did my son. It didn't happen overnight. I found out from this experience the undeniable proof of the ancient Chinese proverb that states, "One moment of anger can cause years of sorrow." It took several years to get my son back completely to the level we are at today. I learned how to love even my enemies. Love and tolerance is my code.

The Bible states in Mathew 5:44 to love your enemies and pray for those who persecute you. Matthew 5:46 states, "If you love those who love you, what reward will you get?" This means that of course it's easy to love those who love us, however loving those who are unlovable is difficult. This is where true strength lies, and I believe that is the way God intended for us to treat each other. I learned to love my son's father where he was even if he persecuted me. He was doing so out of his own hurt and pain from my thoughtless actions during our marriage. I had to take responsibility for this and start to take direction from others.

One of my sponsors from many years ago said to me, "There is magic in the pen." I indeed found true freedom in writing a journal, taking a personal inventory, and sharing my inner work with my sponsor or therapist. I learned to accept help. I learned to love myself and others in the way that I believe God intended. I learned to be honest with myself and honest with other people. I learned what integrity is and I learned to have a deep respect for myself, my child and other people even when they didn't deserve it.

ABOUT TINA RAFFA

Tina Raffa is a correctional officer of eighteen years and a Certified Success Principles Trainer. She holds an MBA and a Master of Science Degree from the University of Phoenix in Ontario, California. Her passions are sobriety, animal welfare, and helping others. She has fourteen years of active sobriety, is opening her own animal adoption center, and is pursuing her new career as a speaker and coach. When she isn't working she enjoys quality time with family and friends, camping by the beach, and riding her Harley.

Tina's expertise is the prevention and/or reversal of Parent Alienation and Parent Alienation Syndrome. Her mission is to raise awareness about PA and PAS to help co-parents remain close to their children in the event of a divorce or a separation. She has an 8-step method that she used in her own life to reverse Parent Alienation Syndrome, which will be outlined in her upcoming book. She resides in Corona, California with her fiancé, Rick, and their pets, which include her toy poodle, Prince, six cats, and even two reptiles.

To reach Tina or submit your own story, she would love to hear from you. You can write to her at:

PO Box 295 Norco, CA 92860

Or email your submission to:
TinaRaffa@CourageousCo-Parents.com.

For additional resources or to book your own coaching session with Tina, you can refer to her website at:
www.CourageousCo-Parents.com.

GAIA DAWN

Jennifer Roth

I was on my way to the life I had always dreamed of. My husband, Walt, and I put our house on the market and we were looking out in the country for a smaller home. We were ready for a simpler life. A life full of travel, adventure, and family fun. A life away from all that we had ever known. But things weren't going quite as planned. I was homeschooling our three children and our house had been on the market for four months. We'd had more than thirty showings and no interest, and I was stressed and exhausted. In desperation I prayed to the universe for help because I couldn't go on like this any longer. And then it finally happened, we got an offer on the house! We also got the shock of our lives within hours of the offer. I was pregnant …

This was not the plan. A fourth child and starting over? I'd been a stay-at-home mom for twelve years and I was starting to see some freedom within reach. But I didn't have time to process the pregnancy, we just needed to accept the offer on the house and find a new one! The houses we had been looking at would not accommodate our growing family. Gavin at twelve, Autumn at ten, and Astrid at four couldn't be crammed into a tiny house together with a baby. So we started to look at larger homes and increased our budget. We only needed to adjust our plan and figure out details later. Our family's changing needs were most important and we couldn't lose sight of that. The first house we looked at was the perfect fit. I wondered if it could be this easy after the stress of selling. But the sellers accepted our offer and within a few months we moved out to the country and into our dream home.

Soon we welcomed the birth of our baby boy, Griffin, and we were feeling pretty settled in to our new home and surroundings. But as time went on, I began to sink deeper and deeper into a dark state of depression. I completely gave up on self-care and lost sight of what I wanted and who I was. In my mind, I was stuck. My plans had been shattered and I just could not accept and embrace this beautiful blessing of a new baby and new home for what it was. I loved Griffin and gave him all the care and attention he needed, but there was this underlying anger within my heart that I would not allow myself to fully feel, let alone acknowledge. This anger was clouding my mind and growing darker each day. I was only going through the motions of life. Caring for my family of six was taking everything out of me. I was depleted of energy and I began to accept that this was just the way it was supposed to be and that what I wanted didn't matter anymore.

Even though I felt like an empty shell, I knew that I was meant for more than this. Intuitively, something told me I needed to get out of the bubble I was living in and change my perspective. But how was I going to do that? I was feeling called to take my family to Oregon to visit my cousin and her family, so I answered the call and arranged for a trip. The first few days that I was in Oregon I cried. Waves of release just kept washing over me and I didn't even know what I was releasing. I only knew that my body was holding so much pent-up emotion, and once I removed myself from my surroundings it poured out of me. I allowed myself to surrender and let go; I could finally allow myself to just be.

After our vacation I was feeling lighter, but knew I had a lot of work to do. I had just skimmed the surface enough to know that it was time to get on the path to healing. One day while scrolling Facebook I noticed a self-love workshop. I was intrigued … what would that entail? So I signed myself up for this three-part series in an effort to do something for myself. I had no idea what a gift the universe had just delivered to me, because this was the first of many gifts and I was going to keep following my instincts and acting on them. I was ready to allow myself to heal …

As I walked through the doors of this workshop I had a feeling that I had come to the right place. I was met with a team of women who were energy healers and life coaches who became supportive friends. They provided me with the tools, awareness, and community I was so desperately seeking. I began to set intentions, journal, meditate, and practice yoga. I slowly felt myself getting back in tune with my body and soul. I continued to reach out to these women and ask them for support and help when I needed it.

As time passed, I attracted more supportive women and experiences into my life, and I continued to allow myself to accept their knowledge and assistance. The key was committing to finding myself and my soul's true purpose. Each time I journaled or got on my yoga mat I felt closer to knowing.

Yoga had always spoken to me in a profound way and I had lost sight of that feeling when I gave up on myself. Coming back to this practice was the best thing I could have ever done for myself because it led me to eventually commit to a 200-hour yoga teacher certification course. Being a part of the certification process allowed me to deepen my practice and learn to teach others how to heal themselves through this incredible practice.

Through all of these avenues I opened a clear channel of communication with my soul. As each layer of fog was lifted, my inner voice became louder and clearer. I began to release suppressed emotions and allowed myself to sit in the discomfort and not turn to distractions to avoid feeling through them. Experiencing all of these feelings to their very core allowed me to recognize where I was holding myself back and to forgive myself for the many ways in which I had abused myself. I then began to heal my relationship with myself in a way that I had never done before. My inner dialogue began to transform from self-doubt and feelings of unworthiness to believing in myself and feeling worthy of love and abundance. I was ready to step into my role outside of "mother." I was ready to use my gifts and passions to help women feel empowered and show them what they, too, were capable of. And thus came the birth of my business, Gaia Dawn Studios.

I had always loved to make women feel beautiful. As a hair stylist for twenty years, connecting with women and making them feel beautiful was something that came very naturally to me. Also, as a passionate photographer who is obsessed with capturing beauty I am compelled to share the magic I see in the world with others through my photography. I was determined to combine these qualities about myself to provide a unique experience for women. We all deserve to experience the journey of self-discovery and I wanted to be a part of that process for women. I began to look within and ask myself how I could make this happen. I continued to journal about it and turn to the supportive community of women I had manifested into my life for guidance, which was integral in the development of this idea. But, I quickly learned that many other people in my life did not understand what I was creating. I found it difficult to lean on people who I had previously turned to, but this was a gift. It forced me to go deep within and look for the answers and support I needed within myself, only making me stronger and more determined. I believed in this vision so much I was willing to do anything to bring it to life.

I felt called to create symbolic images for women. Images that provoked emotion and empowerment. Not perfectly posed photos that had been photoshopped and polished. I wanted to take photos that captured a woman's true essence and gave her insight into a side of herself that she had never seen. I began talking to women and asking them questions about who they were and what made them feel alive. I wanted to help them see into their souls through photography and bring awareness to them. Just opening these discussions was so powerful and it gave me the right tools to create unique photos. I began to see so much more value in the consultation than the actual photo shoot, so I started to include yoga and meditation into my offerings as they brought this experience to a whole new level. I wanted these women to feel grounded and present when we worked together so that we could create the best images possible.

Learning how to stop negative self-talk and release self-doubt was a big part of this process. They needed to truly feel and know their power, and I was going to do anything I could to help them do that. Photographing these women has been an incredible experience. To see women connected to their emotions, their body, and their soul while I take these photos is extraordinary. But even more powerful is when these women see their photos, and they see their beauty and power, the magic that occurs is priceless.

Out of my own obstacles and challenges I have created something new and I am in awe of the positive impact it has had on my life as well as others. I am finally in alignment with my soul's purpose and I have so much gratitude to the universe for answering my prayer on that day a few years ago. I asked for help and I was sent an angel, my angel baby, Griffin, to remind me that I was off-track. I came into this life to break unhealthy cycles. I am a warrior for positive change. I help empower women with soulful connection and symbolic imagery and I would never have stepped into my power if I hadn't gone through my pain. Through my empowerment I help empower others and the ripple effect goes out from there. Together, we are creating beauty in the world.

ABOUT JENNIFER ROTH

Jennifer Roth is a passionate photographer and certified yoga instructor on a mission to help empower women. She believes that all women deserve a journey of self-discovery. Through her work, she wants to provide the tools to help women transform into a more authentic version of themselves, all while creating symbolic images through photos that represent their beauty and power. By acknowledging limiting beliefs, negative self-talk, and feelings of unworthiness, she uses meditation, yoga, and intuitive guidance to coach women to tune into their inner magic. She also enjoys photographing heart-centered events and creating symbolic images for women entrepreneurs that tell their story in a unique way.

As an entrepreneur with many passions, she also owns a family photography business, *Jennifer Roth Photography*. She focuses on capturing natural and candid photos with an artistic flair. She is a believer in the healing powers of nature and capturing nature landscapes brings her joy. She strives to capture emotion and connection in her photos and that is what makes her art unique.

To connect with Jenn and learn more about how you can experience this self-love journey, go to:
www.gaiadawnstudios.com
www.facebook.com/GaiaDawnStudios
www.instagram.com/gaiadawnstudios

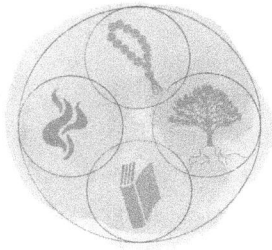

PUT ON YOUR SUNGLASSES!

Erin Kreitz Shirey

Many parents complain about teenagers while I double fist pump the air and say, "YES! Thank you so much for my feisty, storytelling Makenzie who keeps me on my toes! YES, YES, YES!" Could sound like I'm crazy to some parents, but it is honestly that I am high on life. My girls' lives that is, because they each have one; all three have been given a second chance at life. I am a Mom of three out of three medical miracles.

Let me introduce myself. My name is Erin Kreitz Shirey, married to my soccer-loving, perfect girl-Dad, Jack, and Mom to Makenzie "Kenz," Emerson "E-Bomb," and Finley "Fearless Finnie" or "Fin." I am a triathlete, Irish gal, entrepreneur, and complete middle daughter, eager to keep everyone happy and smiling. I was raised in the '80s, in love with Christian Slater and Tony Hawk, and have been in the health and fitness industry since I was eighteen. I own Inspirator Coaching & Fitness, a fitness, retreat, inspirator and professional empowerment coaching and motivational speaking business. My focus has always been to empower women and teen girls with their self-esteem through sports. An inspirator is an inspiration and motivator in one.—a word Emerson created when I was pregnant with Finley, while creating new boot camp circuits in the back yard. It was a word that transformed our entire lives. Who knew that fitness and empowerment would be what helped me up when I truly needed it most.

Makenzie was a blessed surprise! We were living in sunny Playa Del Rey, a beach city outside of Los Angeles, enjoying our twenties. I was training for a half Ironman and was unusually tired. I found out it wasn't from the long training runs, but I was actually nine weeks pregnant with our little miracle! The birth control baby who wanted to shine her way into the world on her own timeline. Beyond surprised, nervous, and blessed, my then-boyfriend and future husband Jack said, "Erin, this is our time. This baby is meant to be here!" While I'd wanted to be a mom since I was a little girl, I had no idea how much I wanted to be a mom until she was growing inside me.

At the time she was born, I chose to not go back to corporate fitness and stay home with her mapping out a future fitness business we could do together. When Makenzie was shy of four months old, we flipped a coin to decide where to move next, landing in Portland, Oregon. When Makenzie was shy of one, I began a pre- and postnatal fitness business empowering women to exercise with their babies. It was a blast, every class a fun new adventure. The business was building our new community and deep-rooted friendships. At that time, I had no idea how much being a community builder would mean to our family. Thank goodness I have always been a talker and community creator! Check marks in school equate positive check marks in life when we needed it most!

My husband and I live a massively healthy lifestyle. We are both athletes, have always been nourishing our bodies with exercise, healthy food, travel, and positive energy. It was my job to inspire other women in fitness and wellness to take care of themselves. Thus, you can imagine how shocked I was that we were the ones whose family's health was challenged not just once, twice, but three times with Makenzie and her younger sisters.

We welcomed Emerson McCafferty Shirey to the world on January 25th, 2008! She was a delightful, sweet baby who filled our hearts.

Makenzie loved being a big sister and would sing to her any chance she got. Being a winter baby, Emerson taught us about RSV. She prepared us for Makenzie and Makenzie prepared us for their younger sister Finley's medical challenges.

When Emerson was seven weeks old, I was just home from the hospital fighting pneumonia. She seemed weak and listening to my mom gut, we went to the hospital and they did a myriad of labs. Our poor infant girl was hooked up to one x-ray machine that had her between two plastic walls, holding her upright to see into her lungs. Her screams still haunt me. She was diagnosed with pneumonia, pertussis and RSV. Within hours, Emerson was filled with many tubes to help her breath, eat, and function. Our sweet little baby, who we were just getting to know, was about to teach us a massive life lesson: that of being in the moment. Emerson's doctors told us, "Pray hard! She is fighting for her life, so keep strong. Only about one to three percent of babies actually get pertussis, so get sleep to have the energy you will need."

Easy to say to a newly postnatal mom, who is recovering from being in the hospital herself, trying to mother an almost four-year-old and, oh, whose dad was also in the hospital with a new heart condition! But that's a story for another time. For us, we showed up every moment. Our friends and bootcampers showed up with meals, sent love, and helped us just BE.

How often do you just "be" without a timeline?

I invite you to begin now. It will change your life.

Forever grateful for miracles, Emerson was home after three weeks in the hospital. We celebrated her first St. Patrick's Day and Easter in the hospital, doing easter egg hunts in the hallways. Fast-forward two-and-a-half years, and Emerson would prepare us for Makenzie. We had moved from Portland back to the San Francisco Bay Area, where we grew up. Having rebuilt our life in Alameda, I was excited to visit friends in Portland for a few days. I was nervous to leave my girls, but a girls' trip was in order. On the second day, I had a feeling something was off. I called Jack and he shared that Makenzie was vomiting. She had a stomach flu, but seemed to be in good spirits. We talked again the next morning, and he said not to worry, that she would be ok, but they had to go to the pediatrician since she was still unable to keep food down. At that moment, I knew something was off. When running with my dear friend Sheri, I remember saying, "Sheri, I am scared. Something is off and I am worried about Kenz."

September 23rd, 2010, is Makenzie's Marker Day. I flew back to Alameda, ran into the girls' room and Makenzie was in my mom's lap. She didn't recognize me. She was foaming at the mouth, extending her arm out towards my eyes and rotating it as if twisting a lightbulb into a socket. My mom said she had done everything the pediatrician said, and with that I told my dad we had to go. We rushed to Children's Hospital, with me talking to Kenzie in the backseat. She didn't recognize me at all. What did that mean? Where was my girl in this sick and weak body?

At the ER, they rushed to get her vitals. While holding Kenz, the nurse was taking her blood pressure and she had a seizure. Kenz was immediately rushed into the ER operating room. They called over the PA system for more doctors to join the room. Having no idea what was going on, Makenzie looked like a lost alien with her eyes rotating from face to face. I was rubbing her leg while they started pumping tubes into her body. She still was unable to keep anything down and looked scared, but without a voice. What had happened to my baby girl? What was going on? Why couldn't she recognize me, her mom, the one whose voice is to soothe her always? The RN asked me if she was bit by a dog or bat, since she was foaming at the mouth. YES, that is what happened. We hang out with bats all the time in the Bay Area, right? They did a spinal tap, then found out that her organs weren't working. They said they had to start more work, stat. After what felt like hours, with a team of more doctors and nurses than I could count, I thought my baby was gone. The fear trickling through my bones, for "What is going to happen?" was overwhelming, but I remained calm. I kept trying to soothe Kenzie with my words, believing she could hear me even without recognizing me. Finally after eight to twelve hours, Kenz was transferred to ICU without any diagnosis, but multi-organ failure. They had no idea what happened or why. Sometimes the lesson learned is, it's not the how or why it happened, but how you step in and deal with it.

Kenzie finally recognized me forty-eight hours after being admitted, which was one of the best moments of my life. She was in ICU for three weeks. Our friends were scared to visit, which was hard. Was she contagious? What happened? People asked what we did, so they could ensure to not do the same. It was horrific. It made us question our parenting and whether we had done something to harm our baby girl. Yet all we had done was love on her when she had a stomach flu.

After two weeks in ICU, they finally diagnosed Makenzie with acute necrotizing pancreatitis and multi-organ failure. She had tons of infections continually, and despite being told by doctors that, "this never happens, don't worry," it would always happen to her. No reason how, nor what to expect, but told they had to revive each organ one by one and pray that she would survive. Our pediatrician came to check in andtold us they were all rooting for Makenzie. I asked what that meant, and she said "The CHO team told us they don't know if she'll make it home, she has a low chance of survival." At that moment, I chose to not listen and believe in my gut that Makenzie was to be the one percent again. I rushed to the hospital chapel, dropped to my knees and said to my God, "I promise, God, I will do whatever you ask and work hard every day. Please, please save my daughter. I am scared and need your hands on my back to hold me up."

Unbeknownst to me at the time, my God listened. Our community rose up and became the hands on our backs, holding us up. From meals, to food, to raising funds to assist, since I was not working except for some early mornings teaching my boot camp to feel that life was "normal." They did fundraisers and showered Makenzie and Emerson with love, more cards and notes than we could post to the walls. Makenzie's room was beyond welcoming, with artwork from classmates, cards from all over the world, gifts from friends, and friends of friends. Kenz went from fifty-six pounds down to thirty-six in just three week's time. My sweet girl with a little booty was suddenly skin and bones, but always with a massive smile. She couldn't walk, was in diapers again, but would smile and charm the nurses and doctors with her detailed stories. I became her tutor, her teacher, her physical therapist, her nurse, and most of all her massive advocate. The years of empowering others to use their voice was my lesson to learn how to use mine when I needed it most.

I also relied on my own fitness. We learned that you can't be stressed on what you don't know to be true, but you can hold yourself up and take care of your spirit. It isn't what happens, but how you respond to the unknown. When family came to relieve me and stay with Makenzie, I put on my headphones for loud music to escape hospital noises and used the stairs. I would run across the street to the top floor of the parking garage to do circuits and sprints with bands in fresh air. Every workout, tears would stream down my face and my muscles were exhausted, but I knew I had to stay strong for my daughters. Sometimes, when back from a run, I would curl up into a ball and cry my eyes out in nerves and depletion before entering her hospital floor. But I would go back to the room having left some weight of the world from the sweat in my workout.

Responding to life-challenging situations is integral to one's success. Emerson wasn't able to visit Makenzie for four weeks, so we had to get clever. We used Skype and prepped Emerson that her sister would look different with the tubes. Tears streamed as their sister-love flowed through the computers. Our girls were close and while nurturing Makenzie, I missed the ease and silliness of being around two-and-a-half-year-old Emerson. One visit, my mom brought her to the hospital with the jogging stroller. We ran to BART, popped on, and went to San Francisco. We ran all over visiting the Sea Lions at Pier 39, ran to our favorite Mermaid fountain at Ghirardelli getting her an ice cream cone, and ran up and down hills forever. When we got to Chrissy Field, I remember looking at the Golden Gate Bridge and Emerson happy in the sand, thinking I didn't want to go back. I wanted to stay there with Emerson pretending that life was normal and all was right. What I didn't know then was that all was right, and what was happening to my daughters was our life's mission.

As an advocate, I worked hard for a second opinion for Makenzie. This is something that at first I was worried would hurt the doctor's feelings at CHO, but knew it was my daughter and non-negotiable. As women, we often stay quiet instead of speaking up. We are afraid to use our voice for fear of offending someone. I invite you all to use your voice and power forward. Your voice matters, and while an advocate for Makenzie, the second opinion saved her life. We had an appointment at UCSF the day before her surgery at CPMC. They were operating at the adult hospital since the pediatric surgeons hadn't done the procedures before. I am grateful for that push as Makenzie had internal bleeding and would have died on the operating table. In the room with Dr. Kanwar at UCSF, he said, "You have a very sick daughter and she can't leave this hospital until she is 110 percent ok." Again, Kenzie was rushed to the ER, mummy-wrapped to hold her down for more IVs to add with her PICC line. Makenzie was saved by UCSF. There for a total of another six weeks, she was able to go home for the final time right before Christmas.

The irony in having kids with medical challenges is when people say "Why me, why me again?" we would say, "Why not us?" We had the community and support. We had our faith. We had a focus that powered through. I wouldn't wish being part of the Hospital Mom's Club upon anyone, however I know there's a reason I'm a gold star member.

When life was finally normal, our marriage stayed strong with much work, and I had said yes to some work goals again. We decided to have a third child. Wildly, everyone thought she was a surprise, being almost six years younger than Emerson. However our Finley Roberta was a planned-for child. The family's baby, we didn't know if she was a boy or girl. I just wanted an easy and healthy baby to nurture and love, which she was, until she was nine months old. After a special getaway to Mexico, Finley couldn't keep food down. She was vomiting continually, had spiking fevers, and was in and out of the hospital. They had no idea what was happening or why. She started to lose more weight, was barely on the weight chart, with her platelets and her white blood count numbers skyrocketing.

For two years, I was Finley's advocate. We had more appointments, procedures, and labs than I could count, and I would never listen to what the test was for. She was tested for three different cancers, cystic fibrosis, and rare conditions, among others. Every appointment or procedure, we'd take the ferry to San Francisco and run together. When in the hospital, I would pull her in the red wagon down the hallways, the wagon handle in one hand, her IV pole in the other, and do lunges with the nurses. We would laugh and play games, making the best out of each visit. I learned from her sisters to be in the moment, make memories where we could and to take care of myself so I could take care of them. To laugh and be present. After countless procedures, and a few surgeries, when shy of three years old, Finley was diagnosed with a low immune system and eosinophilic colitis.

Makenzie has a seventy-five percent chance of getting pancreatic cancer, and Finley may never be able to eat dairy, gluten, and soy. And when other kids get sick, she may get it and end up in the hospital. In our family's mindset, Kenz has a twenty-five percent chance of NOT getting cancer, and Finley may outgrow her issues. You cannot live in fear. You cannot live with nerves of "what if's." You cannot think the worst, but think and focus on the best outcome possible. You can't be stressed on what you don't know to be true, but have the power to own the positive joy and focus on what is TRUE!

What is true is that in my life, the power of being present is the most powerful gift. While many complain about not having enough time to go for their dreams, I invite you to think about that thought. YOU own your time, your time does not own you.

You have the power and ability to make each moment count, even when living in the hospital fighting for your kid's life, like I did times three. You have it in you to step up, to not stress at what you cannot control, but to work hard at what really is true. To let the fears taking energy away from your dreams go to the side, as your life does not have space for fears. It has space for you, living as your Inspirator self!

Moms often put themselves to the side. They put their kids' needs first and themselves last. They lose their spark and desire to live life adventurously. They put their dreams to the side in order to support their family. However, when they live a dream life, the ones they love feel more inspired to live fully, too. Having trained thousands of women over the years, I truly feel I am three for three in the Hospital Mom's Club to empower you.

To empower YOU to live feeling strong, empowered, capable, courageous, and in the moment. For you to be inspired to BE, to own your voice and love on the one body you have. For that body is what serves you best when you need it most and have taken care of it every day. This is not a dress rehearsal. All three of my daughters have been given a second chance for a reason. As a mom, I have been given a first, second, and third chance for a reason. That reason is to empower you to live like your OWN Inspirator every single day. You have the ability to develop more intrinsic motivation than you know what to do with. You have the power to go for the massive dreams, to push your limits physically, to challenge yourself professionally, to nourish your body inside and out with healthy foods and soul-based living. You have the ability to power through the challenging times in a positive manner, with a fierce faith that the end result is better than you anticipated. That it is in your power to embrace life's challenges—aka ELC—as with every challenge, you have a greater ability to own your life!

Thus, shine, ladies, shine. I invite you to shine so bright that the world needs sunglasses when you walk into the room!

ABOUT ERIN KREITZ SHIREY

Erin Kreitz Shirey is an award-winning Personal Trainer, Inspirator Coach, Motivational Speaker and Athlete. *Red Tricycle* named her Mom on a Mission in Health, while Alameda & Portland Magazines awarded her the Best Personal Trainer. Erin has been Featured in *Shape*, *Parents*, *Competitor*, and *Men's Health and Fitness*, among others. A panelist for ESPN, she has been interviewed by NBC, ABC, Disney, FOX, and the Fitness Editor for the nationally syndicated Better TV show. Erin is often found training with her husband, Jack, for her next Ironman 70.3, or hiking with her three dynamic daughters in their adventure city of Boise. Erin is an outside gal who loves to laugh until she cries.

Through experiencing all three of her daughters' medical challenges, the Shireys took on the phrase "Dream Life" and turned their entire life around. Recently moved to Boise, both parents working from home, hours scheduled around kids' schedules, they live fit, travel, and adventure to Kona, Hawaii, as often as possible!

Erin is a sought-after Motivational Speaker, Business Mentor, and Empowerment Coach. She loves empowering women to take care of themselves andgoal up in life's adventures, training from the inside out so they can be energized to take care of those they love. It is her family's mission to empower everyone to live like their own Inspirator.

Connect with Erin via her Facebook community, Empowered Inspirator Life, the Inspirator Academy, Inspirator Fitness & Empowerment Adventure Retreats, or via private coaching or corporate speaking.

Learn more at ErinKreitzShirey.com & InspiratorLife.com
FB- @erinkreitzshirey
IG- @erinkreitzshirey & @inspirator_life

MADE FOR SOMETHING BETTER

Kara Thompson

If you asked me a year ago what I loved and was grateful for in my life, I would have told you about my wonderful family, the dance studio that I co-own, my love of camping and the outdoors, or my new venture into real estate. But my personal health was not something that I would have mentioned, mostly because I took it for granted.

In March 2018, I was hit with shocking news. At thirty-eight years old, my life story changed late in the evening with one phone call and four little words, "You have melanoma cancer." I don't know if everyone diagnosed with cancer feels the same dizzying effects I did when I heard those dreaded words. Cancer is a diagnosis that you only read in articles written about other people's lives, or hear in conversations pertaining to other people, not yourself. Suddenly, those words belonged to me and were about to become a part of my story.

However, this story isn't about my actual cancer, rather it's what this diagnosis has taught me that I find to be so much more important. We all encounter hard situations in life. So when this diagnosis hit me from out of the blue, I drew upon all I had learned from dealing with my difficult experiences up to this point to see if there was a bigger picture that would help me make sense of this situation. At first I felt everything but strong. I was scared more for the people who loved me than for myself. I was paralyzed by the thoughts that came rushing through my head. I was grief-stricken about how this would affect my boys and heartbroken for my husband. I could see the pain in my parents' eyes every time I looked at them. I quickly realized that I had the power to decide how I would handle this situation and that the decisions I made after I received the diagnosis would determine my frame of mind and the impact this journey would have on my life and the lives of those around me. The path I have taken since my diagnosis draws greatly from my past experience and the events that have brought me to this point.

We all have sadness and traumatic experiences that we've had to endure and overcome. Looking back at my "pre-cancer" life, I think about the events that shaped my viewpoint on the world. I was fortunate to grow up in a loving environment surrounded by many happy childhood memories. I was raised in an average 1980s household where we made up dances to our favorite new Paula Abdul tune, we played outside a lot, my grandparents lived next door, and my cousins were my very best friends. We spent hours in my grandparents' pool or gathered around as my grandfather, Austin, made his signature homemade ice cream. Warm summer nights were spent down on the shore with my Grandmom Peggy and Pop, or playing flashlight tag in the cemetery next door. Simple birthday parties surrounded by those you loved, presents, and cake. Singing "Oh, You Can't Get to Heaven" with my Grandmom Shirley and Pop John, or spending hours with my brother super-gluing my mom's "knick knacks" back together before she came home from work and noticed that they were broken while she was out. My parents and grandparents never missed a dance recital or sporting event. I had a wonderful childhood.

However, there were low points as well, just like with any family, and these experiences also help shape us into who we are today. I was touched by true grief when I lost my grandfather. I watched this man, my best friend, take his last breath while I was a college student. Starting with that event, my family continued to experience loss year after year, and I was saddened by the loss of all of my grandparents, whom I loved and adored, in a short period of time. My grandfather was a special man who always had a smile and never let anything get him down, yet from his loss I learned the importance of a positive attitude and outlook, something that has served me well during this journey. My grandmother truly thought I could change the world and was always one of my biggest cheerleaders. From her loss I learned to listen to my soul and follow my dreams. I was touched by true heartache when my parents separated, and I felt that everything in my world was coming undone. Yet from this, I learned the importance of inner strength and the steadying force of my parents' love in my life. I experienced the devastation of losing a baby during my first pregnancy. Yet from this I learned that life is precious, and I've since been blessed with two amazing sons who are the center of my world.

Each of these experiences touched me in a very specific way, leaving lasting impressions on my heart and mind, and reinforcing how important the bonds of family are to me. These experiences are all part of the story of my life and what has made me into the strong and resilient person I am today.

Looking back, I always knew I would be an entrepreneur, I just wasn't sure what it would look like. I have always found joy in creating something and having others enjoy it. As a young child I spent hours teaching my brother his ABCs, giving thought out presentations to my favorite dolls, and even my imaginary friends were lectured on my seven-year-old passions. Perhaps this was an early indication that my future would involve sharing my passions with others in some type of teaching role, but it would be years before I followed my heart to make that a reality. As I grew older, I found myself in a series of jobs after college, but I discovered that the corporate journey was not fulfilling to me. I found myself repeating a pattern of making sure everything looked good on the outside, while everything on the inside was not always quite right. I was feeling unfilled and unsatisfied with my career.

However, staying at a job and in a career that wasn't making me truly happy was the easy and comfortable thing to do. Taking the jump into uncertain spaces was not so easy, especially when I wasn't clear on what I really wanted. But I knew I yearned to do something bigger, to have a greater impact. What I needed was to take a gigantic leap of faith to create something that made a difference and brought me the fulfillment I desired. I needed to get out of my comfort zone, get out of my head, and get out of my own way to make that change possible. That's when the dream of opening a dance studio started to take form.

With my desire to be a business owner and impact the community along with my past experiences as an athlete, coupled with my sister-in-law's amazing talent in dance and choreography, our dream soon became a reality and Fit to Dance Studio was opened in 2011. We spent several years building up the studio to provide high-quality dance instruction and adult fitness classes, and in the process, we ended up creating so much more. From the start we knew we wanted to make a big difference in our community. We never wanted to simply have a dance studio where students came for classes, instead, we wanted to build confidence and self-worth in our students, and create a warm, inviting atmosphere. What we didn't fully expect was the extent to which our dance studio would became like an extended family and change our lives in ways we had never imagined.

In the years since, our studio has become a place where families feel like they are at home, where our staff feels like a sisterhood, where students learn dance and make lasting friendships, and a place where parents and grandparents can connect with their children over a shared love of dance. We have helped to build young dancers who have self-confidence, who are kind and caring friends to each other, and who have gone out and made a difference in the world. Friendships bloomed among our staff, between staff and parents, and among parents. People who didn't know each other before stepping through our doors are now lifelong friends. While we expected that the children may find friendships within our walls, I certainly didn't expect that our dance families would become such cherished friends. Shared conversations about products to feature in the studio's boutique, easy conversations about wine and crafts in the lobby, connections over similar interests related to dance and beyond. These relationships that were formed have led me to some of my most cherished friends. The studio has become a social circle, a place where people show up each week, or several times a week, where it's ok to be themselves. Who would have thought that in the process of creating this dream of ours, this atmosphere of acceptance and comradery, it would turn out to be one of the major supports in my life when I needed it the most.

Immediately after my diagnosis, I was faced with the choice to endure quietly and keep it to myself as much as possible, or to share it with those around me. It didn't take long for me to realize that I needed to be true to myself, which meant that I needed to be authentic and real with this new journey. While everyone needs to face their challenges in the way that suits them best, I know in my heart that sharing my story with those around me was right for me. The family within our studio has been a major force in helping me navigate through one of my most challenging chapters in life. As someone who focuses on serving others, it's been a difficult transition to let people help take care of my needs and my family's needs, but there's something very powerful in accepting and being open to help that brings people even closer together.

The outpouring of love and support from our dance studio family, as well as all of our family and friends has been amazing. Especially through the dance studio, being able to show up as my authentic self and share the day-to-day challenges with the staff, students, and families has been so liberating. It's taught me that everyone has bad days, and that's ok. You don't have to be strong every day. And it's ok to let these people, who I have tried to serve to the best of my ability since the opening of the studio, be there for me in ways that I never imagined. Comfort and support, phone calls, texts and Facebook messages, warm meals, carpools for the boys, covering aspects of work to remove added workload from me, help cleaning my house, rides and companionship during treatments, long conversations, and even longer hugs. I've been blessed to realize that cancer doesn't change who I am or what I was put on this earth to accomplish. There is always so much going on as a busy, working mom, and we all find ways to make it work and to be strong, even on our darkest days. Before this diagnosis I was always sure I could figure it out on my own and felt that I had things under control. But being sick was out of my control, and it forced me to relinquish some control over all aspects of my life and allow the people who love and care for me to step in and help.

It's easy to ask, why me? Why did this happen to me? Yet for me, it's helped bring many aspects of my life into clearer focus. If I only focused on being sick, I would have lost sight of the positive things in my life. Perhaps cancer didn't happen to me, it happened for me, to remind me of all of the good that surrounds me every day, and to strengthen my commitment to living my life with meaning. A good friend has reminded me throughout this journey that God only gives us challenges to make room for more good things to happen in our lives. I know I will be ok throughout this ordeal because I have a network of people who truly care and show compassion for each other. I can show up at the studio and be authentic. I do not need to hide my struggles. This is a place where I can fully show up as myself and not only be accepted, but be surrounded and enveloped by love and support.

This disease is only one piece of my story. And after getting to where I am right now, at a place where I'm proud of my accomplishments, personally fulfilled, and excited about what's still to come, I tell myself that I didn't come this far only to come this far. This part of my journey isn't what I might have chosen for myself if I'd been given the choice, but I am grateful for what it has shown me. Sometimes through grief, heartache, or loss, we're forced to begin a new chapter and we can either enter it with resentment and apprehension, or with faith and love. I am choosing faith, love, and the abundant support of friends and family.

This journey has taught me that even when you're at your weakest, you can find your strength in the support around you. It has reinforced my passion for helping others, even with very small acts of kindness that make a huge impact. It has brought me to the very hard realization that you never know what tomorrow will bring, but you must face each day with courage, confidence, and a dream in your pocket. It has showed me that sometimes people with the biggest smiles are struggling the most. It has proven to me that I'm going to lose special people in my life (this one's for you, Marisa), and I've realized that no matter how much time I spent with them or how much I appreciate them and told them so, it will never be enough. It's made me realize that it's ok to express how you feel and cry hard, but surround yourself with people that let you cry on their shoulder and then make you laugh harder than you cried.

I have learned that even at age thirty-eight, I'm still a work in progress and there's something new I can learn every day. It has taught me to be honest about my experiences and to be my true authentic self, regardless of those who might not like the real me. To show up and be authentic, even when authentic means showing your vulnerability. It has shown me not to be afraid of losing someone who doesn't feel lucky to have me. People who are meant to be in your life don't leave, or will somehow find their way back. I've learned that you never know when your story can make an impact for others, even if their situation isn't exactly the same.

I'm sharing the details of my journey in the "My Mountain ~ Kara's Cancer Journey" Facebook group both for myself and to help others. Not everyone has cancer, but everyone has struggles, and I hope that the feelings and thoughts I voice through this page bring different meanings to different people depending on where they are in their lives. It has taught me to embrace the challenges and keep moving forward using my experience to guide me. I've learned that today is the day to swim into uncertainty and move forward to the next great chapter, because tomorrow is never promised.

There is meaning to the story that you were made for something better. You are the only person who is in charge of what happens next. So even if you aren't sure what your ultimate goal is just yet, take those leaps of faith and trust that you will land exactly where you were meant to be. You never know how a decision you have the courage to make today could be the basis for what you find out you need later down the road. My next chapter is just beginning to unfold …

ABOUT KARA THOMPSON

Kara Thompson grew up in Mullica Hill, New Jersey, and has always been fascinated with health, nutrition, and fitness. As a child, she was a dancer and gymnast, and in high school and throughout college she played softball and was part of the swim team. Kara pursued another passion in college and received a B.A in communications from Rowan University, but always dreamed of starting her own business.

Kara and her sister-in-law, Megan, started Fit to Dance Studio with the dream of bringing a love of DANCE and FITNESS to families in their community. They are thankful every day for the F2D family of students, FIT clients, and staff. It is a pleasure to watch people young and old alike grow and express themselves through dance and fitness.

Kara's love of helping people achieve their dreams, and her passion for home interior design, have recently led her to pursue a part-time career in real estate as well. Her Next Door Homes real estate team services the South Jersey area. In her free time, Kara enjoys spending time in or on the water, hiking, and camping with her husband, Tom, two sons, Garret and Reid, and dogs, Harlee and Tex.

You can continue to follow her cancer journey on Facebook at https://m.facebook.com/groups/469781906787905, keep up-to-date on Fit to Dance Studio happenings at fit2dancestudio.com, or let her help you find your next door to call home by emailing soldbykara@gmail.com.

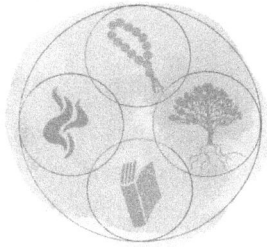

MOVE FORWARD

Dr. Wendi Wardlaw

As I thought on this title, *Women Who Impact*, I first wanted to thank my Lord and Savior, Jesus Christ, for allowing me to be a usable vessel. It is only through the power God gives me that allows the service for an impact. I mentor young people and future doctors and, recently, a young future doctor asked me how she could "make an impact" in this world. My response was "Move forward and take YOUR next step." I told her a little about my journey to encourage her, and I pray that it will also encourage you.

Watching my mom work full-time while going to school at night and raising three kids would be the spark behind the openness of taking my next step. My mother accomplished what she set out to do regardless of the obstacles around her. She always moved forward, took her next step, and taught me to do the same.

Like many, I have the testimony of overcoming my childhood. With a rash—eczema on my face, neck, arms, legs, and hands—ugly, leopard, alligator, and snake were my nicknames. It took me years to learn that success is not in your beauty but in your character. I moved often, changing schools eleven times. I lived in a constant state of change, loss, and starting over. I rarely felt stable, safe, or accepted. By the time I was fourteen, my living situation had drastically changed. I was unable to understand or process what seemed to be daily errors and I found myself feeling homeless many times. I realized that being sent away five times in four years was an attempt to place marks of insecurity in my life. Through disappointment, I eventually learned to stop trying to get help, that my problems were burdens on others, and asking for help was selfish and self-centered. Yes, like most, I had self-limiting beliefs and needed to unlearn most of the lessons of my childhood and re-learn wholeness, which I walk in today. Mom's lessons of taking my next step, stuck. In that season, I felt that telling others of my needs or my situation was not an option and would further alienate me from those I desired love from. 'Smile and bear it' was the rule, so problems real and imagined were hidden.

By the age of fifteen, I had attempted suicide twice. My daily prayer was not to wake up and I felt lost, alone, rejected, and unwanted. At any time, on any day, and for any reason, I could be sent away. I wasn't equipped to process this experience clearly, so I thought suicide was the answer. I just wanted out! I thank God I failed. Hopelessness and abandonment taught me what that looked and felt like. This place of sadness, like most painful places, point to our destiny, calling, and direction of impact. It equips us for the journey ahead and allows us to touch the minds and hearts of those we are called to serve. Childhood can be hard alone … and the big take away to survive it is to know indeed, there IS a next step and you must get through it to get to it. We all have yesterdays, but they do not have to dictate our outcomes. It is only our choices today that can predict our lives tomorrow. Therefore, surround yourselves with wise counselors, mentors, and coaches. People that know more, have more, and want more than you. John Maxwell would say, "Yesterday ended last night." Paul Martinelli would say, "You get what you fight for." Roddy Galbraith would say, "Fear tries to convince you that it is saving you." Les Brown would say, "You can't see the picture when you're in the frame." Throughout my journey, I've learned that people outside of the frame help us move forward, grow, and take our next step.

I learned how to run, sprinting from those attempting to steal my innocence. Sprinting/running was one of my first big lessons. I learned that blessings can come from your pain. Graduating high school, I received three full scholarships to college and ranked at the top in track and field in the state. I was shooting for the '92 Olympics … just running! Unfortunately, I could not take advantage of the hard work I put in for those scholarships because no one would sign my financial aid form. Yes, this was sad and yet it is what I pull from as a mentor today. I had no one to tell me I could've sat out one year, filed as an independent student, and still received my scholarships. I mentor today to be this voice of help, reason, and information.

Moving forward to my next step was the US Army. As private, I enlisted as the lowest ranking soldier in the US Army, seeking opportunity and to finish college. In the Army Dental Corps, we began the day at 4:30 am for physical training (PT) and finished between 5–6 pm, assuming nothing additional was required. Throughout my ten years of active duty, I attended undergraduate evening classes. Yes, this was a very long time if you compare it to most who complete an undergraduate in four years. Evening classes began at 7-7:30 and ended at 10:00-10:30 pm. As I look back now, I realize that today is still today, whether I invested ten years, four years, or no years. The answer to making an impact is in your next step. If I had looked at the big picture, I would have been discouraged. But because I focused on my next step, I arrived. Whether I'm late is up for debate. Stop looking at your mountain and focus on your next step. At two classes from completing my prerequisites for dental school, I was tested for learning disabilities in the Army. I was informed that I had multiple strokes as a child and many other problems, including short-term memory loss. I was told I would never make it through the rigors of dental school and to find another career goal. I was devastated for about two seconds, snatched my results, and never looked back. I was too close to my goal after going to school at night for ten years to stop. I had to move forward and take my next step!

ALL OF YOUR STEPS COUNT

While serving in the Army Dental Corps, God was growing the tools I would certainly need today as a missionary, dental practice owner, teacher, and speaker. I worked on all sides and levels of dentistry while in the Army: the assistant, hygienist, and office manager. I served as an operating room technician, EMT (Emergency Medical Technician), and trained in emergency field medicine. I was being prepared for the field of missions and growing my passion for dentistry and serving others. God gives us passions in our gifts. So, if you are looking for your destiny, look for your gifts. Inside your gifts, you will find your passions. Taking your next step in your passions is how you find your destiny. These steps allowed me to survive the 2008 recession as a startup business and have formed the different layers of Dr. Wendi Wardlaw that exist today. Remember, both the good and the bad, **all of your steps count and have a purpose. Move forward.**

There was only a one month transition between ten years in the Army and being a full-time dental student at the prestigious Howard University College of Dentistry. Calling the cafeteria a "mess hall" more times than I wanted, the transition was challenging, but I was taking my next step. During dental school at Howard, I completed two years of externship at Columbia University School of Dental and Oral Surgery. I continued at Columbia for postgraduate, completing my Advanced Education in General and Cosmetic Dentistry with a focus on accessing the underserved for care. It was here I began missions abroad, with my first start in Nigeria.

Throughout my life, from childhood through the Army, and even dental school, I've felt as if I was led to serve others. You see, I found healing through helping others. I decided early on to give what I felt I needed. This was a big revelation and a big next step.

Through my journey, I learned that people may not ask for help because they may not know how. People may not look like they need help. I didn't. Some may not be able to reach you, so you may need to reach them. I believe God allows us to walk, run, and sometimes crawl through tough seasons for the tools we need to serve others. We are ALL required to serve others. Where do we serve, you may ask? Well, this answer is in your pain and struggles. I sought to be an answer to a pain I didn't know how to articulate. There is no level too insignificant to give back. At every level you find yourself, you find your tools for your next step, a place of need and a direction to serve in. We all have places in our lives we need to share with someone else, equipping them for an easier journey. Share your lessons and truths ... someone needs to hear from you.

THE QUESTION IS, WILL YOU? HOW, YOU ASK? JUST MOVE FORWARD INTO YOUR NEXT STEP.

I moved to Florida and opened Stoneybrook Dental that specializes in CARE with state-of-the-art dentistry, like CEREC one-visit ceramic crowns. I structured my nonprofit, Inspired Purpose, Inc.; the vehicle God allows me to serve through in the greater Orlando area and abroad.

Today, I am a dentist, an entrepreneur and business owner of a top-rated dental practice, Stoneybrook Dental. A missionary with a nonprofit, Inspired Purpose, Inc., who has traveled to Albania, the Dominican Republic, Ghana, Haiti, Jamaica, Nigeria, South Africa, and more. I am DrWendiDDS, six days a week on syndicated radio with "A Healthy Mouth is a Healthy You®." This segment reaches thirty-five cities in over 100 countries around the world—and growing. I am an Executive Director on the John Maxwell team, a mentor, a teacher, a certified speaker, and a coach. I have a beautiful family full of love and acceptance.

If I had known it would take ten years to complete undergrad, do you think I would have tried? What is it that has convinced you that it takes too long to complete, or you will never finish, or it's too late? Who told you that you weren't smart enough, strong enough, creative, or beautiful? What voices stop you from moving forward? We don't need to have the whole picture, we just need to give 100 percent to our next step. I pray you are encouraged to take yours. Just do it ... move forward and take your next step!

Time will pass whether we are growing or not ... so move, go, and grow into your destiny! Do not give yourself so much on your plate you become overwhelmed. Place all your focus on your next step. Take it, own it, do it, and when you are done, do it again.

Where is your next step, you may ask? I promise you, you do know. You may not know how to cross your mountain, but you do know how to take your next step. Look in your gifts. There, you will find your passions and your next step. Move forward right there. Every step is a good step if it's your next step. **Move forward.**

I am on the road with you moving forward in the scripture God has given Inspired Purpose, II Corinthians 9:8, and it says, "And God is able to make All grace abound toward you, that you always have All-sufficiency in All things, may abound toward every good work." He said we would have everything we need all the time and, in every situation, to accomplish what He has called into our lives ... Let's go, trust God, **move forward and take your next step!**

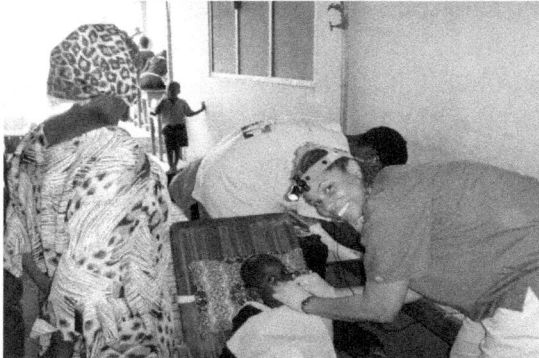

Inspired Purpose Missionary Trip to Ghana, Africa

266

ABOUT DR. WENDI WARDLAW

Dr. Wendi Wardlaw began her dental career as a private in the United States Army Dental Corps. While attending school at night she went from dental assistant to doctor from private to sergeant. Dr. Wendi credits her diverse background as steps for the foundation, passion, outreach, and dentistry of today.

Reaching higher, she received her doctorate from the prestigious Howard University College of Dentistry. Motivated with an inspired purpose, she went on to complete a post-doctoral degree in Advanced Education in General and Cosmetic Dentistry with an emphasis on community health, outreach, and access to care from Columbia University, Dental and Oral Surgery, NYC.

Dr. Wendi Wardlaw is the owner of the award-winning Stoneybrook Dental in Winter Garden, FL. She is the founder/president of Inspired Purpose, Inc., a non-profit serving through education and dental missions both locally and abroad. She's heard internationally six days/week as Dr. WendiDDS, "A Healthy Mouth is a Healthy You®" educating on the largest access to the internal body, the mouth, and its systemic health connections. Dr. Wendi Wardlaw is a sought-after speaker and trainer and an Executive Director on the John Maxwell Team, motivating, coaching, and growing individuals and teams.

Through Inspired Purpose, Dr. Wendi is a missionary serving in Nigeria, South Africa, Ghana, Dominican Republic, Haiti, Albania, Jamaica, and Uganda. Along with local outreach efforts, Dr. Wendi walks out her Inspired Purpose with love. She attributes God's grace to every step taken and those moving forward. She was featured in several magazines as one of Orlando's top dentists: Orlando Magazine, #1 Orlando's Elite Doctors and Woman of the Year 2016, Orlando Style Magazine. She has also been featured in "O" Oprah Magazine,

Entrepreneur, and Fortune magazines. Always striving for excellence, Dr. Wendi was awarded the Distinguished Alumni Award from Howard University College of Dentistry, 2017. With God in front, she accepts her marching orders as 2nd Corinthians 9:8 and understands it is truly blessed to be a blessing. She believes Love is an action word and does it.

REPRINTED WITH PERMISSIONS

Lisa Nichols
Enna Aujla
Laura Husson
Stefanie O'Polka
Terrie Peters
Cristina Rodriguez
Patty Staco
Stacey Friedman
Katie Jefcoat
Michelle Lee
Denise McCormick
Debbie Pettit
Violeta Potter
Donna Wald
Katherine Wolff
Carole B. Young
Jessica Amaro
Sagoo Arora
Jodie Baudek
Natalie Citarelli
Megan Datz
Cameo Gore
Amy Hehre
Stacey Kirkpatrick
Tina Raffa
Jennifer Roth
Erin Kreitz Shirey
Kara Thompson
Dr. Wendi Wardlaw

Are you a woman who ignites?
Are you a woman who inspires?
Are you a woman who influences?
Are you a woman who impacts?
Are you a woman who illuminates?
Then we want to connect with you!

The Inspired Impact Book Series is looking to connect with women who desire to share their stories and serve the world. If you have dreamed of publishing a book, then this is for you. If you have dreamed of bringing your message to a larger audience, then this is for you. If you have dreamed of exposing your business through a new platform, then this is for you. If you have dreamed of inspiring women all over the globe, then this is for you.

We want to hear your story!

Visit www.katebutlerbooks.com to begin your journey on becoming a Best-Selling Author that impacts women around the world.

May your soul be so inspired that you are moved to inspire others,

the women who impact

www.ingramcontent.com/pod-product-compliance
Lightning Source LLC
LaVergne TN
LVHW051224080426
835513LV00016B/1399